P9-CLC-116

Sissinghurst:
an Unfinished History

Happy Birthday
with much love

Judithxxx   Davidxx

9th December 2008

Eighteenth-Century Sissinghurst

A remarkable eighteenth-century picture of Sissinghurst has surfaced in Ontario. For years nobody has known which house it portrayed and its owner, Derrick Bradbury, recently started to circulate copies to see if it could be identified. It was finally recognised as Sissinghurst by Nicholas Cooper, the architectural historian, in May 2008.

This watercolour was intended as a picture of a double murder, but it is also by far the best portrayal ever discovered of Sissinghurst as the Elizabethans intended it to be.

An onion-domed prospect tower-cum-gateway was centred on a distinguished courtyard, at the far end of which an elaborate doorway opened into a passage which in turn led through to the medieval court beyond. Small banqueting houses to the north and perhaps to the south had large windows overlooking the park. Dignified barns stored the hay necessary for the park deer in the winter. A great garden was laid out between the middle courtyard and the moat to the north and east, of which the paths and beds can faintly be seen in this picture. It was on the site of the lower left-hand bed of this Elizabethan garden that Vita Sackville-West discovered the unknown gallica rose, now called 'Sissinghurst Castle', when she arrived here in 1930. It now seems at least possible that bushes of the particularly persistent rose had been growing in this garden continuously since the sixteenth-century.

By the mid-eighteenth century, Sissinghurst was burdened by debt, the park was in ruins and the place was let out to the government because no one in the Baker family cared for it. It became a camp for French naval prisoners during the Seven Years' War. About three thousand of them were held there, guarded by detachments of various English Militia regiments.

The prisoners trashed the buildings, destroying the Elizabethan panelling and marble fireplaces, burning the pews and altar rails in the chapel, leaving the garden without a stump above ground. After the war was over, most of the buildings shown here were demolished. Only fragments, including the tower, the long front range and one barn, now remain. These were the damp and poignant ruins in which Vita Sackville-West and Harold Nicolson made their famous garden.

On 9 July 1761, the terrible incident shown in the painting occurred. Its details are known from the evidence given to an inquiry later that year. Early in the morning, three re-captured escapees were being led back to Sissinghurst through the fields, outside the frame of this picture to the top. 'A Number of P[risoner]s ... having the curiosity to see which of their comrades they were that were retaken, did all make towards the Fence but with no other intent.' The sentry on the far side of the moat, a soldier of the Kent Militia called John Bramston, told them not to come near the fence, or he would fire at them.

Bramston was already known to be off his head. He seems to have loaded his musket with three balls. One of them lodged itself in the wall surrounding the garden (shown pale pink on the left of the garden), but one hit a Frenchman, Baslier Baillie, and wounded him. (He is shown here being attended by two of his friends.) The third hit and killed Sebastien Billet, shown here lying dead, with his blood spattered on the ground beside him. Baillie would die later from his wounds in the hospital – a toxic sink of disease and filth – which was in the barn at the bottom left of the picture.

Bramston was far from contrite, swaggering around the prison that morning saying 'If he had killed more it would not have given him any uneasiness.' In the general shouting and commotion after the shootings, another Frenchman, Claude Hallet, was wounded by a militiaman with a bayonet, and the artist shows that outrage too.

Nicholas Cooper thinks the picture may have been painted by a Frenchman, or perhaps by an opportunist Englishman as a form of visual journalism. Certainly the architectural details are made to look a little more French than they appear in other pictures made by Englishmen at the same time. The lanterns on posts are eighteenth-century security lighting; the little building by the moat with steps up to it is the 'necessary house' or privy; and the wheeled carts attached to the barns in the bottom left of the picture are for the night soil.

Sissinghurst:

an Unfinished History

ADAM NICOLSON

Harper
Press

HarperCollins*Publishers*
77–85 Fulham Palace Road
London w6 8jb

www.harpercollins.co.uk

Published by HarperCollins*Publishers* 2008
1

A catalogue record for this book is
available from the British Library

ISBN 978-0-00-724054-8

Set in Postscript Linotype Adobe Caslon and Monotype Photina by
Rowland Phototypesetting Ltd, Bury St Edmunds, Suffolk

Printed and bound in Great Britain by
Clays Ltd, St Ives plc

Mixed Sources
Product group from well-managed
forests and other controlled sources
www.fsc.org Cert no. SW-COC-1806
© 1996 Forest Stewardship Council
FSC

FSC is a non-profit international organisation established to promote the
responsible management of the world's forests. Products carrying the FSC
label are independently certified to assure consumers that they come
from forests that are managed to meet the social, economic and
ecological needs of present and future generations.

Find out more about HarperCollins and the environment at
www.harpercollins.co.uk/green

for Sarah
with all my love

and

for Sally Bushell, Jonathan Light,
Sue Saville and Fiona Reynolds
with many thanks for
their longstanding support and encouragement

CONTENTS

ONE

Sissinghurst

I HAVE OFTEN DREAMED of Sissinghurst on fire. I am in the house, on the middle floor, and above me the boards are cracking. The tiles are falling away on the outside. Smoke pours into the night. But there's no rollocking, licking flame. It's more like a fungus eroding the timbers, a slow and inexorable eating away at the most precious thing I know.

As I see it burning, I am sure I am dreaming of the framework of my life rotting in the heat. It's a form of dissolution, of a valuable thing coming to an end. Sissinghurst is the shape of what I am. I do not own it but it is my place. Anything else can only ever be an approximation to it.

I have lived here, on and off, for the last forty-five years. For my entire conscious life it has been what I have thought of as home, even when living away, in London, or abroad. For all my attachment to other places, Sissinghurst has always seemed like the root. I belong to it. It is the land I have walked over, looked out over, driven through, smoked my first cigarette in, planted my first tree in, bicycled over, slept in and lived in all my life. It is where I came to understand what a tree was, what a friend was, what a hideout was, what a landscape was, how entrancing streams were as they made their way in and out of the margins of a wood, and what solitariness, nature and love might be.

If I think of a view, or of mist on an autumn morning, the way it lies in a valley like a scarf, or the way a stream when blocked makes a reedy place upstream of the blockage, where after time willows grow in the wetness and make a dark summer tent over the bog; if I think of the way wild flowers peak and then collapse as spring deepens into summer; if I think of geese belling across winter fields; or of being alone, or of the transition from childhood to adolescence, of the relationship of a place to its history or its future: every one of those things, strung out across my life, like lights marking a channel, is tied to and founded on Sissinghurst. When I was a boy, it entered my mind as a model of a place, the place against which to measure what the world could be.

There is a tree in the garden, an oak, growing on the edge of the moat that my sister Juliet and I planted together when she was four and I was one. It is nearly fifty years old but, in its tree-life, still in its teens. One or two of the lower branches have been pruned, to improve its shape, and the bark of the oak is creeping back, in pillowed, almost animal ridges, across the scars that the saw has left. But the rest of the tree – it is a strange hybrid, a sycamore oak, which has oak leaves but drops sycamore seeds in the autumn, the single wings helicoptering to the autumn grass – the rest of the tree is in the first glowing moment of adulthood, no leaning in the trunk, a full head of hair, if you can say that about a tree, a kind of bushy-brushed wholeness to it, its trunk like the trunk of a young man. It is now part of the Sissinghurst landscape, rooted, solid, essential, inevitably there, and I feel in my heart as much part of this place as that tree. My nutrients come from this soil.

When I was a boy here in the 1960s, my father used to take us, my sisters and me, down to the stream that runs through the wood, usually after lunch in the winter, to have a boat race. We chose small, fat sticks for boats, to be thrown into the stream where it entered the wood below a marshy patch in the Dog Field. He cut long wands from the hazels for what he called 'hoikers' – the only way, if your stick got caught in the deep trench of the stream, that you could hoik it back into the main flow. No cheating was allowed, nor hurrying on of your stick if it happened to be drifting in a treacle-slow section of the current. It had to be stuck and immobile before you could push it back into the race with the hoiker. The finishing line was the chestnut bridge by the outflow from the lake. All of us cheated when he wasn't looking.

Or there were clearance weekends and bonfires, the brambles and dead wood lopped and slashed away with billhooks and bow-saws, all piled on to a smoky fire, the smoke finding its way out through the roof of the coppiced chestnuts as if through the thatch of a medieval hall. He would send me down to the wood sometimes to start the fire on my own before he came to join me. Start it small, he said, but make it as big as you can. Once he raced me to Bettenham, the neighbour farm to Sissinghurst, half a mile away, him on foot, me on a bike. I remember him now, stampeding down the track ahead of me, uncatchable and distant, however hard I pedalled. Or on a summer morning, at breakfast, on the bleached and knotty deal of the kitchen table, he would pore with me over a 2½-inch map of the Weald, the gridlines pale blue, the occasional contours a browny orange, the stipple of the scattered farms, the fleck of Kentish civilisation, a grey background to it all, each with the blue spot of a farmyard pond. Why don't you go and see what the Hammer Brook is like here – a bridge four miles away down-stream – or here, where it joins the Beult? You see where it says 'Roman Road' there, where it goes down the contours of that hill? Or look, a Roman ford – miles away, south of Benenden, into another parish – why don't you see if you can go and find that?

So I did, alone on my bike for hours and days at a time, looking for these places that he had made precious and important to me. I learned to read the map, which I kept folded in my pocket. I found the Roman road dropping south through woodland beyond Benenden: he must have known it but never told me he did, a place reverberating with the past, a huge trench as straight as it should be, just wobbling here and there like a piece of furniture two thousand years old, half a mile long, exactly preserved and deeply creased into the Wealden hill. I remember it now, its runnel filled with autumn leaves, the hornbeams and hazels on its banks, unvisited, unknown, the most wonderful and vivid antiquity I had ever seen. At the bottom of the valley, on a tiny tributary of the Rother no more than two feet wide, trickling to the south, with ferns and moss around them, I found the smooth dark stones of the Roman ford, scattered in the stream bed, as neglected as they had been since the Romans left 1500 years before.

I would return from these expeditions, excited and exhausted, unaware of the riches I was gathering. Only now do I see this as the best education a child could have: the private discovery of a stretch of country rich in buried meanings, so easily and fluently to hand, to be discovered with nothing more than a map and a bike. Seeing, I suppose, how much I loved it all, the finding of the way, the connections made in three dimensions which the map had hinted at and led one to, we started going on longer expeditions. One June morning, early, when the world was heavy with summer and greenness, we went for a long walk together through the flat, oak-hedged grasslands of the Low Weald towards Biddenden. I was about eleven, my father had a copy of Pevsner, and we walked from one fifteenth-century Wealden farmhouse to another, through the cold morning, the leaves grey with dew, the sun blinking through them, maybe twelve miles or so, admiring the close-set studs, the pitch of the roofs designed for thatch, now tiled, the rooted richness of this country.

It is not the buildings I remember, though, but a long hay meadow on the Hammer Brook, a mile or two upstream, just the other side of Hammer Mill, which we came to as we circled back to Sissinghurst and breakfast. I had never guessed that the world could be so beautiful, that an air of perfection was not something to be dreamt about, but could be experienced on your skin, as a living, seen reality. I thought then and can still imagine now that the meadow was the most beautiful thing I had ever seen. One side of the long narrow green space, perhaps four hundred yards from end to end, all of it walled in by the fresh green of the springtime wood, followed the brook's meandering path. The other took a long straight line against the trees. We were there the morning after the farmer, Mr Hall, had mown the grass. He had begun by following the stream in his tractor and had laid his swathes in repeated, rippling slices which mimicked the stream itself, as if the wavy hair of the field had been combed flat but kept its wave, gleaming early that brilliant morning, like oiled braids, with the pale stubs of the shorn grass between each mown tress, the buttercups laid in with the grass as a summer wreath, a vision of perfection for that moment only, before Mr Hall came back with his tractor later that morning and began to turn and stir the grass with his tedder into the lifted ridges in which he needed it to dry.

We did other things: my father bought a double canoe and for three days we followed the Hammer Brook from where the Bettenham track crossed it, along its winding trench to the River Beult and then on to the Medway until we reached salt water at Rochester. We did the same on the Stour from Great Chart to Sandwich, taking with us this time, in a deliberate act of matchmaking, my cousin Robert Sackville West, so that we would become friends, as we have remained for life. We walked to the North Downs across the Low Weald and then along the Pilgrim's Way. We went to see where William the Conqueror had landed and then Julius Caesar. It was as if my father was conquering Kent for me, not the Kent of commuter modernity but an older place, one in which nature and culture were more intimately bound together

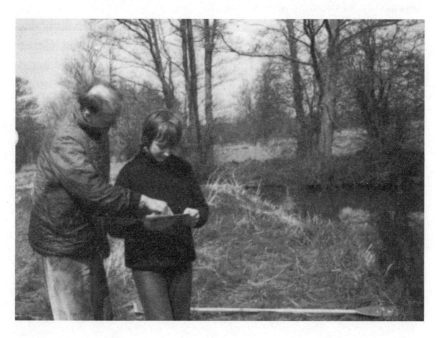

and of which Sissinghurst itself always seemed to be the centre and the exemplar.

Nowhere felt deeper or more like a vein under the skin than down in the bed of the Hammer Brook. It was an entrancing and different world, a green, wet womb, a place of privacy and escape. Going down in there, when I was a boy, was like pushing in under the surface of Sissinghurst, not looking for the large surveying view, or any form of flash display, but for the consolations of closeness and intimacy, secrets and shelter, getting away not by getting out but by getting in. Along the banks, the alders and hazels were so thick that the wavering line of the stream was like a strip of wood run wild. Once beneath them, you were in a liquid tunnel, arched over with leaves, gloomy in its hollows, suddenly bright where the sun broke through, seductively cool when the day was burning on the fields outside. Where the shade was particularly thick, in the depth of the little wood, the sunlight still found its way between the alders and the maples, making spots of light no bigger than a hand or a face, dropped across the darkness as if by a brush, looking like the speckling on the skin of a trout, or those pools of light hair you find on the flanks of a young deer.

The water flowed in riffles over the shallow bed, the gravel banks stained orange with the iron seeping from the ground. Green hanks of starwort sprouted from the stream floor. Occasionally, a small group of trout found its way from pool to pool, dark bodies in the sun, where curtains of the light dropped through the speck-filled water. In this tiny Wealden river, they were not the slick creatures of Wiltshire chalk streams, but flighty, on the edge of viability, darting away even from the shadow of a big dragonfly, a skimmer, manoeuvring in the air not far above them. There were pike here and they must have been fearful of those jaws, but I have stood on the bank and watched a family of about twelve trout, the spotted bodies in the golden water, not hanging as they do in a big stream, but actively seeking prey, a gang of fish on the hunt, the big swaying adults, the slighter young ones, all of them rootling like pigs in the stones of the bed.

It was a world that encouraged slowness, detail, attention.

Downstream of each of the gravel banks, at the head of the still pools, I watched the current circle back on itself in tiny transient spirals, no more than a millimetre deep, slowly whirling through the leopard-spot patterns of light and shade. Nothing showed that the water was moving unless there happened to be the fleck of a seed pod or a fly caught in the surface, making its waltzing, turning progress downriver. Through it all a drowsy current moved, with amber-lit sandbanks far below, and sometimes a drifting leaf caught under a stone, waving up from its bed.

Then, rarely, as a treasure from nowhere, something different: I remember the first time I saw it here. I was standing in the river, the water running up against my boots, and dragging at them, so that the rubber was wobbling with the pull of the current and the tops of the boots were opening and closing like a pair of lips. I had the dog with me, splashing in the shallows, shaking the drops from his muzzle so that his own lips were slapping against his teeth. Then from nowhere it came past us: a kingfisher searing through the gloom, making its turns along this river sunk beneath the fields on either side, a soundless riff played on the river air.

That swerve, a taut, cut line of wing through air, with so much verve to it, as if running the length of an electric wire, was a form of quickness the life of a plodding mammal could never approach, a magnesium strip in the light and dark of the river, travelling through those patches so that it seemed to flash as it passed, a stroboscopic flicking on and off of the colour, but with a continuity, a driven line, leaving only an afterburn on the mind's eye, an under-surface glamour in the shadows of the stream.

I used to leave the house in my windcheater and gumboots and head out to the woods and tracks that cross Sissinghurst from north to south and east to west. These were the places I loved to sink into, away from the noise and business of the house and garden. I dawdled in the wood, under the dark of the leaves; when scarcely a hundredth of the light in the air outside penetrated to the wood floor, the whole place was as cool as a church. The air in springtime by the streams was thick with wild garlic, and later with the sweeter, gentler smell of the bluebells. The swallows and house martins dipped on to the lake and the woodpeckers yaffled in the distant trees. The grassy banks on the field edges were dense with archangel, red campion and stitchwort, before the brambles and the nettles, always the winners in this annual race, strangled and overwhelmed them. All of these were the deep constituents of home. For days at a time, I circled the house and garden, all the public places at Sissinghurst, through this other hidden world, and never, or so it felt, emerged into view. It was as if out here, concealed from the public, the real thing existed, and that other place, over there, was an ersatz version of it, prepared for public view, with public, adult concerns dominating it in a way they wouldn't or couldn't in a distant field or wood.

The only person I ever met in the wood was the woodman. I never knew his name; neither he nor I was exactly adept at conversation, but I liked his thin, silent, pensive presence, as narrow as a rolled cigarette, intensely solitary, shy, turning away from any question to bend over his work. Every year in the winter he would buy the growing timber on an acre or two of wood, an area Kentish men have always called a 'cant'. In a system of management at least as old as the Stone Age, a broadleaf tree if cut (or 'coppiced', the Norman-French word) would sprout again from the stump or stool. Within ten or twelve years, the new shoots would have grown thick enough to be usable for firewood or fencing and could be cut again. In this way the wood yielded up a steady harvest, cant by cant, twelve years by twelve years, and each part of the wood was at a different stage in the cycle: the tall smooth poles ready for cutting, the dense scrubby younger growth, or the cant just cut, shorn and freshened, like a stubble field after the harvest.

Each year the woodman bought his cant, and alone, with his rough shed made from spare poles and a tarpaulin strung across them, he would fell the chestnut, cut the trees to length, split them and peel them, so that by the end of the winter huge piles of clean, shaved lengths and grey shaved bark came to lie around his shelter. The waste he would burn in big fires whose smoke trailed out over the head of the trees like a picture, it always seemed to me, of medieval England. You could have stood in the field outside the wood five hundred or even a thousand years ago and seen precisely that, even heard – if you edited out for a minute the repeated whining and relaxing of the chainsaw – the same sharp-heavy falling of billhook on wood stem, a clunk-cut, half heard across the distance, the same sudden crackle of a flame as it caught.

Then one day late in the winter, he would be gone, sometimes leaving his tractor there, wrapped up in tarpaulins, the rubbed places and hollows still worn around his shed where he had been working, but the chestnut poles gone, leaving only the clean faces of the cut stools. As the spring returned, the anemones flowered in the cleared wood and those coppice stools began to sprout again for their next cycle. Above them, the trunks of the oaks stood out in the air for the first time in years. And in the new openness of the cleared cant, the emergent dagger leaves of the bluebells pushed through the leaf litter as if from individual silos. That sense of purpose was everywhere: the primrose leaves crinkled like a Savoy cabbage, with the flowers just then unfolding; the cow parsley in low soft-edged pouffes about the size of a dinner plate at the foot of the hedges; dog's mercury everywhere in the woods, as well as lords and ladies above the brown wood floor like the blades of soft-bodied spears.

Following that, in the great annual unfolding, the nightingales arrived and sang, as they do now, in two patches of thickety wood, one in an abandoned loop of the river, towards Bettenham, another a third of a mile to the south where the Hammer Brook is joined by the boat-race stream coming down through the Sissinghurst woods. The nightingales sing so loudly that you can hear them half a mile away in the garden by the moat, but faintly, like the weakest of signals picked up by the most sensitive of antennae. I remember that as a teenager once, on a warm night, after dinner, with half a moon shining, when everyone else had gone to bed, I went out towards them, walking and stumbling across the fields to where they were singing in their little moonlit thickets, bubbling and trilling, a song interrupted now and then by long, ecstatic, deep-throated slides into the bass register, which seemed to come from somewhere deeper within a body than any bird could manage. Those notes sounded as if the ground itself were singing. I lay down on the warm earth next to the thicket, in the field by the trees, and listened to one on my left, unseen in the bushes, and the other answering him six hundred yards away up the little valley, first one and then the other, a duet or duel, I couldn't tell. I have read that it is the males who do the singing, and they sit on the ground inside their protective thickets. That is scarcely what it sounded like then: men, for sure, but more like the lords of two manors, shouting from their tower tops, each proclaiming the virtues of their wives and lands, their need for dominance and love of possession, the deliciousness of this thicket, the ridiculousness of the other, the hilarious beauty of this life, all its sorrows and all its wonders. I fell asleep and woke an hour later, with the stars turned in the sky above me, and the two of them still singing away, blow for blow, note for note, their sliding, gurgle-ecstasies exchanged across the moonlight, and I left them there, walking back through the bright blue fields, listening to the sound of the birds slowly weakening in my ear.

Sissinghurst then, in the 1960s, as well as a house, a family home and a garden open to the public, was a fully working farm. James Stearns, the farmer, a big, tall, young man, with enormous hands and a way of looking down at you from a vast height, lived with his wife Pat in the Victorian farmhouse. Seven or eight men worked under him, milking a Guernsey herd, keeping chickens and renting some ground out for Ned Farris's sheep, growing hops, wheat, barley and oats. There were two orchards, one of Worcesters, one of Bramleys, but they soon went. They made hay, still cut faggots from the wood and carted enormous quantities of farmyard manure out on to the fields at the end of every winter. Year after year, ploughing, rolling, harrowing, pruning, hedging, woodcutting, sowing, hop-stringing, sheep-dipping and shearing, mowing, haymaking, baling, clearing the streams, harvesting the cereals, picking the apples and then the hops, year after year, the farm was an intensely worked and busy place.

As a boy, I felt this was only how things should be. The cattle pushing into the yard to be milked, their dung flopping out on the concrete, their sweet, milky breath, the massive stodge of mud and straw they made in their winter housing down by the big Elizabethan barn, the sound in the summer fields of their teeth tearing at the grass, the rough sandpaper lick of their tongues through the bars of a gate, the feeling that they might eat you if they could; the pigs and their own version of stodged-up chaos in the shed where the National Trust shop now is, and Copper, the chauffeur-handyman, telling me that they were the cleanest and neatest of animals; the chickens pecking their way around the pats in the cow field; the flock of Jacob sheep which lived in the field by the lake and were always, it seems, afflicted with foot rot; the harvest moment in the summer when the tall laden carts came back up to the barns from Frogmead and Lodge Field, piled high with straw bales, the men who had been stacking them riding on top, ducking under the branches of the oaks where they came past the moat; the hay harvest in the park, where the lines of cut hay swerved to avoid the ancient trees, leaving eye-shaped lozenges of uncut grass around each trunk, as though the trunks were the pupils of those eyes; the white clouds of blossom in the pear and apple orchards and then the autumn smell of the apples coming wafting to the house on the wind: these were the ingredients of the world as it was meant to be.

Down in the southern end of Frogmead, there was a hop garden. It was only ten acres but seemed huge then, the hops growing in towering alleys stretching miles away into the dark, as if they were the creepers of some Amazonian forest. I scarcely dared go in. But in September, when the hops were ready, they were harvested, the bines cut from the network of wires and string, loaded into trailers, which were then hauled up the track to the oast houses for drying. I used to bike up behind them, a Bisto kid pulled along by a smell that once smelt could never be forgotten: sweet, acrid, vegetable, mineral, woody, flowery, odd, heavy, heady, druggy, earthy and sharp, a taste more than a smell, its acidy resins catching at the back of the throat. I can taste these hops as I remember them now. As the trailers bumped along the track, bruised bodies of individual hops were left lying behind them like little green birds. As I rode over them the air turned green. There is something alien to the smell, not what you might expect from a plant that is native to England. It is more outlandish than that. It is a relative of cannabis, one of the *Cannabaceae*, and the air that hangs about it is smokily dopy in the same way, a subtle and combined smell, a blended soporific that would be more at home away on the other side of the Mediterranean, hidden in the souks of Aleppo or Isfahan.

The tractors came up to the oast house, where gangs of men and women dragged the bines off the back and pushed them into the stripping machines on the ground floor, jiggering and sifting the cones from the leaves and string and stalks, and then feeding them through to the gantry, where they were taken to the kilns.

From below, for eight hours or so, giant diesel boilers dried the hops, which were stacked a yard deep above the slatted floor in the big round oasts. When dry, they were shovelled out on to the upper storey, the hop loft, which was sheeny with a century of resin gelled into place, burnished and sticky with it. Hop lofts are always dark, with small windows, because light degrades a hop, and the only illumination comes sharply in at one side, from the open doorway, as if from the wings. It was a beautiful scene: the walls and beams whitewashed, the fresh hops going into the kilns lime green, the dried hops transformed, their colour, as my grandmother once described them in this same loft, 'a cross between ash and gold, the colour of dust motes, of corn in moonlight'. In the worn and darkened wood of the room, the men brushed the dried hops into piles with birch brooms before pushing them with canvas shovels called scuppers towards a hole in the floor. A giant press stood over the hole, and underneath it, on the floor below, a giant sack, called a pocket, was hung from the beams. Into it the hops were first deftly shovelled and then, as a man turned the giant iron wheel on the press, a weight dropped into the pocket and pressed the hops into their bag. So tight were they in a full pocket that the two top corners of the sack, where it was tied, stuck out like bullocks' ears. Each pocket had stencilled on it the horse of Kent, the Invicta county motto, the name of the farm and of the farmer, still here called A. O. R. Beale, James Stearns's grandfather. At the end of the season, the number of pockets achieved that year was painted on the whitewashed beams above our heads.

I loved the farm as it was then. I loved its detail and business, the sheer fullness of what happened there, the way the young men in the summer with their shirts off would chuck the tractors down the lanes between the buildings, throttle open, work to be done; or the shoving and jostling of the cattle, the business in the hop gardens, the orchards and the arable fields, the way that the men with their Jack Russells would stand around at the door of the barn, sticks in hand, smoking and laughing, waiting for the rats to run, the quivering dogs on the edge of the group, suddenly jumping for the rat in the dust and the loose corn, gripping it by the neck and shaking the body to death, while the men joked and rolled another.

I loved the roughness of that world, the thorns and elders

pushed up against the side of the buildings, the way that tractors would be left parked at loose and unconsidered angles by the garages, the nettles behind the pig shed, the stacks of logs in from the wood, waiting to be sawn in the saw shed next to the piggery, the sense of unregulated space and the freedom that came with that. This was not somewhere that was made for show, but had evolved this way because of what it did. All parts of the wider Weald that I was coming to know on my bicycle; the streams and the wood, the huge beech trees whose outer tips would come down so near to the wood floor that you could climb on to them and walk all the way up to the main trunk; the variety, multifariousness and vitality of this world on my doorstep – all of that was at the root of what seemed good here.

In the middle of it all was the house and garden, where we lived. Our part of the house was in the southern half of the long front brick range, built in the sixteenth century, part of an enormous palace, most of which had long disappeared. My grandparents had not lived here: they had slept in the South Cottage, my grandmother Vita Sackville-West had worked in the Tower, their dining room and kitchen was in the Priest's House, their sitting room in the old stables and their sons' rooms in the old brewhouse. Our house had been adapted in the early 1960s from two cottages, where Mrs Staples, the cook, and the chauffeur, Jack Copper, and his wife, had previously lived side by side. They had now moved to flats in the other half of that range, north of the arch. My mother had installed a new, clean pine kitchen, with dark blue Formica surfaces, and a big six-burner gas stove in the centre of it. Mousse-moulds in the shape of curved fish hung from the wooden ends of the shelves, and there she cooked warm and delicious food, enormous cartwheels of mushroom quiche, sole in creamy sauces, giant pieces of roast beef, and roast potatoes which she fried to make crisp. One summer, when some people we hardly knew came to lunch, they said to her how delicious peas were when they came straight out of the garden. She and I knew they were frozen, Bird's Eye, from the village shop. I had opened the bag earlier for her and poured them rattling into the pan. She thanked our stranger guests, agreed with them and then looked at me and smiled. I see the smile now, her crinkled laughing eyes, our precious secrecy.

That dining room was lit with silver sconces which Vita had brought from Knole. They were fixed to the umber hessian of the walls, and between them hung a large portrait of a Sackville ancestor, the Puritan first earl of Dorset, who had been chosen by Queen Elizabeth to give Mary Queen of Scots the news of her impending execution. His rheumy, pink-edged eyes followed me around the room. Beside him were two pictures by John Piper of Knole in a rainstorm, and a snake strangling a horse, somehow made out of sand. There was a large carved chest, inlaid with mother-of-pearl, which I think may have been Spanish, to hold the glasses, and one or two odd framed things: a drawing on a menu from a London restaurant in 1919, which was Edwin Lutyens's first sketch of the Cenotaph, made for Vita over lunch; a poem of Verlaine's written in high calligraphy on vellum, *Je suis venu, calme orphelin*, an offering to Vita from one of her lovers; and a battered medieval wooden Spanish saint called Barbara, Harold's first present to her when first in love. The place was full of memorabilia, fragments salvaged from earlier lives.

For all that, there was no heaviness about it, nor any atmosphere of gloom or ancestor worship. The very opposite: noisy, talky, warm, engaged, alive, nothing formal. I remember as a boy sitting at the long oak table, my back to the frightening earl, on the tall 1890s faux-Jacobean chairs, with flat wine-red velvet cushions on the cane seats, my father at one end, my mother at the other, my two sisters, our nanny Shirley Punnett and I along the sides, feeling in one of those rare moments when, however fleetingly, you imagine you see your life as it is, in its present form, exactly how it is, with all its parts combining and colluding, that here, at this table, with these people, in this house, with the farm beyond it and beyond that the woods and lanes of Kent – the onion skins of my world – I was happy and even blessed, that no one could properly ask for anything that I had not been given.

Across the other side of the garden, in the South Cottage, my grandfather lived alone, or with the series of young male nurses who looked after him. He had lived there ever since he and Vita had come to live at Sissinghurst in 1932. By the mid-1960s, when he was almost eighty, he was in a sad and pitiable state, broken by a series of strokes and by his grief after Vita's death in 1962. I remember nothing of her. Or what I do remember has been overlaid by books, films and photographs, so that I can no longer distinguish what I remember from what I know. Of him, I knew only his fragility, his sticks, his slow, shuffling progress down the garden paths, his weeping silently as he sat at the end of the lunch table, his gobbling of his food so that he had finished before my mother sat down, his strange clothes, left over from an earlier age – huge white or cream summer trousers with turn-ups, the broad-brimmed hats he always wore, plimsolls looking too small below those trousers, always a tie, however ragged. When he looked at us, it was with an unbridgeable distance in his eyes, as if we were scarcely there. In private and occasionally, he had moments of lucidity, particularly with my mother, in which he told her how much he hated the humiliations of his condition, how much he wanted to die, how much he missed Vita. With us, though, he seemed to be looking through a screen.

The garden then wasn't treated with the sense of exquisite preciousness it is today. My friends and I used to bike around it and invent racetracks through it. The start was at the front of the house, between the nineteenth-century bronze urns and the floppy arms of the old rosemary bushes: down through the medieval gateway into the upper courtyard, sharp right in front of the pink brick Elizabethan tower swathed in clematis, across the lawn and through the narrow gateway into the Rose Garden – a terrifyingly spiny acanthus bush on the corner there – a zigzag through the alliums and the mounds of old roses before hitting the fastest of all straights through the Lime Walk and under the branching hazels of the Nuttery, where I would finally skid to a halt outside the Herb Garden. The whole thing, which is slightly downhill, could be done in just under a minute. If you had left the gate open there, you could cut through it, along the far side of the moat, up the tail end of the Bettenham track and back to the front of the house to complete the lap: three minutes if you were on form.

There were no exclusions. Our dog, Rip, a terrier, chased cats down the Yew Walk and through the Rose Garden. In the evenings my father used to stand on the lawns with a tennis racket and hit a ball as high as he could, sixty, eighty, one hundred feet in the air, and ask one or other of us to catch it as it came down, stinging our fingers or smacking our palms, all for increasing double-or-quits money, starting with sixpence, going up sometimes to the heights of thirty-two shillings, sixty-four shillings, before crashing to zero when you dropped one. We did three-legged races from one end of the courtyards to another. And it wasn't only us: children from the village used to come and play hide-and-seek in the garden. All the gates were always open. There was scarcely a lock on the place. I had a friend, Simon Medhurst, the son of a skilled mechanic and blacksmith who lived in a cottage on the farm, and together we used to make bases for ourselves in the attics of the long range and in the ratty barns. One day we found a pink cardboard box, filled with lead knights and their horses, both men and horses armoured, and plumes on their heads. They had been Vita's toys from the 1890s. Simon, his sister Alison, Juliet and I played in the hay barns, making terrifying tunnels through the bales, filled with the threat of collapse and suffocation. There was a frighteningly dark air-raid shelter in the orchard where we played naughty games of show and tell. More politely and more publicly we had a gypsy caravan where Juliet played at tea parties for our parents and their friends. Or we used to stand all morning in the fruit cage, eating the red and green gooseberries from the bushes and pulling the raspberries from the canes. Above the piggery, Simon and I made a den which no one guessed was there. We dragged chairs up the ladder and made a table from boxes. From there, through the warped gaps in the weatherboarding, we could spy on the world outside.

All of this looks in retrospect as if it might have been a dream of happiness and integration. It wasn't entirely. Inside this beautiful outer shell was a pool of unhappiness. Harold's grief was explicit, but at least that was a symptom of his love for Vita. Between my own parents there was no longer any love. My father no longer slept in the same room as my mother. Very occasionally, their mutual frustrations burst out into the open. I remember one evening at the table in the kitchen, with all of us, as well as my nanny Shirley Punnett, who had been born in the village, sitting around the scrubbed deal, when the two of them began to shout at each other, from one end of the room to the other, a terrifying, exchanging, shouting barrage in the air above us, as if shells were exploding inside the room, and we ran away upstairs to our own rooms in tears. At another time my mother threw precious plates the length of that table, beautiful nineteenth-century plates on which early balloons were painted – they had belonged to Vita – while my father stood there fielding them as if at slip practice.

She couldn't bear to be alone with him and, inevitably, another man fell in love with her. She was sad, beautiful, in her late thirties, and looking for someone who would give her a warmer and more comfortable life than the distant, unsexual and reproachful super-vision that was all my father could offer. She left in April 1969, when I was twelve, and went to live in a flat in London while my father continued to live alone at Sissinghurst.

The warmth left Sissinghurst that day. The warmth left with her. The kitchen there never smelled good or right again. It became cold and inert. My father replaced the old double gas stove with a cheap upright electric thing and had the gap filled in with the wrong-coloured Formica. The house was never warm again. My father shrank into a feeling of hopelessness and despair. He heated the room he worked in with an electric blower, and the room with a television in at the far end of the house with another. The rest of the house remained fridge cold. The cold clung in the walls. Cold seemed to hang behind the curtains and seep up from the floor. If the heating was ever turned on, it would take days for the warmth to penetrate the depths of the house. Getting into bed was like getting into a sea.

My mother had removed some furniture and my father re-arranged what was left to fill in the gaps. He made himself instant meals and boil-in-the-bag kippers. Entire weeks went by in which he ate nothing but bananas and cream, occasionally relieved with a Findus fish pie. If anyone came to lunch, he would get the caterers in. One Christmas, when I was there with him alone, as I had asked to be, we exchanged our presents at breakfast and he went up to his room to work. I spent the morning picking books from the shelves and reading a page or two before returning them to their place. At lunch we had half a pound of sausages each and half each of a side of smoked salmon someone had given him for Christmas. Then we watched television and scarcely spoke. A few years later, when my sisters all came to warm up another Christmas, he went to bed on Christmas Eve and stayed there until we left a week later, his meals being brought to him on trays and a few muffled remarks passed through the door. He could not live with the reality of human engagement. It was as if his need for love, real enough, had never been quite unlocked. I did not know it at the time, but he felt he had failed. Any confidence he had once enjoyed now drained out of him.

He worked in the meanest and pokiest room in the house, with no view from the windows, using a varnished modern table from a shop in Tunbridge Wells, sitting on an old and dirty chair. He rarely turned the hot water on. Was it somehow gratifying to combine this private despair with his charming life outside? I doubt it. His repeated nightmare was standing on the stage in his prep school, while the audience and the rest of the cast waited for him to speak his lines, but no words came and he was left standing there, his mouth silently opening and closing as if he were a fish.

Just at this moment, in June 1976, Jim Lees-Milne wrote about him in his diary, and in what Jim wrote I suddenly see my father not in the clawing, anxious way that children attempt to understand their parents, but from the outside, and through the eyes of an acute and informed observer. 'What an odd man Nigel is,' Lees-Milne wrote.

Affectionate, fair, honourable, just, dutiful, hardworking, a first-class writer, an exemplary parent, an aesthete, exceedingly clever yet modest. At the same time, is he quite human? He speaks didactically, in a precise, academic manner. He is a cold man who wants to be warm, and cannot be. He has humour and understanding, being totally without prejudices. Discusses his parents' love lives as though they were strangers. Asked me whether Harold picked up young men of the working classes. No, I was able to tell him. Asked me if I had an affair with Harold. Yes, I replied, but he did not fall in love with me for longer than three months. Nigel told me he was in love with James [Pope-Hennessy] at the same time as his father was and had an affair with him. I know more about this incident than he thinks. For Jamesey told me he was in love with Nigel and used to lie with him without touching. That has always been Nigel's failing, the inability to make close contact. I expect he regrets it in middle age.

That is not the sort of thing anyone tells their teenage children, and so my sisters and I orbited around the sad and central absence of our father, his regret-filled cold, without ever quite seeing it for what it was, and all of us saddened and angered by it in our turn.

More than anyone I have ever known, he came to polarise the good and the bad in his life: social, warm, delighted, graceful, generous, successful and hospitable summer openness; solitary, unseen, parsimonious, gloom-ridden, cold, unwelcoming winter despair. If we came to stay, he would long for us to leave. I said to him once that he treated his books and everything he wrote in the way that most people treated their children, with endless, careful nurture; and his children in the way most people would treat a book – look into it, see what it has to say and put it back on the shelf. Sometimes, he seemed like the enemy. In his files, he kept the letter from the head-master of my boarding school, saying that I was the most neglected boy the school had ever had. Did he not realise that boys needed visiting from time to time?

He certainly wrote, wonderful letters, which made me cry with longing for home. Only many years later would I come to distrust them, and through them everything about our family's word obsession. Sissinghurst floats on a sea of words. Shelf after shelf in our house was filled with the millions of words a family of writers has produced over three or four generations. Filing cabinets stood around in our corridors and our landings of my grandfather's letters to my father and to his brother Ben, my father's and Ben's letters to their father, my father's letters to me and to my sisters, and all of ours to him. There are hundreds of my father's letters to my mother, if few from her to him, not to speak of the thousands of letters from Harold to Vita and her to him. Harold's diaries and my father's diaries occupied complete cabinets of their own. Yards of shelf were filled with the books they had all written. Tin boxes stood stacked in the corner full of Vita's letters to her mother and her mother's in return. And so there was another landscape here, written and rewritten, sheet after sheet, a whispering gallery of family meanings, lasting more than a century, from my great-grandparents to us, a layered tissue of communication. You could make a mattress of those papers, lie back on it and feel the past seeping up into your flesh like a kind of damp.

But for all the volume, all the drawers and files, there seemed to be something lacking. So much was written but so little seemed to have been said. If I think of those filing cabinets standing there in the corridors, what I see is a world that is said to be private and intimate but is in fact coloured with performance and display, a show of bravado and communication laid over the anxiety and apprehension underneath. How much of it was real? Was this world of written intimacy and posted emotion, of long-distance paternal and filial love, in fact a simulacrum of the real thing? A substitute for it? Nicolson closeness had been a written performance for a hundred years. And that unbroken fluency in the written word made me think that it concealed some lack. If closeness were the reality, would it need to be so often declared?

My father's social life consisted not of a steady stream of friends and visitors but bursts of smart sociability in the summer, what he called The Season. I remember one lunch party he held in which everyone had a title. I looked at it all in the unworldly, unforgiving way of adolescence and as I remember it now I can feel the chill of my own regard. Without pause, for what seemed like weeks at a time, they would discuss the Bloomsbury Group. I deliberately learned nothing about it. There were waitresses and cooks, bottles of Riesling, conversational sallies. In each of the guest's bedrooms my father would provide short, semi-complimentary CVs of the other guests. Only once, thankfully, did he put the wrong list in the wrong room so that one man found himself described as 'past his best'; another as 'patronising.' I looked at my father and thought he was living each day for the account he could write of it the following morning in his diary. After that summer show, he retreated to boil-in-the-bag TV dinners, a sense of diminution and failure. This polarised spectacle, the deep disconnection in him, troubled me then as it does now. I remember accusing him once of 'dishonesty' – the only word I could bring to address this troubled core of unhappiness – and he of course asked me, cold, angry and forensic, for examples, of which, in fear, I could provide none.

As a teenager, I remained both devoted to him and angry for what I thought of as his selfishness, his hiding of the truth, his weakness, his lack of practical love, the theatricality of his life, the way in which he would do little or nothing for us and demonstrate so much vivacity, charm and engagement to those people who hardly knew him and who can have meant little to him. His love of America was the encapsulation of all that: visit after visit, in which he would act 'Nigel Nicolson' in front of adoring audiences to whom the edited version could be presented, before returning to the cold of Sissinghurst, to be that other, self-despising person, living, as he put in his private memoir written in 1985, in 'the morass of self-reproach I feel'.

In that memoir, written when he was sixty-eight, he summed himself up:

> The two great deficiencies in my make-up are lack of judge-ment, and an incapacity to feel deeply, in anger or in love. A mushiness of temperament, a short-cut mind, indolence, no power to execute, a copy-cat mind, poverty of intellect and spirit, constantly wishing myself more rich in scope, self indul-gent, and selfish were it not that I take pains not to appear so,

my generosity fake, my gentleness an excuse for lack of vigour.
It's not a pretty self-portrait.

He was so lonely that he could feel comfortable only with people who scarcely knew him. Anyone who came at all close was, to use the word he used in his own memoir, 'menacing'. Intimacy itself was menacing.

He and I were always different. I liked roughness and in-completeness, the wrinkled suggestion of things, Romanticism, the seventeenth century and authenticity. He liked Palladianism and neatness, the Augustan vision, Chippendale not oak, Jane Austen not Shakespeare, tidiness and the effective display. He couldn't contemplate the idea of religion or psychology; he developed an overt distaste for sex or even any talk of it. I played Bob Dylan loud on the record player but he was unable to listen to music, thinking instead that he should read a book about the workings of the orchestra. He once said to me that if anyone was ever moved by music, it was a symptom of sentimentality.

All he wanted was clarification and tidiness. He was in many ways disgusted by mess and increasingly fearful of the anarchic or the spontaneous. But it is one of the consolations of age that the anger and incomprehension of the adolescent can turn to sympathy and love. I feel towards him now as a father might feel towards a son who seems curiously stuck in his relation to the world, who has not let himself emerge, who has not in some ways let himself *be*, to be the immediate creation of flesh and appetite he, at least in part, might have discovered. It is as if my father spent his life not existing but making himself up, endlessly fashioning a papier-mâché skin to cover the hollow he both knew and dreaded beneath it.

In his later years he cleared, ordered and sorted Sissinghurst. Everything found its place. No letter was written without a copy being kept, none received without being filed. He burned a great deal of the lumber in the attics. All our childhood toys were thrown away. I didn't see any of this for what it was at the time. I was away at school, university and work. I didn't realise that this process of clearing up, of cleaning, sorting and clarifying, not only represented my father's attempt in the outer world to cure the sense of worth-lessness and dirtiness within him, it also coincided with some kind of ending of the world I had known as a boy.

Of course, other factors were in play. The landscape historian Oliver Rackham has called the central decades of the twentieth century 'the locust years'. It was the period when a hungry and powerful simplicity, a rationalist clearing away of the mess, was imposed on the world, when logos was substituted for mythos, the rational fact for the imaginative idea, something rather blank and reasonable for the complex and wavering story. In the outer world, the demands of modern agricultural systems meant that the same simplifying, tidying up and 'making efficient' was occurring across the entire farmed

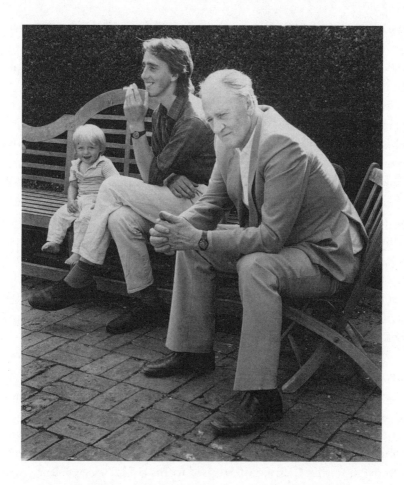

landscape of England. Mixed farms were giving way to more profitable monocultural systems.

Sissinghurst had been open to the public since the late 1930s, and for us the visitors had always been as much part of the place as customers in a shop. A Sissinghurst without visitors would have felt odd and incomplete, as if a play were being performed to an empty house. But in the 1960s and '70s, as Sissinghurst became more famous, the ever-growing numbers of visitors had to be accommodated in new ways. So the hops went, as their market collapsed, and the hop gardens were taken out. The oast houses went silent, to become first a tea room and then an exhibition space. The black tin hop-pickers' sheds, whose pale, light blue interiors were like the miniature parlours of London houses, were demolished. The orchards were grubbed up and grants were given to bring that about. I still remember the lopped branches of the trees lying on the autumn grass and the stubs of the trunks standing there in their orderly rows like an abandoned cemetery. The cattle went and then the farmhands. The tractors went: there was no more of that familiar open-throttle chucking of the tractor through the gap between the pig shed and the garden fence. Then the pigs went and their place became a series of carports of which my father was particularly proud. The Jacob sheep's foot rot became worse than ever and they went. The chickens went. The hay was no longer stored in the brick barn and the old Dutch barn outside it was demolished. The woodshed and the pig shed became a shop. The old granary, where the wood of the partitions was worn by the heavy usage of filled sacks, men and labour over three hundred years, so that the wood inside looked as if it had come from the groynes on a beach: all that was taken out and converted into part of 'The Granary Restaurant'.

Jack Copper died, his garage was taken down and a smooth mown piece of grass with elegant parkland trees replaced it as though a slice of an American campus had taken up residence in the farmyard. My father had the rough, shed-like buildings removed from around the perfect arch of the sixteenth-century barn. The thorn trees and most of the elders that grew next to the oasts were removed, so that their uninterrupted forms could be seen clearly, out and in the open. The cart shed became a ticket office, the dairy and bullpen a coffee shop and plant shop. The stony track was tarred and smoothed. Neatness, efficiency, modern systems and a certain absence and emptiness replaced what had been the lifeblood of a lived place.

No longer was any dung carried out to any field. Dung in fact entirely disappeared from Sissinghurst. No produce from the fields returned to any of the buildings. No animals lived here. No one worked on the farm full time. 'I look at this farm now,' Mary Stearns, James's mother, said to me one day, 'think what it once was and almost weep.' The old veins and arteries of the place, the routes going out into the land from the cluster of buildings at its heart, were not used any more except for ladies taking their dogs for a walk. Only the widened busy arterial lane which is Sissinghurst's umbilicus to the outside world remained an active, living route. Along it came the hundreds of thousands of visitors, all supplies, all the food for the restaurant and all the oil for the central heating. Back along it, all the visitors left and all the rubbish with them.

I scarcely saw this change for what it was, but that is how the real losses occur: invisibly, cumulatively, in a way one cannot grasp or measure. Only afterwards you see that the snow has melted, that autumn has somehow become winter, that the evening or the past is over. Time doesn't slide away from underneath you, as though it were a river moving easily under a bridge, the heavy body of one single thing moving from one state to another. It evaporates, its substance floating off not as a body but atom by atom, unfelt and unheard. Look away and the world changes.

When my father was ill in 2004, Sarah, I and the children came back to live at Sissinghurst. He was fading but outside Sissinghurst was throbbing with its new life. It had become one of the most successful 'visitor attractions' in the south-east of England (180,000 visitors a year, turning over £2 million), and in doing that had slowly and invisibly lost its soul. Remembering what had been here, I came to realise what had gone: the sense that the landscape around the house and garden was itself a rich and living organism. By 2004, all that had been rubbed away. An efficiently driven tourist business, with an exquisite garden at its centre, was now set in the frame of a rather toughened and empty landscape. It sometimes seemed as if Sissinghurst had become something like a Titian in a car park.

I walked a lot around Sissinghurst, its woods and fields. Some-times it filled me with despair. It seemed as if the country was over. It had become a bogus version of itself: thin city, tied together by cars. Get up in the morning at Sissinghurst and you heard the pulse of rural England: not wonderful, variegated birdsong; but traffic – the seamless, unitonal, flat and flattening noise of tyres on tarmac. This ubiquitous presence of traffic in the morning was for me a sudden and terrible measure of what had happened in the twenty-five years I had been away. The traffic laid a lid of sound on everything else. Sissinghurst on those exquisite mornings would be beautiful only if you were deaf.

As I took the dogs for a walk in the wood, the mist lay along the stream in the valley, threading itself in and out between the alders that grow there in a woody marsh. The early sun was pouring honey on the trees and over the fields of the Weald beyond them. Between them, just appearing over the wooded shaws, the tile-hung farmhouses and the white cowls of the oast houses looked, as my father always used to say, as if nothing had happened here since the first maps were made at the end of the eighteenth century. The dogs sniffed for nothing in the grasses. But behind and over it all, the traffic roared, and the traffic was the new reality.

The sound of traffic is the great eroder, the dominant signal that although, in some aesthetic way, little may have changed, in reality everything has. The planning system might have guaranteed that farmers have not sold off garden-sized plots for bungalows. No motorway has been cut through here. But that noise means the old meanings have gone. Was I sentimentalising this? Was it ever different? I feel sure it was. I can remember hearing, as a specific instance, the sound of motorcycles burning up on the road that runs along the ridge above the wood, like a slice cut through the air. That can only mean that the air itself was silent, or near silent. Now it was filled with this aural otherness, a thick substance of the not-here laid all over the here, like woodchip wallpaper slapped all over the walls of a room you used to love.

There was nothing now to be done about that. Nevertheless, I knew in my heart that to look across this landscape now was to see something that was not as it should be. The house and garden were no longer connected to a working landscape. There were no animals here, no farmer who considered this farm his own, no farm building used for farm purposes, no sense that this place was generating its own meaning or its own energies. The fields were inert, with no movement or life in them.

And so, on these morning walks, while my father lay in bed, asking about the garden, the flowers, I could see only a kind of voltage gap: between everything I had, emotionally, invested in this place, inadvertently or not, and the lifeless collection of fields and buildings on which my eyes fell. It looked like façadism to me, an eviscerated pretence, not really a farm any more, scarcely even a place any more: just a beautifully maintained garden dropped between a café and a shop, with some fields somewhere in the background. Is there any atmosphere sadder than an empty, dead barn? Or a field that used to glow with health now simply the sterile medium in which highly chemicalised and industrialised crops could be produced? Christopher Lloyd used to say that there was nothing sadder than a garden path that was not used. But here I saw something sadder still: something which for perhaps forty or fifty generations had been fully alive, now maintained in a condition of stilled perfection. There was no longer any relation of life to place.

The afternoon of the day my father died, late in September 2004, I went up to a hill on the edge of the land that surrounds and belongs to Sissinghurst and for the first time in ten years, and for the only time since, smoked some cigarettes. They were delicious. The burnt matches smelled sweet and woody in the sunshine and the smoke filled my throat and lungs like a drug. It was settling, being there and doing that. I smoked and looked, picking the tobacco from my lips, as nothing much happened in the five hundred acres of wood and farm in front of me, the trees dark blue, the stubble pale with age, a kestrel hanging and then falling into a long curving cruise above the grasses on the edge of the fields.

The top of that hill, only half a mile away from the house and garden which five million people have visited in the last thirty or forty years, is almost private. From there a track drops down the field to the Hammer Brook and then across the cornfields before making its way through a pair of hedges, one old, one new, to the moat, buildings and lawns of Sissinghurst itself. From time to time a man and his dog came past. There was a woman on a grey horse. And a polite couple in green anoraks. A wind from the north-west was blowing across us all, as it would for the next few days, and the flag on the Tower, at half-mast, stood out like a noticeboard of my father's death. The kestrel, now over the alders by the stream, hung and flickered, that steady eye, slid away ten or twenty yards and hung again. Pigeons flustered out of the big wood to the south and flogged their way across the open ground.

Death itself is more than welcome after the strain of dying, and the air that afternoon felt light and heady, as if a clamp had been released. I looked across the fields and felt I could breathe at last, not because my father had died – not at all: I had come to love him – but because the many months of his lying in bed, gradually thinning under his bedclothes, the sheets becoming tents across his bones, as he made inordinate efforts to be polite for his visitors, even for us his children, leaving him slumped and exhausted afterwards, alone with the humiliations of age, the shame you could see every day in his eyes – at last all of that was over.

For all the sense of relief, even if you are in your forties, the death of a father leaves a feeling of orphanage in its wake. A fixed point in the landscape had been removed and the flag flying from the Tower, and extraordinarily bright in the sunshine, was all that remained. I was suddenly responsible for my life in a way I had never been before. I was both free and loose, as if a limb, the limb of my own life, had come out of its socket.

When he died, early that morning, very calmly, his nurse, my two sisters, Sarah and I were all with him and it was, in the end, the steadiest and gentlest of moments. It felt simply, in the quietness of his breathing having stopped, as if the race was over. Only the week before, typically of him, he had given me the *Oxford Book of Death* to read. He had reviewed it when it came out in the 1980s – slightly offended that the literary editor of the *Spectator* had considered him a suitably aged candidate to be its reviewer – and had quoted in the review Henry James's words as he felt death approaching: 'Ah,' the novelist had murmured, 'the distinguished thing.' That is what it felt like the morning of my father's death.

My elder sister Juliet said we should pick some flowers for him: three of the late Iceberg roses from the White Garden, their second flush of the year. We cut them with scissors and put them on his chest near where he lay in his narrow, single bed, with the nineteenth-century drawings of Athens given him by his mother when he was a boy on the wall beside him, a photograph of his brother Ben on the bookshelf, next to a jacket of a new edition of his father's diaries, the window open and the cold September sun coming past the magnolia outside. The doctor arrived and then the undertakers. They carried his body downstairs on a stretcher from which a set of wheels could come down, turning it into a trolley. They wheeled him along the stone path in the upper courtyard and out through the entrance arch. They had brought a blanket and put it over his body and face, but you could see the outline of a person beneath it. The hearse – not a hearse but a white Volvo – was parked by the entrance. It was a Thursday and the garden was closed, as it usually is in the middle of the week, with little chains strung between posts. As I was unhooking them to allow the undertakers to put him in the car, an Italian came up to me, tall, a little agitated. 'Is the garden closed?' Yes, I am afraid it is today. 'But we have come from Italy.' Yes, I'm sorry, it is always closed on a Wednesday and Thursday. 'Why is it closed today?' Because it needs a rest every now and then.

The undertakers had opened the boot of the car and were manoeuvring my father into it. 'But we have come from Milan. Could we not just for a few minutes . . .?' His body was in and the boot down. The Italian seemed not to have noticed what was happening. I am so sorry, I said, there are one or two things going on here today. 'Just ten minutes?' No, I'm sorry, no. The undertakers got into their car, saying they would be in touch later, and drove quite slowly away. 'Five minutes?' asked the Italian, now with his wife smiling kindly beside him.

No, I said, not today.

I thought about my father as I looked at Sissinghurst. All I could feel then was gratitude for his love and affection, for the way, out of his own fragility, he had loved us. Fathers inevitably forget the most important moments in their relationships with their children. There were many, but I remembered one in particular. I talked to him about it one day when he was ill in bed, and of course he had forgotten. I was small. I must have been about seven.

We were at home, looking out at the grass on one of the lawns at Sissinghurst where a mulberry tree used to grow. Gordon Farris, the gardener, was hoeing the beds under the lime trees, and my father described to me the difference between Gordon's work and the work of what he then used to call 'a city slicker'; and the contrary difference in what they earned, and their status in the world because of it. In that tiny parable was bundled up an entire universe of liberal political and social ideas, a kind of moral baseline, a yardstick against which the acreages of life could be measured. There were many other things – more than he knew: the importance of love and work, of treating people properly, of not giving up, not cheating, of friendship, efficiency and honesty; of the love of nature and the landscape; of buildings, history and archaeology; and above all, as the defining frame for all these things, a love of and attachment to Sissinghurst.

I was thinking of this, this gift of a place, with all that word means, as I sat and smoked that long afternoon, looking across a piece of England, of Kent, the Kentish Weald, which I knew better than anywhere on earth. I listened to the traffic booming on the road to the south and looked at the bobbled roof of the woods, on which the sun was just laying its coat of afternoon light, the scoop of hedged fields between them, the shadows of the trees drawn out across the stubble, almost from one hedge to another, the dust lying in pools on the track at my feet. Was this my socket now? Was Sissinghurst, this picture of rooted and inherited stability, to be the frame for the remaining half of my life? That afternoon I thought so, and felt its arms closing around me.

I went down to the Hammer Brook. It was a quiet and windless afternoon. The stream, at the end of summer, was low and the feet of the alders exposed, but here and there along its length, over some of its darkest pools, so deep that there is no telling where the bottom lies, the big, old oaks were standing on the banks and stretching their arms out across the river to the other side. One by one, quite regularly, every now and then, the acorns fell from the trees into the river, a slow, intermittent dropping, occasionally hitting a branch on the way down and ricocheting through the tree,

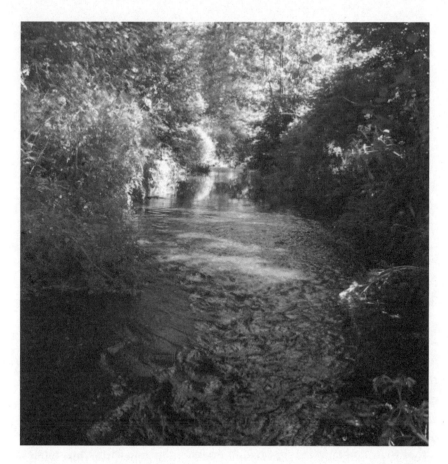

but more often a steady, damp, percussive music: a plum-like plop, a silence, and then another, *glop*. The acorns didn't float, but sank into the depths of the pool to join the piky darkness of the river bed.

When there was a gust of wind, some of the leaves came floating and zigzagging down to the water, where they landed on the surface as curled boats, to be carried away downstream, or more often caught in the banks, or on the logs and branches that stuck out from them, where in the damp they started to rot, already becoming humus, returning nutrients to the soil from which they had sprung. Meanwhile the soft, slow oak-rain continued, a glugging, swallowing cluck or two each minute, the dropping sound of history and time, mesmeric as I listened to it, the twin and opposite of fish rising, the gulp of a river swallowing seed.

'The past is never behind,' John Berger wrote in *Pig Earth*, his great collection of tales and meditations on life in a small village in the French Alps. 'It is always to the side. You come down from the forest at dusk and a dog is barking in a hamlet. A century ago in the same spot at the same time of day, a dog, when it heard a man coming down through the forest, was barking, and the interval between the two occasions is no more than a pause in the barking.' That is what I have come to understand about the acorns dropping into the Hammer Brook. Nothing is intelligible without the past, not because it is the past but because it is the missing body of the present. The bed of the Hammer Brook has always seemed to me like an ancient place, where without effort one can see and feel what it was like here in the distant past, but Berger's point is more than that. In places like this, at this level, time has not passed at all. The dropping of the acorns is how things are.

I came to realise what I was hungry for, not that afternoon, but in the weeks and months that followed. It was to revive a landscape that had been allowed to forget its past. That desire, my attempt to make it a reality and a belief that it was something that had significance beyond Sissinghurst, is what this book is about. I knew that to understand it I first had to go back to some roots and sources, to the beginnings of this place, to establish some of the foundations, to understand what the historical beginnings of Sissinghurst had been, to discover its hidden meanings. But even as I began to think about them, I understood that the place I remembered, with all its multifarious life, was the last of the great continuities that stretched back from here deep into the past. By chance, just at the moment it was coming under the knife, I had been allowed to see it, before the locust years ate away at its body. In the light of that, those years, the years of 'modernity', seemed now to have been an aberration. The lasting fact was the system as it had been. The new sanitised monoculture was a short wrong turning. All I wanted was to rejoin the main path.

How to make these landscapes live again? How to sew back

together the very things that modern life seemed to have severed: people and place, good food and good environments, what was done now and what had been done here before? How to reconnect? That was the all-important question: how to reconnect the deeper meaning of the place with the way it existed today. That need for connectedness became the driving motive for me. If I could help steer Sissinghurst towards a richer condition, that would be a form of reclaiming it, of moving it on to another stage in its existence. Sissinghurst had to be restored to a fullness of life, but how to do it? That was the task and the question.

TWO

Inheritance

SISSINGHURST BELONGS TO the National Trust. In a cabinet on the first-floor landing, my father had left a file for me. All the relevant papers, carefully arranged in chronological order, some of them marked with Post-its, told the story of how and why he had given Sissinghurst to the Trust in the 1960s. Soon after he died, and after I had replied to the five hundred condolence letters we had received, I sat at his desk and read through the file. I knew that if I was going to do anything for Sissinghurst I had to understand the relationship with the Trust in detail. Nothing would happen here unless the Trust came to share the ideal.

By June 1962, when Vita died, the Trust had already become a complex organism, well into its middle age. It is a profoundly English institution, in love with the past and with the natural world, polite in its ideals and civilising in its aims. As David Cannadine has written, it had its beginnings in a period at the end of the nineteenth century when along with 'royal ceremonial, the old school tie, Sherlock Holmes, Gilbert and Sullivan, test match cricket and bacon and eggs' a whole clutch of institutions was established which have survived and have come to define a certain kind of Englishness. The Society for the Protection of Ancient Buildings (1877), the *Dictionary of National Biography* (1885), the Royal Society for the Protection of Birds (1889) and *Country Life* (1897) are all the National Trust's contemporaries. It had begun in 1895 with a high-minded, liberal, philanthropic desire to bring the solace of the untouched natural landscapes of England and Wales to the multitudes of Britain's industrial cities. The properties it owned – largely pieces of beautiful landscape – were to be 'open air sitting rooms for the poor'. After

1918, that liberalism morphed into its conservative cousin, a Stanley Baldwinesque longing for the perfections of a forgotten age. In the late thirties and even more after 1945, that reactionary glow to the Trust deepened once again into the phase that still marks it in the minds of many. With a helping hand from the Old Etonian Labour Chancellor Hugh Dalton, the Trust was able to acquire a string of country houses and their estates, not through buying them, but through the Treasury transferring these precious places to the Trust in lieu of death duties and as a memorial to the dead of the Second World War. As a central part of this Country House Scheme, the donor families, as they were called, were allowed and encouraged to remain in the houses which they no longer owned.

Presided over by the spirit of the charming, arch-conservative, gentry-loving Jim Lees-Milne – one of my grandfather's most devoted lovers – the Trust became an elite oasis in which a version of old England was able to survive. It was, until the mid-1960s, a club for aesthetically inclined grandees. Its all-important Historic Buildings Committee was made up almost entirely of peers. When a man called John Smith (who later founded the Landmark Trust) was proposed as a member, the chairman, Viscount Esher, said, 'I suppose it is a good thing to have a proletarian name on the Committee – anybody know him?' 'Yes,' said the earl of Euston, 'he is my brother-in-law.'

The curators and designers who formed a (largely gay) coterie at the centre referred to the muddy-booted agents and land managers in the regions as the 'mangel-wurzels'. There was little concern for the realities and subtleties of landscape ecology. What mattered was the elegant view and the general sense that here at least the inroads of the vulgarising masses had been resisted. Enormous liberties were taken not only with historic interiors (where the favoured decorator, John Fowler, devised a kind of all-purpose National Trusty loveliness) but with historic gardens (Hidcote had its authentically vulgar cherry trees removed) and important landscapes (the great if battered avenue at Wimpole in Cambridgeshire was needlessly cut down and many of the Trust's ancient woods were planted with conifers). Angry reports by the conservationists springing up in the

1960s regularly condemned the organisation for an indifference to the things that really mattered.

The 1960s saw the beginning of a fourth phase: more efficient, less introspective, more commercial, pushing for large-scale membership and large-scale visiting, publishing more, opening up the previously hidden parts of their properties, getting serious about nature conservation. This was just the moment Sissinghurst engaged with the Trust. It had become a classic English organisation, riddled with tensions: moneymaking against high-level aesthetic appreciation; wide-scale access against conserving the fragile and the delicate; purity against populism; a grandee vision against popular need.

Both Vita and Harold had a long relationship with the Trust, serving on its committees and writing its guidebooks, even in Vita's case the guidebook to her beloved Knole after the Trust had taken it over in 1948. Harold had eventually become vice-chairman of the governing council. Sissinghurst and the Trust were always in each other's orbit, even if, for Vita in particular, its value was ambivalent. It represented for her both the preservation of what was precious and the very forces of bureaucratisation and mediocrity against which the precious needed to be preserved. When in 1954 my father, rather bravely, first mentioned to her that he thought the Trust might be the ideal owners and managers of Sissinghurst, it did not go well. 'Never, never, never,' she wrote in her diary that evening.

> Au grand jamais, jamais. Never, never, never. Not that hard little plate at my door. Nigel can do what he likes when I am dead, but as long as I live no Nat. Trust or any other foreign body shall have my darling. Over my corpse or my ashes; not otherwise. It is bad enough to have lost my Knole, but they shan't take S/hurst from me. That, at least, is my own. Il ya des choses qu'on ne peut pas supporter. They shan't; they shan't; I won't; they can't make me; I won't; they can't make me. I never would.

About ten days after Vita died in June 1962 my father met the Trust's secretary, Jack Rathbone, 'all casual like', for a drink in the

Travellers' Club in Pall Mall. Would they be interested in taking Sissinghurst on? Vita's estate was worth about £100,000, on which there was £38,000 of inheritance tax to pay and hardly any cash to pay it with. Harold was chronically in debt and Vita had spent almost everything she had on the garden and buildings. My father's only options were to sell the whole thing, sell everything else he had or give Sissinghurst to the Trust. Only by giving it to them could he guarantee that his parents' life-work, far more lasting than anything either of them had written, would have a chance of surviving. Rathbone agreed to a visit.

He and Sir George Taylor, the head of Kew, came down by train on 5 July 1962. My father was with them, at his most Tory MP charming. He gave them copies of the Sissinghurst accounts. It all looked neat, the books balancing satisfactorily year on year. Money from the garden visitors, farm rents, timber sales and the sale of plants just about covered the costs of the six gardeners, the secretary, the chauffeur-handyman, the cook and Mrs Honeysett, the daily. Rathbone and Sir George – described by my father in his diary as 'a big bluff man, rather like an Australian who has discovered an unknown gentian in the Andes' – arrived at Staplehurst station in a good mood. There they were met by Jack Copper, the chauffeur-handyman, famous at Sissinghurst for two things: the home-made hand grenades he had prepared during the war in case the Germans arrived; and the cider press he kept at the back of the garage for a swift one whenever any of the gardeners or farmhands felt a thirst coming on, as they did most afternoons. A famous incident involved Vita walking out of the garden and down to the garage, to find George Taylor, one of the gardeners, coming towards her.

'Drunk again, George,' Vita said.

'Are you, madam?' George said. 'That's funny, so am I.'

A companion story, which has lurked for years in the Sissinghurst undergrowth, never mentioned by my father, tells of Vita, after a glass or two of sherry in the Tower, being taken by the gardeners in a wheelbarrow to her bed in the South Cottage.

Here, immediately, was a signal of that other Sissinghurst world: rough around the edges, idiosyncratic, authentically itself,

not smoothed or sheened, not tightly controlled but a little im-
proper, alcoholic, not quite respectable. That morning, the grandees
from the Trust wanted to see something of the estate, and so my
father told Copper to drive round by Bettenham. Leafy lanes, lovely
views, everything going very well until Copper pulled over. He
had got himself lost in the four miles between Staplehurst and
Sissinghurst. I can imagine my father's clearing of the throat. 'We'll
have to go round by Horse Race.' Eventually they arrived, having
lost the way again, coming in over the 'smooth shorn grass between the orchards' to find the secretary, Ursula Codrington, who
had some thwarted dramatic ambitions, coming out of the entrance
arch 'looking like an Andalusian peasant with a striped apron'.
She was followed by the two head gardeners, Pam Schwerdt and
Sibylle Kreutzberger – both impeccably and utterly English despite
their names – who were desperately anxious at the threat of a dead
managerial hand being applied to the place they loved. They had
been getting ready for a fortnight, sweeping and preening the place
so that it looked as perfect as they could make it. Nervous intro-
ductions, then the slow walk round: upper courtyard grass and the
purple border, the Tower lawn with pink and lemon-yellow roses
trained against the walls, the Rose Garden, in which the ancient
damasks and gallicas were erupting in slow vegetable fountains,
the Lime Walk and the Moat Walk, the Herb Garden with its
view out to the wood, the orchard, the White Garden, the stony
half-Mediterranean Delos, the greenhouses, the vegetable garden,
while the two great men tested the competence of the gardeners at
every turn.

Then a pause, and the secretary of the National Trust turned to
Nigel and said, 'Do you know the thing I like most at Sissinghurst?'

'No,' said Nigel, looking anxiously at Pam and Sibylle.

'I just love the fact that it is quite so untidy.'

'Untidy?'

'Well, you know, that relaxed look, as if no one has bothered to
tidy up.' Nigel rushed them all up the Tower. 'The whole Weald
was bathed in sunshine,' he wrote to my mother in London that
evening. 'I have never seen it so clear. I pointed out the boundaries

of the estate. The clock struck one. It was at that moment I think that the fate of Sissinghurst was decided. It will pass into the hands of the National Trust.'

Or so he hoped. Rathbone and Taylor recommended acceptance of Sissinghurst but only 'subject to finance'. Their previous acceptance of houses and gardens without thinking hard enough about the money had landed them in trouble. Nigel's first breezy suggestion was to give the house and garden to the Trust, sell most of the farmland to raise an endowment and keep the nearest fields and woods for himself. To this Rathbone replied that Sissinghurst represented 'a very difficult financial problem'. In October 1962, he warned Nigel that 'this is likely to be a long business'. My father wouldn't have that. In December 1962 he was tugging at Rathbone like a terrier. 'Don't you think we should take this a stage further. It would be nice if we could have the thing agreed before the opening of the garden in April [1963].' Rathbone: 'It may take a little longer than that.'

By January 1963, my father had refined his proposal: house and garden to the NT, plus some surrounding farmland, most of the rest sold off to raise cash with which to endow the property with £15,000 and a couple of fields kept for himself. He and 'any descendants of mine' would have the right to live there for free. He would act as the Trust's unpaid manager and have the right to be consulted over any decision affecting Sissinghurst. Any income at Sissinghurst would remain at Sissinghurst. Its coffers would never be drained for general National Trust purposes – this profoundly valuable clause made at the suggestion of the National Trust itself.

The proposals were to come up before the NT finance committee that July. They looked at Nigel's figures for income and expenses and reached a set of gloomy verdicts. After Vita's death, they were sure that visitors would fall away. They had no inkling of what would actually happen: that Vita's Sissinghurst, which seemed a little out of date in the early sixties, would come to represent for hundreds of thousands of people a lost world of romance and beauty. It is as if the Trust in the early sixties were not quite aware of the hunger for the past which would build so powerfully over the next thirty years. Kipling's house at Bateman's in Sussex, which the Trust had owned since the 1930s, had never been popular with visitors. Why should anyone be interested in the garden of a minor poet, long since unfashionable and 'back-number' as Harold had called it? The Trust also thought that the beauty of the garden itself would slowly and inevitably diminish as Vita's inspiration sank into the past. It was, anyway, going to be increasingly expensive to keep the buildings going. The Trust had standards of maintenance which were higher than a private individual's. Besides, Vita had been underpaying her garden staff and wages would now have to rise. There had to be allowances made for disasters and contingencies. There were management costs. The Trust had accepted responsibility for Knole without an adequate endowment and now they were suffering an intolerable financial burden there. Their 'realistic forecast for the future' at Sissinghurst saw a heavy ongoing annual deficit of £3625. If the Trust were to take Sissinghurst, Nigel would have to provide an endowment big enough to make up that annual shortfall. On top of that, he would have to pay a market rent if he was not to fall foul of the Inland Revenue. As it stood, there was no way the Trust could accept my father's offer.

Nigel wrote to Ivan Hills, the Trust's area agent:

> Your draft budget is appalling. If the logical consequence is that the Trust could not take Sissinghurst without an endowment of something like £90,000 [the amount required to generate £3,625 a year; about £1.5 million in 2008 terms] then very regretfully we would have to abandon the idea, for I haven't anything like that amount of money in the world. I haven't any idea where this amount of money is to come from. Annual repairs, contingencies, £800 a year for a management fee, a gardens advisor ... And now you tell me that, in addition to that, I shall be expected to pay a rent. Really I can't do this.

Three-way negotiations between my father, the Trust and the Treasury dragged on through 1963 and 1964. Nigel remained convinced that the Trust had overestimated costs and underestimated income. He wrote to my mother: 'It is difficult to see why they need £3000 more than we have ever spent on it ourselves. "Oh," says Jack Rathbone, "the Tower might fall down." "Well," I say, "it won't fall down every year."' Negotiations were opened with other government departments and by January 1965 the Trust had managed to extract from the Ministry of Works the promise of an annual grant to cover the expected shortfall. With that in their pocket, the Trust decided to accept Sissinghurst if Nigel could provide a £15,000 endowment. He was earning £3000 a year at the time but the sale of Bettenham and Brissenden farms could raise the cash.

Rather gallantly, at the same time he had embarked on a new conversion project for turning the southern end of the front range into a single family house. Neither he nor my mother wanted to spend their lives, as his parents had done, traipsing between bedrooms in the South Cottage, sitting room in the old stables, dining room in the Priest's House, workroom in the Tower, children's rooms in the brewhouse. It was to be one warm, centrally heated, hot-watered house for a single happy family. By 1965, he had spent £17,000 on that, inserting a beautiful new oak staircase, my mother's modern kitchen, a big sitting room and eight bedrooms into what had been the two cottages occupied by Mrs Staples and the Coppers. I remember moving in that summer, the physical pleasure of the big new oak doors, my bedroom up in the attic, one dormer window looking out to the poplars at the front, the other to the Tower and the wood, my mother at home in the kitchen, and the dreadful leaving of it that September as I went away for the first time to boarding school in Oxford.

He loved Sissinghurst more than anything in the world. He adored his father and in a more distant way admired his mother. The remaking of Sissinghurst was the best thing they had done, they had done it together and its preservation was, for my father, an act of intense filial duty and care. Sissinghurst was them. He could never have let it go or cashed it in and still looked at himself in the mirror in the morning. He needed to preserve Sissinghurst, he wanted for me not to have to sell it, and by the autumn he had become desperate. He offered the Trust everything he owned: all books, pictures, silver, the small islands he owned in Scotland, if only they would take Sissinghurst off his hands.

> Sissinghurst is somehow kept going while my resources are running out. Everyone here is gradually losing faith in the deal coming off at all. Meanwhile our finances are very delicately balanced and there are almost no reserves. The weekly wage bill is large for a private house. There is no income from the garden throughout the winter months. I am taxed on the income I get and the rents. I pay interest to the Treasury. All this is draining what little I have left. I shall simply not know what to do if the negotiations are not completed soon.

Faintly, in my memory, looking now at these blurred carbon copies of his letters, I see myself then, aged eight, that Christmas, putting my head around the corner of the door into his workroom, his anglepoise light down low over the surface of the table, smoke from his cigarette curling up into its beam, a yellow biro in one hand, and the fingers of the other pushing back over his scalp through his hair. Briefly he looks up at me and smiles.

The uncertainty dragged on for the best part of another year. Treasury officials did not respond to letters for months. Civil servants moved jobs and the details of the case were forgotten or pushed to the back. My father's attempts at a viable budget became ever more agonised until, at last, in August 1966, a breakthrough, a very English solution. He realised there were strings to be pulled: he had been at Balliol with Niall Macdermot, the Financial Secretary to the Treasury. Nigel wrote to him: 'My dear Niall'. Surely he could get something moving on this? Within a month the juices started to flow and the Treasury accepted the offer of house, garden and farm. The sale of Bettenham and Brissenden raised quite enough money for an endowment. There was no talk of a rent. Nigel would not have to give the Trust everything he owned. The Ministry of Works would give an annual grant for five years to cover the expected deficit. By Christmas 1966, it was settled. A solution that had seemed inadequate for years now for some reason seemed to be perfectly fine.

On 6 April 1967, the metal plate saying 'National Trust Sissinghurst Castle' arrived from the Royal Label Factory. On 12 April, my father wrote to the new secretary of the Trust, Jack Boles:

> My dear Jack,
>
> This is just a note of thanks from your newly adopted child. I heard today that everything was completed according to plan and the announcement will be made this afternoon.
>
> So ends happily negotiations which have lasted almost five years. I have a real affection for the Trust, deepened by this experience, and to me it will cause no pang when I raise your metal plate this evening at our gate. I feel only gratitude and thankfulness that Sissinghurst will thus be preserved for ever.

Juliet and I went up with him to the top of the lane that evening to see the new plate on its new oak post, which Jack Copper had set up that afternoon. It meant nothing to me then, but everything to him. He felt, I think, that he had done his duty to this place, that he hadn't wrecked it, or simply disposed of it, or betrayed his inheritance. The National Trust was a resting place, a cradle from which threat could be warded off and change kept at bay. It had come at some emotional cost. That April, my mother wrote to him:

> It's time you left this place for a while. It's wrong for you to stay here all the time. You become confused and muddled as to how you and I should regard Sissinghurst. Finally, now you've achieved the assurance of its protection, you may have to worry a

bit how you care for and protect your family. But away from us all you may be able to consider this rationally.

A few days later he set off for a four-month tour of Europe, writing a book about great houses of the Western world.

My father had saved Sissinghurst. He had bound together house, garden and most of the farm in a single quasi-public ownership. By doing that he had made it inviolable and established our own family's presence here for ever, at least in theory. And the process of how he did it was at least in part a model for me, forty years and a generation on: engage with the world as it is; keep pushing; don't be put off by the sluggards; keep your sense of humour; don't be afraid to show your teeth now and then; but don't hold grudges; be generous and grateful; always have the goal in mind; but remember too that Sissinghurst isn't everything. He had done it well, with all the qualities required: doggedness in a corner, love of Sissinghurst, acumen, persistence. The National Trust had shown itself too: as a rational operator, prepared to be patient, in for the long term – it was to own Sissinghurst 'in perpetuity' – financially cautious, dedicated to an ideal of beauty, not afraid to say no and not be swayed by emotion or romance.

I had never before embarked on any enterprise that involved steering a large corporate body in a new direction. I had worked for newspapers, broadcasters and publishers, I had founded and run with my cousin Robert Sackville West a small publishing company. But each of those involved making something new and self-contained. This would be different: a change in ideals and practices for something which already felt it was doing fine. The systems at Sissinghurst were heavily dug in and highly evolved. They would have bucketfuls of answers to any proposal I might make. It would be a case of uncorporate man meeting corporate life and both, inevitably, being changed in the process.

I realised if I was going to propose something to the Trust I had to know in some detail what had happened on the farm here in the past. In 2005, there was no farmer at Sissinghurst. The land was let out to four separate farmers who had the bulk of their businesses elsewhere: a pair of brothers, the Pipers, who were expert arable men from Hawkhurst; two different graziers, June Munday and Ian Strang, who kept sheep and cattle here; and a man and his son, the Farrises, who owned a wood on the northern edge of the farm and rented a couple of Sissinghurst fields next to it, on which they grew game crops for their pheasants. It was a place that had been cut in four. It was the landscape equivalent of low-maintenance gardening.

From the 1920s until 1999, the very opposite had been true. A dynasty of outstanding men, their wives, sons and daughters, had been the farmers both on Sissinghurst Castle Farm and at Bettenham, its neighbour. Captain A. O. R. Beale, known as Ossie, a decorated hero in the First World War, had been the tenant here in the 1920s and '30s. In 1945 he had gone into partnership with his son-in-law, a Canadian pilot from Coastal Command, Stanley Stearns. After Stanley's death in 1967, a partnership between Stanley's son James Stearns and his uncle John Beale had taken on the farm and continued with it until James's retirement in 1999, when the present four-part system was set up. James and his wife Pat still lived in the big Victorian farmhouse, which they ran as a bed-and-breakfast. James's mother, Mary Stearns, Stanley's widow and his sister Linda, with her husband, Brian Clifford, still lived side by side in the two halves of Mount Cottage on the north-west corner of the farm. His uncle, John Beale, and cousin Nick lived in the Priest's House.

The Beales-Stearnses were long-standing Sissinghurst families quite as much as the Nicolsons-Sackville-Wests. It was clear that in them there was a deep reservoir of understanding about how this place might work as a single, integrated farm again. So I talked to them all. One morning early in 2005, James walked me round the fields. All the generalised nonsense that people talk about landscape fell away with the farmer's eye, with James's big bass voice and his gentle, half-hesitant, half-adamant air. The engine room of the farm, as he called it, was in the northern half, the big arable fields called Lodge, Large, Frogmead and Eight Acres. 'You could get four and a half tons an acre of wheat off all of them in a good year,' he told me, looking at me with his huge bloodhound eyes. Some of Frogmead lay a little frosty and so 'you would need to be careful if you were thinking of putting fruit in there'. In other words: don't. The hops did well in Frogmead but only a madman would consider setting up a hop garden nowadays. The economics of hops were in tatters, destroyed by a combination of lager (which needs no hops) and chemical substitutes, which were said to flavour the beer just as well.

The whole of the rest of the farm was, in James's view, rather subsidiary to that northern arable block. He had never been a great man for animals, and all the photographs his mother showed me of him when he was young had him sitting on a tractor, ploughing or bringing in the harvest. The belt of grazing around the Castle and garden, the four wet fields, known as the Well Fields, in the far south-western corner of the farm, and the very rabbity Horse Race and Nine Acres, all varied in his mind from 'too small' to 'clogged' and merely 'rubbish'. Only the Park and the Cow Field next to the old dairy survived James's general verdict that the arable engine room was what counted. What was so good about the Park? It made 'beautiful blue soft hay', especially at the far end. And the Cow Field? 'It's the best bit of dirt on the farm. The cows were always turned out on to it and it would grow anything now. It's wet along the southern edge and up in the northern corner. I think there might be a broken drain there. But the rest of it: you couldn't look for anything better.'

I had never heard anyone talk about Sissinghurst like this before. No one here had ever talked to me about dirt as a lovely thing. It was as if James was a voice from the past, from a time that understood the reality of something I only half remembered, a reality beyond the reduced condition of the modern world. I loved talking to him, and I could see he loved talking to me. I don't think anybody had talked to him like this for years.

Even so, I knew this emphasis on heavy arable cropping was not quite the whole picture, or at least it was a picture that had already come down from the high point it had achieved a little earlier under his grandfather. I went to the National Archives in Kew. During the war, confidential reports were made to the government about the state of every farm in the country. I looked up the Farm Survey Record made at Sissinghurst and Bettenham on 4 June 1941. The two farms were being run in tandem and the farmer was listed as Captain A. O. Beale. Here at last, in all the sterility of a ministry form, was the picture I had been looking for, the concentrated meaning of a place complete in itself, quite straightforwardly listed in the printed boxes and dotted lines of an airmail-thin, sky-blue government form.

The mixed and variegated fields were laid out in front of me: 93 acres of wheat, 7 of barley, 11 of oats, 1 of rye, 5 of mixed corn and

23 acres of beans, into which the animals could be turned at the end of the year. There were 3 acres of first early potatoes and 5 of main-crop. (These the Beales used to sell to local schools and individuals, bag by bag.) There was kale, a little rapeseed, an acre of turnips and 2½ of mangolds. There were 10½ acres of hops in Frogmead and 46 acres of orchard with grazing below the trees. The 15 acres of peas were to go for canning. Fifty acres of meadow were to be made into hay and 144 acres of grass to be grazed by 45 head of cattle and 600-odd sheep, ewes and lambs. There were 12 pigs and 27 piglets, 110 chickens, 4 horses and 21 people, men and women, boys and girls, working here.

It was no fantasy, then: here at one level farther down than James's memories was his grandfather's farm at full stretch at the height of the war. All of it, according to the report, was in a near-perfect condition: rich, busy and complex, with piped water to the farmhouse, fields and buildings, all fences, ditches, drains, eight farm cottages and the farmhouse itself in good repair, with no infestation of rabbits or moles, rats or mice, rooks or wood pigeons and with no derelict fields. Two 22-horsepower Fordson tractors as well as five fixed engines powered the work on the 450 acres Captain Beale rented from Vita. Messrs S. J. Day and L. Holland, who compiled the report, wrote that 'This farm is being farmed to full capacity in a most excellent manner. The present arable crops being especially good.'

I looked through the neighbouring farms. There was no scrimping of criticism there. Captain Beale's neighbours would have been crushed to read the verdicts written on them and their farms: lack of energy, insufficient attention, no good with hedging and ditching, illness, ignorance, lack of experience and ambition, lack of modern knowledge, 'not enough pains being taken with the arable', 'I do not think the occupier has much idea of how to manage land', poor ploughing techniques, their farms infested with magpies, anthills, docks and charlock, thistles, their ditches clogged, their fields too small, their drainage hopeless, their houses reliant on wells and without electricity. Almost alone in the entire parish, Bettenham and Sissinghurst Castle Farm stood out as a joint model of completeness.

'The Hon Mrs VM Nicolson' filled in her own form, listing her half-acre of maincrop potatoes, 6 acres of orchard and grass, 1 acre of vegetables for humans, her 3 cows, 18 ewes, 42 chickens, '1 motor mower for lawns (not used yet this year)' and '1 engine to drive circular saw for wood'. I knew that engine, still there when I was a boy, connected with a long wobbling belt to the naked saw-wheel which would spin to a blur when Copper started it up with the crank and make its own repeated animal whine as he pushed one log after another past its revolving teeth. Vita could not 'give the best estimate you can of the annual rental value' because 'much of it is a pleasure garden'.

There are moments when you realise that what you had only been sleepwalking towards has suddenly acquired a substance and a materiality. That is what it felt like at the varnished beech desk in the National Archives, looking at these forms, which I am sure no one had looked at since the 1940s. I do not need to have the fields at Sissinghurst in front of my eyes to see them in every detail, but that morning I saw them as I knew I wanted them to be.

Linda Clifford, James Stearns's sister, gave me something even better: her grandfather's farm diary for 1954. Here, fourteen years later, in the peak of the 1950s boom, were the same pair of farms still pursuing the same wonderful, variegated, polycultural ends. Captain Beale, now in partnership with Stanley Stearns, still had seven men working for him, not to speak of the thirty or forty hop-pickers who came down from London in the autumn and stayed in the sheds beside the Hammer Brook, where their foundations and bits of corrugated-iron roof are still to be found in among the brambles. There was a herd of dairy shorthorns at the Castle, and another of Guernseys at Bettenham. There were pigs and sheep, all the same cereals, as well as plums, pears and two sorts of apples. The breathtaking part of it was the work programme for the year. I made an abstract of the year's tasks:

Ploughing (Jan 20; July 23 Tassells; Oct 4)
Defrosting pipes (Feb 1)
Litter yards (Feb 1, 2, 11)
Snow clearing with dung lifts (Feb 2)
Sawing (Feb 5)
Shooting foxes (Feb 8)
Hedging (Feb 9)
Pruning (Feb 9, Nov 5)
Woodcutting (Feb 9)
Sowing (Peas 12 March; Barley 13 March; Wheat 15 March; Clover under barley April 13; Kale July 30 (Bettenham); Oats Oct 6; Wheat in Banky Nov 3)
Hop dressing (15 March)
Moving poles in hop garden (28 March)
Rolling (April 9, 13)
Harrowing (April 13)

Hop stringing (April 14, May 17, 29, June 1)

Sheep dipping (April 14)

Faggot carting (30 April, May 17)

Weeding (30 April)

Turning our heifers (30 April)

Gang mowing in orchards (May 15, 18, 29, June 1, 5, 22, 24)

Hop earthing up (June 1, 24)

Mowing (Park June 8)

Hoeing (Kale June 22)

Haymaking and baling (June 23, 24, July 7, 8, 9, 12, 13, 15, 20, 21, 29, August 3, last bale made August 4)

Silage making (Hoppers Hut July 2, Aug 11, Horse Race Aug 13, 14, 17)

Cut clover (Aug 11)

Combining barley (Aug 11, 13–14)

Apple picking (Aug 12, September 2, Oct 4, 27, 28)

Combining oats in Birches (Aug 14, 15, 16)

Baling straw (Aug 16, 17, 19, 21)

Cutting peas (in Banky Aug 16, 17, 18, 21; in Frogmead, Hop Garden Aug 28)

Combining wheat in Large (Aug 20, 21, 22, 23, 25, 26)

Combining clover in Lodge (Aug 23)

Hop picking (Sept 6–30)

Combining Barley in 8 acres (13–17 Sept)

Combining peas (in Hop Garden Sept 19, 20, 21; Banky Sept 23, 29, Oct 4–8)

On top of all this was the pharmacopoeia of treatments to which the crops and fields were subject. Although monumental quantities of farmyard manure were being carted out on to the fields from the cattle's winter housing, any thought that fifty years ago this was an organic farm, as I had fondly imagined, soon disappeared under Captain Beale's busy, often slightly scrawled diary jottings. Chemical imbalances, fertility deficiencies, fungal and pest attack: the tractors were out almost daily applying one potion or stimulus after another. Nitrate chalk, potash and superpotash, Epsom salts and 'Copper colloidal' for the peas, Melaldehyde on the wheat, slag on the orchards, Arcolin on the kale, the kale sprayed for flea-beetle, and the full battery of sulphate of ammonia, Pestox, Blitox, sulphur, copper sulphate and Boclear all applied to the labour- and capital-intensive hop gardens.

All this was clear enough. There had not been a moment when the guillotine had come down. Here was the farm in transition from its old to its modern state. The large workforce, the integration of the dairy herds with the pastures and arable fields, providing their dung and requiring their fodder, was still the old world going at full tilt. Alongside it were all these 'artificials', these answers in a bag. By the end of the decade, Stanley Stearns had bought a hop-processing machine which made the forty hop-pickers unnecessary. By 1968, the hops, which had caught 'wilt', a fungal disease, were no longer worth going in for. The cattle finally went in 1980. Any idea of rotation went with them. There was no longer any need to interrupt the growing of arable crops with a fertility-building clover and grass ley if you could simply apply fertility brought in by a lorry. Artificial fertilisers made mixed farms inefficient. If you could grow 4½ tons an acre of wheat on a field year in, year out, then that was the way to go. Sissinghurst became a mainly arable farm, with some field-scale lettuces and Brussels sprouts grown on the side. It made some money – just – but its 259 acres were too small to compete with the East Anglian cereal barons, let alone America or the Ukraine. The industrial processes that made chemical farming possible had not only removed from this landscape almost everything that I loved about it, by the 1990s they had also made Sissinghurst unviable as a farm.

Given these economic and technological conditions, was there any way of recovering the enriched landscape? Was Sissinghurst caught in a kind of historical bind? Or was there a route out of this, based not on competing in world markets but by satisfying the modern appetite for 'real food'? Could Sissinghurst become, in effect, a retail farm? Could a new version of the high, expert agriculture that Captain Beale, in his tweed jacket and tie, his pipe in one hand, the other in a jacket pocket, had performed so expertly, could that be practised here again?

THREE

The Idea

IN THE WINTER AFTER my father's death I started to feel my way towards a new, or at least a new-old, understanding of how Sissinghurst might be. I wrote to Fiona Reynolds, the director-general of the National Trust, who I knew slightly, to thank her for coming down to his funeral and to float past her a rather public version of the ideas that were on my mind.

> There is only one thing at Sissinghurst I would love to see different – which is the farm not producing commodity cereals in a contractorised and heartless way, as it does now, but becoming a model of polycultural richness as it was 40 years ago: hops, fruit and dairy, to all of which it is well suited, and all of which could become the basis of a rampantly successful Sissinghurst brand of jams and beers and cheeses and all the rest of it. You would have to go a long way to find as good a ready-made brand as Sissinghurst waiting on the shelf. And it would employ people on the place! I am sure I have heard you talk often about a people-rich countryside, labour-intensive and high value-added agriculture and so on. The country needs it and this could be such a good and profitable working model for that idea. That is a long term dream of mine, but it is one I feel in my gut you might share.

She replied nicely but uncommittedly. Long-term was probably the phrase. Anyway, the idea of the 'Sissinghurst brand' is something that would come to seem too thin and wrong. The whole notion of a brand, even if the brand was meant to embody authenticity and richness, contradicted the very qualities it was meant to convey. The idea

I had of Sissinghurst was something that was too much to be encapsulated in anything resembling a brand. I wanted to rekindle the sense of this place as a fully working and integrated whole. To do that, we had to sell something from it. We even had to sell the idea of 'wholeness'. But that didn't mean the brand was the destination. The brand was an instrument not the goal. I wanted a sense here of overwhelming well-being, which could be interpreted I suppose as a kind of brand but could scarcely be achieved if thought of as one. That was the paradox: a brand whose brand identity was its brandlessness.

Perhaps Sissinghurst could be considered a product, and like all products needed to renew itself, to sew together its old self, its particular qualities, with a new kind of response to an evolving world. And perhaps, now I look back on it, that is what I was engaged in: a rebranding exercise. What, in the most brutal terms, was the business here? Heritage horticulture with a lesbian-aristocratic gloss, allied to a tranquillity destination with café and gift shop attached. That was the old proposition. My ideas, equally brutally seen, were to bump that into another market niche by laying over it a holistic real-food agenda which would appeal to the urban ABC1s, precisely the kind of moneyed market the National Trust needed to court. I can write that now, three years later; it was certainly not how I was thinking of it at the time.

Meanwhile Sarah and I tried to settle into Sissinghurst. It was a slightly strange experience. The house was overwhelmingly parental: my father's furniture, his books, his files, his pictures, his whole habit of being. I used to catch myself tidying up, not because I minded the mess our family was making but because he would have. Boots in the hall, old cups of coffee, dog beds, last night's washing-up: all of this would have summoned from him that particular, half-audible, rather sibilant under-the-breath whistling, usually a tune from *My Fair Lady*, which was the signal of contained impatience and anxiety. A shift into 'Lili Marlene' was not good: major dissatisfaction. So I tidied up to avoid the whistling. And then, terrifyingly, I found myself whistling too. 'Why are you whistling under your breath?' my daughter Rosie asked. 'Because I like the tune,' I said, exactly what my father would have said, and just as untrue.

On top of that, we had to deal with the National Trust, which at times was like having a third, even more supervisory parent. We were undoubtedly a difficult new presence for them. Instead of a single, self-contained, beneficent and peace-loving octogenarian, they now had on their doorstep a family consisting of two busy, untidy grown-ups, a Land Rover that leaked oil all over the National Trust cream- and caramel-coloured tarmac, two daughters with bikes that were leant against yew hedges, three dogs that needed to do what dogs need to do, two adult rabbits (brother and sister) and their six babies, which were currently smaller than the mesh of the wire we had put up to enclose them. None of this was within the National Trust guidelines. The rabbit run we created looked like something on the back edge of a run-down housing estate outside Swindon. But what can you do if that is the sort of family you are?

And then in January 2005 the Trust sent me a 'Draft Occupancy Agreement', which seemed to confirm the worst. Sarah and the children were to have no rights to live here if I died. We needed permission to go into any part of the building except the part we actually ate and slept in. We were to 'notify Trust staff if guests of the family will be entering the garden'. Our children were not to go anywhere near the greenhouses or nursery. We could have people to lunch only on closed days and only then 'with the prior agreement of the Trust'. Any photographs we took inside or outside the house were to be Trust copyright. The Trust was to be informed if we were away for more than two days or if anyone came to stay. We were to park our car with the exhaust pointing to the west. The occupation of the house was 'at the discretion of the National Trust' – in other words we could be thrown out at any time it liked.

I reeled from this document, sunk in gloom. I have talked about it more recently to Sally Bushell the Trust's property manager and she has explained it from her point of view. They didn't know us at the time. For them, we were new arrivals. They needed to be careful about security and safety. The yew hedges had to be preserved from exhaust fumes. And it wouldn't have been nice for our friends to have been challenged in the garden. At the time, though, I was in no mood for understanding. I wrote an angry letter to the Trust's area manager, who had signed the document. 'There is no sense that any of my family belongs to Sissinghurst,' I told him,

> nor that we grew up here, that we think of it as home, that we know it and have known it more intimately and for longer than anyone else, that it is a place to which we are deeply attached. This draft agreement might well have been proposed to someone who had just strolled in from Arizona or Mars. Many of its clauses treat me and my family as though we were simply unwelcome here, to be contained and enclosed, and not to be trusted.
>
> I would like you to imagine addressing the kind of proposals you have made to my father. Would you have dared do that? I don't think so. I can see my father now, if I showed him what you sent me, holding his head in his hands and saying it was unbelievable. It is an almost complete betrayal of any spirit of cooperation or trust we might have had. And if not to him, why to us?

This was bleak; it felt like the moment of dispossession. 'How lovely to be at Sissinghurst,' people would say, but it wasn't lovely. Doubly or even triply, it felt like borrowed clothes: first because it was my father's house, then because it was his parents' and thirdly because it was the National Trust's. A three-layered baffle lay between us and any sense that this was home. It made all too obvious the acknowledged fact that the status of 'resident donor' is difficult. Even the phrase reveals the difficulty, as if one were living in a body whose heart had been given away. It's your home but someone else's business, a place that is yours emotionally but very far from being yours in terms of who owns it, runs it, pays for it, works at it and conceives of its future.

I could see the position clearly enough to know that if I had been a National Trust employee, working hard all year to keep the place in prime condition, I might not have liked us either. There is something structurally unlikeable about a 'donor family'. They swan about as if they own the place, but they don't own it. They think they know how things should be but they don't do much to keep them that way. For all the heart-drenching beauty of Sissinghurst, it felt a little cold. At times it felt like living in a theatre. One tends, at those times, to see the mechanisms rather than the show.

The Trust reeled in turn from my letter. I saw Sue Saville, the regional director, who did her best to mend the damage that had been done, smiling at me and rather sweetly touching my arm in reassurance. She said that visitors to NT properties liked the idea of a donor family living there. That the NT liked donor families because they often provided an instinctive feeling for a place which an administrator would have to guess at and feel for. That this occupancy agreement had been a mistake, a failure on the Trust's part to imagine themselves into our shoes. Finally, one day that summer, Sir William Proby, the chairman of the Trust, came with Merry, his wife, to talk to me and to apologise. We sat in the garden together, looking at the azaleas, their honey-scent blowing over us. The Trust had got it wrong and Sir William was sorry. I know, poor man, that part of Sir William's job is going around the country soothing donor families in these situations, but he did it well. There was no more talk of occupancy agreements.

Nevertheless, it hardly changed the atmosphere on the ground. Sarah and I decided one dank evening that we had to leave. What was the point in pouring our energies into this place when clearly it neither wanted nor needed us? Sissinghurst could roll along on its current path and nobody would ever know what hadn't happened. There was another life to be had but I knew I didn't want it. To leave would be a defeat and a retreat. I would be giving up. Surely there was another way, another form of relationship with everything that Sissinghurst meant? Maybe. Sarah was sceptical. What could it be? What way out of the straitjacket was there?

Through the course of 2005, I gradually worked my way to

understanding what needed to happen here. That summer, going for a walk with the dogs, on the path just between the Priest's House and the barn, apropos of nothing, I had an idea. The restaurant at Sissinghurst serves tens of thousands of people a year. Why not grow on the farm the food that the restaurant cooks and sells to the visitors? What does a good lunch need? Some lamb, beef, chicken, eggs, pork, sausages, vegetables, bread, butter, cream, fruit, pastry. If the farm here could supply these things again, as it once had, the place would, almost inadvertently, reacquire the vitality and multiplicity it had lost, not as a smeared-on look, but from its bones. Above all, there would be people working the land here again, people for whom the soil of Sissinghurst was of vital importance, who would get to know it and look after it as carefully as their own children. That stupendous list of tasks performed on the Captain Beale farm would again become at least half necessary. A good lunch would make a good landscape. Grow lunch. That was all it needed.

In the wake of the idea came its drawbacks. This was not a lovely blank canvas. Over two hundred people – employees, residents, volunteers – were directly involved in the working and management of Sissinghurst as it stood. That big and complex business, with its own multiple tensions and high profitability, had to be kept going while this new cluster of ideas – a market garden, an organic farm, a restaurant dependent on very local produce, a labour-intensive use of the land – was pushed into the middle of it, with the same management team having to make the changes. It would not be easy. The new Sissinghurst enterprise would have a ready-made market on its doorstep – the stream of visitors to the garden – but that benefit came at a huge price: the need to convert everyone from the old system to the new. What was good about the idea was also bad.

In October that year, one of the National Trust's committees of the great and good – this was the Gardens Panel, chaired by Anna Pavord, the writer and plant historian – was coming to Sissinghurst anyway, to see how things were going. It was a routine visit, something that happens every two or three years. I decided I should talk to them about my idea. Here was a chance to get change into the bloodstream of the Trust. I rang Anna, slightly with my heart in my mouth, feeling that it was scarcely the role of a member of a donor family to suggest to the Trust how they should go about managing things, and asked whether I could address her committee. Of course, of course, she said. They would be there on Thursday. I could have ten minutes.

I have never written anything more carefully in my life. I knew I had to say it to them with some conviction, but I printed it out as well, so that the committee would have something to take away with them, a physical object which could make the idea stick. The meeting was to be held upstairs in the old granary, whose windows I had shot out with my air rifle one bored ten-year-old morning. It was now part of the varnished pine world of the National Trust restaurant. There were about twenty-five people there, arranged around a giant table, tweed jackets, ties, professional, slightly curious. I distributed my sheets of paper, stapled together, along with copies of the poem called 'Sissinghurst' which Vita wrote soon after arriving here. I then stood to address them.

This is what I said:

> Sissinghurst is more than a garden. It is a garden in the remains
> of a ruined house and that house is at the heart of its own piece
> of Wealden landscape. It is a deeply rooted place and its mean-
> ing and beauty depend on its working not only as a garden but as
> a place that is fed by those wider and deeper connections.

That was code for a major transformation of the place. If connections were what mattered here, then the whole way it worked
had to change. Vita's vision of the place had spread far beyond the
horticultural. Garden, buildings, farm, woods, history, Kentishness,
the land: these were the necessary ingredients. 'This husbandry, this
castle and this I', she called it in her poem 'Sissinghurst'. It was
a place, she wrote, where she found 'in chain/The castle, and the
pasture, and the rose'. That chain, that sense of connectedness, was
what Sissinghurst needed to embody. It was a garden in a farm and
it should seem like that.

I told them about the four different tenants, the lack of anyone
working on the farm full time. No animals attached to Sissinghurst,
no farm buildings used as farm buildings, no one farmer who
thought of Sissinghurst Castle Farm as his.

> The result is a certain, efficient heartlessness, decisions made
> about this land not for the place but in the context of the four
> farm businesses of which it forms a part.
>
> The garden at Sissinghurst is the crowning element of a
> landscape which needs to be polycultural. It once had both soft
> fruit and top fruit, hops, a herd of Guernsey cattle and another
> of Dairy Shorthorns, farmers who were attached to it as a place,
> as well as orchards, cereals, sheep, pigs, chickens and ducks.
> That is the landscape described in VSW's poem, and that is the
> landscape to which we should aspire. I am sure the pursuit of
> such a rich and various landscape would bring the aesthetic
> changes to the landscape which the garden needs. Sissinghurst
> the place would become the poem which Vita envisaged.

How could we do that? By growing the food for the 115,000 people who sat down to eat something in the restaurant and café here each year. Lunch would make its own landscape. And for that we needed a business plan.

The farm would need to employ people. It would strengthen this community and would restore some vital connections to it. I think we have an opportunity here to make something of great rarity and beauty, a poem of connectedness, something of which we would all, in five or ten years' time, be exceptionally proud.

There had been some nodding of heads as I spoke and people clapped when I sat down, but I had to leave the room for the discussion that followed. I wasn't quite sure where the question had ended up. Afterwards, I spoke to Jonathan Light, the Trust's area manager. 'The one thing I am absolutely determined I am not going to do is string an albatross around Sissinghurst's neck for the next twenty years,' he said. 'And there's another point. The landscape looks like it does for a reason and that is because economics and the market has driven it to look like that over the last fifty years. If we try to do something different, we will be swimming against the tide.' Negative then? I asked. No, not at all. 'If we can demonstrate you can have a beautiful landscape, a mixed farm, and make money, then that really will be something we can show to others.'

The next day I had to go to Cheltenham to give a talk. On the way there, in the car, my phone rang. 'I have Fiona Reynolds for you,' her secretary said. I had met the new director-general of the Trust before but being called on the mobile in the car was a first. 'I hear you've set the cat among the pigeons,' she said. Friendly, warm, busy, amused. 'I've had some excited phone calls. Do you think you could send me a copy of what you said? I am not saying anything but it sounds interesting.' It was the best of signs. People on the committee wouldn't have rung her if my words hadn't gone in somewhere. As I drove back home, I couldn't stop smiling. Just think: this thing I had been half-remembering and half-imagining was still alive.

I walked out across the farm that evening, taking the dogs through the autumn woods, kicking up the leaves in the trenches which the old roads had left in the wood floor. A rising moon hung at the end of the long rides and autumn filled the air like a soup. It seemed possible, then, that there might be no disconnection between the future and the past here, that the passing of time wasn't mere diminution. In the car I'd heard a woman on the radio say that we met the world only once, in childhood, and that everything afterwards was only memory. I knew well enough the attractions of that idea, the Wordsworthian regret, the sense of significance being invested only in the past. But here now, maybe, there was something else: the ability to fold the past over into the future, like turning the blankets and sheets over at the top of a bed, or digging over a piece of ground, turning the sods, grass down, and breaking the exposed soil to make a new tilth. Walking through the wood that evening, with the dogs prodding for rabbits among the chestnut stools, and that moon climbing through the branches, I knew I had never felt such buoyancy, such deep and rooted buoyancy, and I wished my father had been there to tell him.

FOUR

Origins

IT IS AN ARTICLE OF FAITH with me that a place consists of everything that has happened there; it is a reservoir of memories; and understanding those memories is not a trap but a liberation, a menu of possibilities. The richer the knowledge, the wider the options. Multiplicity is all. The only enemy is narrow, singular definition. And Sissinghurst, perhaps like any place that people have loved, is layered with these multiplicities. Even now, anyone who lives or works here soon develops an intense relationship to it, none of them quite the same, none quite distinct, none of them quite secure. Our different histories are buried and half-known but we all think we own the real thing, or at least want to. It is a place drenched both in belonging and in the longing to belong.

I always knew that its foundations were in clay, silt and sand – clay at the bottom end of the farm, through which the Hammer Brook runs, sand on the higher ridges above it and silt scattered through all of it. The clay is late land, always lying cold and reluctant, heavy and wet. It is where the fertility lies and where cereals do have some kind of a chance, at least with modern equipment. Hops, which are hungry plants, were always grown down on the heavy land by the Hammer Brook. In summer the clay is capable of turning to concrete – and then dust – as soon as the sun starts to shine. In winter, it makes for thick and cloggy ground. If you walk across one of the clay fields when it has been ploughed, it gathers in lobed elephantiasis clumps around your boots. Teams of six or eight oxen were always needed to pull a plough through these fields, and when

Queen Elizabeth and her court came here in August 1573, Lord Burghley, who was with her, said it was worse than travelling in the wilds of the Peak District. Even in midsummer the roads were 'right deep and noyous'. If heavy goods had to be brought in – in particular the bells for the churches – or timber taken out, the oxen laboured for days. I asked a farmer who had worked all his life on the clay lands to the north of here what his farm was like. 'Not boy's land,' he said.

Clay, born in the wet, remains a friend to it. Surface water turns into streams. The streams cut away at the clay country, leaving the better-drained sand and silt standing proud as ridges. It is that physical difference which has cut the physiognomy of Sissinghurst. High is open and relatively dry; low is wet, secret and thick with clay. A hole dug in the clay ground here becomes a pond. No lining is needed. Clay smeared with the heel of a JCB bucket seals itself. In the 40,000 acres of pure clay lands to the north and east of Sissinghurst, I have counted on the map very nearly four thousand ponds. They are usually no more than the holes where farmers have dug, more often than not for the slightly limy clay called marl, which was used from the Middle Ages onwards to sweeten these generally acid soils. The holes have simply filled with water, but each has its character: overhung with ancient oaks, the outer fingers of their lower branches dipping into the dark surface; smartened in the garden of a newly gentrified farm; or eutrophic, clogged in the middle of an arable field with all the green slime that comes from too much fertiliser draining into it.

The sand is the clay's opposite: thirsty, capable of drying out in anything resembling a summer, without the nutrients on which good crops rely but making for easier and lighter country. Clay and sand are the polarities of the place, although in reality the situation is not so clear cut. The two principles mix and muddle across the whole of Sissinghurst. The soils roam from silty sands and sandy silty clays to silty clay loams and on to solid clay itself, perfect for the bricks that were made at least since the eighteenth century in the Frittenden brickworks just to the north of Sissinghurst. Patches of lightness appear here and there in the middle of heavy fields, and sudden wet clay sinks can be found in the middle of soils that are otherwise good and workable.

Only here and there do the two extremes appear as themselves. On the hill above Bettenham, there is an old sandpit, perhaps where the sand for the mortar used in building Sissinghurst was dug, and where now you can find little flakes and pebbles of the sandstone pulled out by the rabbits. It also appears in another small pit in the Park, just next to the old road going south, a friable, yellowish stone which crumbles between your thumb and finger. Here and there are thin iron bands within it. But play with a pebble for a moment and all you are left with is smooth, talcum-like dust on your skin. There are small pieces of this stone, included as yellow anomalies, among the bricks next to the entrance arch at Sissinghurst. On the high dry ridge at the western edge of the farm, there is a field still called Horse Race because that is sandy, well drained and had the best going for the gentry in the seventeenth century and the officers of the eighteenth-century militia who used to race their horses here up until the 1760s. But it is not as building stone that this sand is significant. It is for the lightness it has given some of the soils here, far lighter than many places in the Weald.

At the top of the big wood there is a light, almost purely sandy patch, where a big group of sand-loving beeches grows. They are the most climbable trees at Sissinghurst, and not one of them appears down in the damp clay land. A third of a mile away, at the other end of the ridge, a cluster of sand-loving Scots pines was planted here in the 1850s by George Neve, the improving Victorian tenant. It was here that my father, as an anxious young man in the 1940s, proposed to the beautiful and entirely alluring Shirley Morgan, the only girl he ever loved and who would never accept him, despite a campaign lasting years. It was a well-chosen spot: if he had decided to lay her down on the damp sticky clay soils at the bottom of the farm, he wouldn't have had a chance. At least he got the geology right; but geology wasn't enough. How much easier it must be for men who live on perfectly drained, downland turf, with endless vistas across their spreading acres, to convince the girls they love. My poor father could only point to distant views scarcely visible between the trunks of the surrounding trees. Over there, on a good day, he would have said, you can almost see the tower of Canterbury Cathedral. It wasn't enough; Shirley married a brilliant and handsome marquess whose beautiful house in North Wales has a view across its lawns of mountains and the glittering sea. My father never ceased to love her.

Sissinghurst, in its roots, is a little second rate. It has never been part of smart England, and its deepest of origins, the sources of its own soil, are decidedly murky. I love it for that. This is ordinariness itself: no volcanoes and no cataclysms, just a slow, deep gathering of what it was. The first moment when Sissinghurst came into being, when the stuff you can now hold there in your hands was there to be held, was about 120 million years ago. Britain was at the latitude of Lagos. Dinosaurs walked its river valleys, and a range of old and stony hills lay across the whole of England to the north. Forests of horsetails and giant ferns shrouded the valley slopes. Two steaming rivers flowed south out of those hills, their tributaries grinding away at the old rocks of which the hills were made. The rivers ran fast and carried with them a load of coarse-grained sand. As they emerged from the hills, just south of London, they flowed into a huge and swampy delta, covering perhaps 30,000 square miles, stretching from here far to the south of Paris, a dank, tropical place with many soft islands within it. Here the current slowed and dropped the sand in wide banks across the estuary. These, in their origins, were the sands on which Shirley Morgan lay immaculate and the officers of the Hampshire Militia, the young Edward Gibbon among them, raced their sweating horses.

As the rivers coming south from the uplands in Hertfordshire and Essex wore away at their hills, they slowed and became sluggish, carrying now only the finest of grains. What had been delta sands turned to thick grey mineral mud. The grains settled closely together in a gluey morass, a brackish and hostile place. It was a fossilised quagmire, impenetrable, a trap for anything that wandered into it, burying entire trees and whole animals, a graveyard of gummy secrets. This was the origin of the Wealden clay. Of course, my father didn't try to kiss Shirley Morgan there. They would have sunk into it, slowly disappearing, as if into the jaws of an insect-eating fungus.

When I was a boy, I used to play with the clay in the summer. You could dig it out of the side of the lake banks, wet and slithery in your hands, your fingers pushing into the antique ooze. If you held a small ball of it in your fist and wetted it and squeezed it, two slimy snakes of clay, like a patissier's piping, would emerge top and bottom, curling, ribbed, while their miniature cousins came out between the joints of your fingers. It felt like ur-stuff, stuff at its most basic, as good as dough or pastry, squeezable, makable, lovable. Occasionally, we moulded it into pots, one of which I still have sitting on my desk, unglazed and unbaked, a rough lump from the basement of existence. Your shorts and shirt after one of these mornings would be unwearably filthy, your hands and legs washable only under a hose.

This was the clay which in the sixteenth century gave modern Sissinghurst one of its essential substances and colours: brick. No record survives of the great brick building programmes here, either from the 1530s or the 1560s, but there can be no doubt that the clay for the pink Tudor and Elizabethan palaces at Sissinghurst came from the stream valley just to the south. When Vita and Harold wanted to put up new garden walls in the 1930s, they commissioned bricks from the Frittenden brickworks only a mile away on the other side. But the bricks of those walls never looked right: too brown, without the variable, pink, iron-rich, rosy flush the sixteenth-century builders had found. Even from a mile away, the brick Vita and Harold used was obviously not from here. It was one of their mistakes.

If the Sissinghurst process followed the pattern elsewhere in the Weald in the sixteenth century, the clay itself would have been tested and selected by an expert, a travelling brickmaker. In the autumn or early winter, gangs of labourers would then have dug the raw clay out of the valley and spread it out over what are now the Lake field and Long Orchard, so that autumn rains could get into the lumps and the frost split them. All winter the clay lay there on the fields, a dirty orange scar, like the embankment for a railway or bypass under construction. In the spring, the clay was rewetted and then, with more gangs of day labourers, trampled underfoot. Raw clay is full of little stony nodules. If they are left in the clay when it is fired, they overheat and split the bricks. For weeks, probably in large wooden troughs, the clay was kneaded and the little stones removed so that the brickmakers were left with a smooth and seamless paste which could be pushed into wooden brick-sized moulds, usually here nine inches long, four wide and two deep, the long, thin, smoked-salmon sliver-shaped bricks of sixteenth-century Sissinghurst. I remember seeing moulds of exactly that form in the Frittenden brickworks when I was boy, but they have disappeared now. The clammy raw clay bricks were then turned out of the moulds and left to dry in stacks for a month. In Frittenden there were long, open-sided wooden sheds for this, with oak frames and tiled roofs, but the scene in the fields of Elizabethan Sissinghurst would have been more ad hoc than that: bricks drying in what sun there was on offer. The whole process would have relied on a good fine summer.

Only at the end of the drying, when the bricks would already have developed some of the cracks and wrinkles you can still see in Sissinghurst's walls, would they be fired. Specialist brickmakers would arrive again, hired for the purpose, and build temporary 'clamps', clay-sealed kilns in which the bricks were baked in a wood fire. It was a local and not entirely consistent process. Those bricks that were at the windward end of the clamp were more thoroughly fired than those downwind. The clay itself had wide variations in iron content. Different clamps, some with drier timber than others, some even using brushwood, burned at different temperatures. And so the flickering pinkness of Sissinghurst's walls emerged from the ground, everything from red to black, the near-white pink of flesh to the pink of camellias, wine red, apricot, even where it is rubbed a kind of orange, but in sum, across a whole wall, always with a rosy freshness, a lightness to the colour which denies its origins in damp and fire, and scarcely reflects the whole process, the transmutation of an ancient eroded swamp. Not that the Elizabethans would have liked the variability. They would have admired and required precision and exactness. It was only because there was no stone here with which to build that they turned to the clay. The idea of bringing any quantity of stone from the quarries in the greensand ridge eight miles to the north was unthinkable, in time and expense, on the wet clay roads. Clay ground, thank God, meant a brick house, a subliminal joining of a high-prospect tower to the ground it surveys.

Even since human beings first arrived here, 750,000 years ago, seven ice ages have come and gone, driving the people, the animals and the plants far to the south, to their refuges in the warmth of southern Europe, and leaving this place, if not ice-bound, at least a frozen tundra, bleak and treeless. If I shut my eyes, I like to see it then, just at its moment of emergence, at the end of the last ice age, about twelve thousand years ago. It is a rolling windswept plain, continuous into Europe. Nothing coats the horizon but the grasses and the moss. There is cold to the north. Storms cross it in winter. In summer, as it does the steppe, the sun dries and burnishes it, a Ukrainian pelt concealing the earth. Ten thousand years ago, the average July temperature in Kent was already in the mid-sixties Fahrenheit. With that warmth, into this huge savannah, more developed forms of life come rippling up in the wake of the retreating cold. First, the great herds of grazing animals, what may appear now like a North American scene but was indeed the case in northern Europe as the ice withdrew. Roe deer, red deer, no bison but the huge wild cows called aurochsen (of which the last, a Polish cow, died in 1627, and one of whose horns is still used as a communal drinking cup in a Cambridge college), elk or moose and herds of wild boar: all of these in their hundreds of thousands thrived on the great grassy treeless plains, where the wolves and lynxes pursued them. Bears would have fished for salmon and trout in the Medway and the Beult, the Hammer Brook and its glittering, unshaded tributaries. Foxes, cats, martens, otters and beavers would all have been making their way up from the south, a spreading tide of appetite and complexity.

A sense of openness and fullness would have been there at the very beginning of Sissinghurst. Even now, wild animals in these situations are not afraid. The first European visitors to the great American plains found the herds wandering up to them with fearlessness and curiosity, a look in the eye from a stag, a straight sniff from a moose. Charles Darwin killed a fox on the South American island of Chiloe in 1834 by walking up to it and hitting it on the head with his geological hammer. Those paintings of Douanier Rousseau's in which wild animals put their noses into the faces of men asleep on the ground are not romantic fantasies but descriptions of how the world once was. Eden was a reality here. And the first domesticated animals accompanied the men. The children of the native Americans kept bear cubs as their pets. All those paintings on cave walls clearly bear witness to animals seen close up and in numbers. A drawing on ivory from the Pyrenees of about ten thousand years ago shows a horse's head in a harness. People and their animals walked up into the oceanic widths of the grassy savannah. This moment is the oldest of the Wealden folk memories. I have my grandmother's copy of the first great book written about Kent, William Lambarde's *Perambulation*, published in 1570. She must have had it in the 1920s when writing *The Land*, her long Virgilian epic on the Weald, sidelining in it the passages she liked. The Weald, Lambarde had written, and she marked, 'was nothing else but a Desart, and waste Wildernesse, not planted with Towns or peopled with men, as the outsides of the Shire were, but stored and stuffed with heards of Deer and droves of Hogs only'.

The birds came with them and with the birds the trees. In the pollen record, those trees whose seeds are dispersed by birds are the first to appear in the wake of the shrinking ice. Snow buntings, the Lapland bunting and the shore lark all now spend the summer in the tundra on the edge of the Arctic and the winter farther south. They would have carried the first tree seeds up to sub-arctic Sissinghurst, perhaps the blackthorn and hawthorn, whose berries they would have eaten in the Dordogne or the Lot and would have dispersed here to make the first shrubby patches in the grasslands. The nutcracker has been found carrying hazelnuts ten or twelve miles from the trees where they picked them up, and perhaps, ahead of the wind, the nutcrackers were responsible for the big hazel woods which were the first to grow on the grasslands here. A thousand miles at ten miles a year takes only a century.

Quite slowly, with the help of the warm south wind, the wood thickened. First, the willows, the pioneers, set up in the damp patches, the fluff of their seeds drifting up in the summers. By 8000 BC the birch had arrived. Five hundred years later, the oaks came, their acorns almost certainly carried north by jays. The elm had also come, growing only on the dry land, not down in the damp of the clay. ('The oak unattended by the elm,' J. M. Furley, the great nineteenth-century historian of the Weald, wrote, 'betrays a soil not prized by the agriculturalist.') By about 6000 BC alders had colonised the stream margins, where they are still to be found, reliant on the water flowing steadily past their roots. The ash came at the same time. Not until about 5000 BC were there any beeches here, and then only, as now, on the drier hills. The hornbeam came even later and the chestnut not until the Romans brought it.

All of them had come north from their ice age refuges in France, wandering up on the wind into the increasingly friendly environments of Kent. It is like the cast of a play coming on to the stage and finding a seat there. As you walk through the woods and stream margins of Sissinghurst today, it is of course possible to listen to the ensemble, just to drink in the flecking green light of the wood in summer, but you can pick out individual lines of the actors too and find here now, perfectly articulate if you listen for it, the story of their arrival.

The thorns were the early pioneers. In a rough and neglected sliver of Sissinghurst Park Wood, where some giant alder stools have overgrown themselves and crashed down on to the wood floor, leaving a hole in the canopy behind them, blackthorn has invaded to make a thick and bitter, self-protective patch. The long sharp thorns are poisonous. If one of them pricks you and breaks off in your flesh, the red-flushed wound festers for days. The blackthorn patch is everything the word 'thicket' might imply, tangled into a hedge-hog of denial and involution, clawing at itself, a crown of thorns thirty feet across. A big hawthorn standing coated in mayflower in a hedgerow is one thing – and well-grown thorns certainly make outstanding firewood – but the essence of a thorn is this thickety resistance to all outsiders, a miniature act of self-containment which the medieval English called a spinney, a spiny place, designed to exclude.

As children, we were always taught that you must try to sym-pathise with the spiky and the spiny, to understand what it was that did not allow them the open, displaying elegance of the beech or the confidence of the oak. Why are thorns so bitter? What can be the point, in such a calm English wood, of such unfriendliness? You feel like asking them to relax, even if relaxation is not in their nature. But everywhere in the woods at Sissinghurst there is one repeated clue to this foundation-level exercise in tree psychology: at the foot of almost every oak there is at least one holly nestling in the shade. Why? Why is the spiky holly drawn to the roots of the oak? What sort of symbiosis is this? But the question, it turns out, may be the wrong way round.

Why does the oak live with the holly? Because the holly, when they were both young, looked after the oak. Its spiky evergreen leaves protected the young acorn seedling from the browsing lips of the ever-hungry deer. The oak had a holly nurse, and only after a while did the young tree outstrip the protector that now shelters in its shade.

That too was the role played by the early spinney thickets. In an England filled with roaming herds, new trees needed to adopt one of three or four strategies to outstrip the nibbling lips. Either a spiny blanket which would mean they weren't eaten themselves. Or sheltering within someone else's spiny blanket, so that by the time they emerged from it they were big enough not to be eaten. Or, like those other pioneers, the willows, growing so fast that at least one or two of you could outstrip the ubiquitous mouths. Or finally, like the birch, just as much of a pioneer of new ground as the willow or the thorns, colonising new areas in such numbers that at least one or two would escape the enemy. The browsing beasts were at war with the trees and the tree strategies were clear enough: hunker down (the thorns); borrow a friend (oaks, elms, beeches and ashes); keep running (the willows); or blast them with numbers (the birch).

Every one of these post-ice age theories of defence – spike, cower, rush or proliferate – is there to be seen in the Sissinghurst woods today. A few years ago, one of the great beeches on the high ridge of the big wood collapsed in a gale. Nothing was more shocking to me than to find it one autumn self-felled and horizontal, its stump a jagged spike ten or twelve feet high, looking more ripped than broken, as if someone had taken a pound of cheese and torn it in half. My father always used to bring us here in springtime when we were small and lie us down on the dry bronze leaves and mast below the tree. The new leaves sprinkled light on our faces. Each leaf was like a spot of greenness, floating, scarcely connected to the huge grey body of the tree. My father always said the same thing: how wonderful it was that this duchess, each year, dressed herself like a debutante for the ball. I cannot now look at a beech tree in spring without that phrase entering my mind.

Later, I climbed it often enough, chimneying up between its forking branches, avoiding the horrible squirrel's dray in one of its crooks, finding as you got higher that limbs that had seemed as solid as buildings farther down started to sway and shift under your weight and pressure. Then coming up into the realm of the leaves, as tender as lettuce early in the summer, acquiring a sheen and a brittleness as the months went on, until at last, in the top, like a crow's nest in a square-rigger, where the branches were no thicker than my forearm, I could look out over the roof of the wood, across the small valley, to the Tower, whose parapet half a mile away was level with my eye and where the pink- and blue-shirted visitors to the garden could be seen by me, while I knew that to them I was quite invisible.

Now the whole tree was down. Its splaying limbs had been smashed in the fall and lay along with the trunk like a doll someone had squashed into a box. I could walk, teeteringly, the length of the tree, as if I were a nuthatch whose world had been turned through ninety degrees. Even then, the beech started to rot where it lay. As it did so, something miraculous happened: in the wide circle around the beech's trunk, to which its multilayered coverage of leaves had denied light, nothing in the past had grown. Now, though, the light poured in, and in that circle hundreds and hundreds of birch trees sprang up, a dense little wood of rigid spaghetti trees, a noodle wood, without any great dignity or individual presence but extraordinary for its surge and hunger, opportunists, like pioneers pouring off their ship into a new and hope-filled land. Within their new wood, the body of the beech lay as a mausoleum of itself, vast and inert, an unburied colossus, yesterday's story, no more than a reservoir of nutrients for the life that was so patently already coming after. The birch surge was, in its way, just as much as the thorn thicket, or the oaks sheltering in the embrace of the holly, or the romping willows on the banks of the lake, a vision of what happened here after the ice age was over, when the cold withdrew, and trees reclaimed the country.

As much as the clay, the trees are at the heart of Sissinghurst. To the south and west of here, the woods of the High Weald make up a broken, parcelled, varied country, thick with tiny settlements and ancient names, all of them in their own nests of privacy, tucked in among the folds of the wood on the hills. It is still possible, even today, to walk for eighty miles in a line going west from Sissinghurst – if you are careful and pick your path – without leaving woodland for more than quarter of a mile at a time. Not until you reach the Hampshire chalk at Selborne does open country defeat you. Weald means *Wald*, the great wood of England, and although it has been eaten into and nibbled at for at least fifteen centuries, and perhaps for more like fifty, it persists. It is the frame of Sissinghurst, the woods, in Kipling's words, 'that know everything and tell nothing'.

Wood to Sissinghurst is like sea to an island. Everything in the Weald, in the end, comes back to the wood. Sissinghurst's parish church, at least until the nineteenth century, was at Cranbrook, about two and a half miles away, a short bike ride. It became an intensely Puritan place in the sixteenth century, and the feeling in the church still reflects that: big clear windows, a spreading light, the clarity of revelation. But in the church, miraculously preserved, are the remains of an earlier and darker phase. On the inner, east wall of the tower are four bosses from a late-fourteenth-century chancel roof which was replaced in 1868. They are some of Cranbrook's greatest treasures. Each is cut from a single fat dark disc of oak, a yard across and a foot deep, sliced from the body of a timber tree. The carving takes up the full depth of the disc so that there is nothing shallow or decorative about the form. Most of the oak has been chiselled away, leaving only the vibrant, mysterious forms. These faces are the trees speaking. The trees have been felled but here they grow again.

Each of the four bosses has a different atmosphere, a different reflection of the nature of the wood, and of the human relationship to it.

There is a conventional, if smiling human face, a young man, wearing a padded hat and a headcloth, surrounded by a mass of curling leaves, a wide border to the face, with no interpenetration between figure and tree. It is, perhaps, an image of reconciliation, of an easiness with the facts of nature, a civilised man (or perhaps a woman?) settled in his bed of vegetation, like half an egg resting on its salad.

The second, which is aged, bearded and broken, as if the boss had fallen from the chancel roof on to the stone floor of the church, was clearly similar, a face with leaves, but more troubled, an arch of anxiety across the bearded man's brow, a feeling that in the luxuriance of his beard there is some osmosis across the human–natural barrier. Already here, the civilised man is sinking into (or is it emerging from?) the vegetation that threatens to smother him.

The other two come from somewhere still deeper, wild and savage things from a world that seems scarcely connected to Christian orthodoxy, let alone to the neatness of modern Cranbrook going about its shopping outside the door. These are the wood spirits that have emerged from the primitive Weald itself:

The first is a huge, near-animal mask, at least twice the size of a human face, with goggle eyes and an open mouth, a face of threat and terror. Between its lips, roughly hewn, uneven peg teeth grip the fat, snaky stems of a plant, which is clearly growing from this creature's gut and from there spewing out into the world. Its chiselled tendrils engulf the head, branching around it, gripping it and almost drowning it, as though the figure were not the source of the wood power but its victim. The whole disc looks like a hellish subversion of a sun god: not a source of emanating life and light but a sink of power, dark and shadowed where the sun disc gleams.

The fourth of the Cranbrook bosses is the most intriguing. The same net of leaves, which are perhaps the leaves of a plant that hovers between an acanthus and a hawthorn, crawls all over the surface of the boss, but without regularity, a chaotic and naturalistic maze of leaf and hollow, mimicking the unregulated experience of a wood itself, highlight and shadow, re-enacting the obstruction and givingness of trees. Within this vivid maze of life, there is something else, a body, winged apparently, with a giant claw that grasps a stem, and beyond that the full round breast of a bird. There is a head here, perhaps of a dragon, curled round to the top and difficult to make out, a presence, neither slight nor evanescent, both solid and unknowable, the wood bird/dragon, which does not even give as much as the green man, with his terror-explicit face and strangeness-explicit eyes.

These four great Cranbrook bosses were almost certainly paid for by the de Berhams, the family living at Sissinghurst at the end of the fourteenth century, when Cranbrook church was embellished, and whose coat of arms was carved on the west face of the church tower. In their bosses, there is a buried and schematic sermon on our relationship to the natural world. The set of four presents four different visions in a sort of matrix, two human, two natural, two good and two bad: a sense of ease among the froth of vegetation (human good); anxiety at its power (human bad); the bird/dragon half seen in the obscuring leaves (natural good); and the peg-toothed wood god grinning in the dark (natural bad). There seems to be no ranking here. Each is equal with the others. Together they are a description of how we are with the natural world (delighted or threatened), and how it is with us (mysterious and beneficent or obvious and cruel). Nothing I have ever seen has made the wood speak quite like this.

Of all the trees that this part of the world was in love with, none was more constant than the oak. In the great rebuilding of the fifteenth and sixteenth centuries, oak played a constant part. The hundreds of big Wealden houses on the farms around here are always crammed with as many oak studs in their façades as they could manage.

At Sissinghurst itself, which is a brick house, consciously set apart from the yeoman timber-framed tradition around it, the timber still shapes the interiors. All my life, lying in bed in the morning or last thing at night, I have stared up at the oak joists and tie beams of its ceilings. In the five hundred years since they were put up there, the oak has lost the orange-brown tang that it has when new and paled to a kind of dun suede, dry and hard, with a sort of suavity to it. There is no way you could bang a nail into this oak now, but it makes no display of its strength. It lies above you as you lie in bed, the grain visible along with an occasional knot, the edges as clean and sharp as the day they were cut. I have slept in every bedroom in the house at different times, and each has its different quirks and wrinkles. In some you can see where the sawyers using a double-handled saw made their successive cuts. A man stood at each end of the saw, one above, on the timber itself, the other, the underdog, in the pit beneath him. Each downward swoop was followed by an upward cut, and each cut moved the saw a quarter or a third of an inch along the joist. Each of those cuts is visible now in little ridges, not quite aligned, some almost on the vertical, some more on the diagonal, where one or other of the sawyers ripped an extra bit of energy into his stroke. The timbers look like a roughened bar-code, an account of two men at work one Elizabethan morning.

Until recently, it was thought that the original wildwood, the wood of England before man began to change it, was a huge and continuous cover of trees, the crown of each tree meeting those of its neighbours for hundreds of miles so that a squirrel could run from Dover to Ludlow or Penzance to Alnwick without once needing to touch the ground. Universal and mysterious gloom prevailed in this ancient picture. Occasionally a giant tree would crash to the ground, it was thought, and light would come down to the forest floor, but for the most part life was said to crawl about in a romantic vision of everlasting shadow.

All of that, it now seems, may be wrong. In the last few years new thinking, particularly by the brilliant Dutch forest ecologist Frans Vera, has begun to challenge this idea of the ubiquitous, closed forest of the ancient world. According to Vera's ideas, the ancient Weald, the sort of landscape that people would first have found when they came to Sissinghurst, may not, strangely enough, have looked very different from the Weald as it now is. If I walk out from Sissinghurst, across the Park, into the wood and out again into the pasture fields beyond it, where the oaks grow spreadingly in the light, I may well be walking through a place whose condition is rather like it was five thousand years ago.

If you take your bike and ride north from Sissinghurst, about seven miles across the clay flatlands of the Low Weald, past a succession of fifteenth- and sixteenth-century oak farmhouses, you come beyond Headcorn to the first rise of the Greensand Hills. Farmhouses, farm walls, barns and piggeries all start to turn here into the pale grey ragstone of the hills themselves. Just north of Headcorn, where the old road is cut deeply into the slope, you climb to the village of Ulcombe. From here you can look back at Sissinghurst from a place on its own skyline. The Weald lies blue and glossy in front of you. Beyond the ground at your feet, there is

nothing but trees. I scanned the whole horizon. In the binoculars –
it must have been five miles away – I saw what I hadn't spotted with
the naked eye: a kestrel hanging and fluttering in the summer air. Its
body was quivering in the eyeglass from the rising heat, a black dot
buried in the distance, making its own survey of the land. Beyond
the kestrel's body, I could make out the ridges of the Weald, one
layer of wood after another, but scarcely a field and no buildings,
except, very occasionally, a church tower. There was no hint of
modernity, nor from this height even the sound of traffic. Only, far
to the south-east and grey with distance, like islands seen from
out at sea, the huge blocks of the Dungeness power stations on the
Channel coast, and the necklaced pylons strung towards them like
toys. Otherwise only the heat, the dot of the kestrel and the blue of
the wood. Even with the binoculars, I couldn't make out the Tower
at Sissinghurst, but the avenue of poplars going down from the
Herb Garden to the lake, planted by Vita and Harold in November

1932, stood out clearly enough, almost the only verticals in the continuous rounded swells of the oaks.

The view from Ulcombe is a vision of the great wood of England. All the hedgerow oaks in the Low Weald come together to give an impression of uninvaded woodland. It is a view that might have confirmed the old theories of the solid, unbroken canopy of the Weald. Now, though, intriguingly for the later history of Sissinghurst, it seems that this picture of the dark, continuous 'closed' forest of folklore may not be the whole story. The critical factor, for Frans Vera and those who follow him, is the large herds of grazing animals. What effect would they have had on the ability of trees to reproduce themselves? Would they not have nibbled the seedlings even as they emerged? Added to that is the strange anomaly of the large amounts of oak and hazel pollen that have been found trapped within ancient muds at the bottom of lakes and ponds. Neither oak nor hazel can reproduce itself in shade. They need plenty of light to establish themselves as trees. If the forest remained dense and dark, with the canopy closed, how come there were so many of these shade-intolerant trees?

Vera's answer combines an understanding of the nibbling mouths with all the defence strategies the trees employ to resist or evade them. The Vera forest is a mosaic of thorny patches in which young saplings are growing; open, park-like savannah in which spreading, many-branched trees stand over well-grazed pastures; fringes of nettle, garlic, sorrel and goosefoot; and in the centre of the spreading woods places where the trees have aged and died and grassland has re-established itself, with its butterflies and all the birds of the woodland edge. It is not unlike the Park at Sissinghurst now, fringing on to the wet alder and oak wood, with thorny patches here and there (which we call hedges) in which the young oaks spring up, protected by the thorns and looking for the light. If Sissinghurst's well-managed parklands were abandoned, and the grazing mouths withdrawn (by a wolf, say, or lynx), then black-thorn, hawthorn, guelder rose, wild apple, pear and cherry, together with lots of hazel, would all emerge, to make buttons of young, scrubby wood. The whole place would be in slow and gradual flux under its ancient tension of grazing mouth and germinating tree: not a constant and continuous place, but somewhere in movement, a shifting of high woodland from one place to another, an opening of grassland, a recolonising of it by scrub.

Seen from a time-lapse camera, suspended over it in a balloon, the country flickers and shifts. The herds come and go, the patches of woodland emerge as thorny thickets and spinneys, become high, leafy canopied oak wood and collapse in time, the animals moving in again, the grassland emerging, the buttercups flowering in the flush of summer. There were beavers here then, and when beavers build dams in streams and small rivers, the roots of the trees rot and the forest collapses. If the beavers then leave, their dams break and the pools empty. In place of the drained pool, a grassy meadow develops and elk and deer come in to graze it. When Western colonists first went to Ontario they often found beaver meadows up to a hundred acres across and used them to make hay for their own cattle. So perhaps this too was happening down in the valley of the Hammer Brook, beaver dams and beaver meadows, the opening of wonderful damp, grassy glades where the herds of deer would come to graze.

I had to ask myself why this other and more mobile vision of the past here had such resonance for me. I know that for others, certainly for people who have come to work at Sissinghurst and to make their lives here, its beauty lies in its fixity, in its resistance apparently to modernity, and as a place that was reassuringly still and even perfect. Why did I not share in that? Why did I want it animated and flickering with life?

Perhaps, I came to realise, because it allowed us a place here too, because a focus on vitality and change, which may look like a rejection of the past, is, if set in this other framework, in fact a continuation of it. It might re-establish at Sissinghurst a sense that this was not a shrine or a mausoleum, but a long-living entity, far older than any one ingredient in it, of which self-renewal was part of its essence.

*　　*　　*

The Weald has never been the best or richest of lands. Throughout human history, the part of Kent that has seen the greatest development, the most people, money, roads, cities and grandeur, has been the strip of land in the north of the county, between the North Downs and the marshes that run along the south shore of the Thames estuary. Even at the very beginning, that would have been the prime land. It was easy to reach from the sea. Endless little creeks run up into it from the estuary shore. Travelling there, on lighter soils, would have been far easier than in the Weald. The soils were good there. It is one of the deep structures of Sissinghurst's history that it is a long way in from that coastline and set apart from that richness.

Even so, at the very beginning, the wild animals of the great wood would have been a draw, and the first signs that people came to Sissinghurst are now in Cranbrook Museum. Gathered in a glass case are the earliest human artefacts from this part of the Weald, flint hand axes and knives found now and then by chance in ditches and postholes, or turned up by the plough. A cluster of them appeared when Cranbrook School made its playing fields. A mile to the south of here, in a field at Golford Corner, a large Mesolithic flake was found which could have been a pick, perhaps belonging to a group of hunters pursuing the deer five or six thousand years ago. Some of the flints had yet to be made into useful tools or weapons; spare parts, elements of a repair kit. One or two had been chipped into blunt 'scrapers', used for separating flesh from skins. I have handled these stones at the museum, and one arrowhead in particular is a perfect thing, made of flint that the huntsman had brought here from the chalk downland to the north and then dropped or abandoned, who knows why. Its edge, scalloped to sharpness, each chipping like part of a little fingernail dished out of the flint, can still cut a slice in a piece of paper. There is nothing primitive or crude about it. It remains as honed as the day it was made.

Even so, these stones are at best fragmentary memories, half-whispers from the distant past, but they do at least articulate one thing: people were here. And they brought something with them. They were here for a purpose, and the fact they were here must

Staplehurst

Exhurst
Manor

Sinkhurst
Green

Maplehurst
Farm

Iden Manor
Farm

Little
Hungerden
Farm

Hammer Brook

Chittenden
Farm

Hollingbourne Weald

Great
Bubhurst
Farm

Ayleswade
Farm

Lovehurst
Manor

Frittenden

Faversham

Lashenden

Great
Wadd
Farm

Buckhurst
Farm

Ibornden
Farm

Hartridge
Manor
Farm

Tolehurst

Weald

Whitsunden

Brissenden
Farm

Noah's Ark

Hareplain

Hammer Brook

Bettenham
Manor

Hazelden
Farm

Hocker
Edge

Hawkridge
Farmhouse

Little
Bettenham

Canterbury

Biddenden

Wye Weald

Friezley

Sissinghurst
■ Castle

Hammer Mill
Farm

Sissinghurst
(Milkhouse)

*Copden
Wood*

Wilsley
Farm

Buckhurst
Farm

Branden

Hammer Brook

Angley
House

Cranbrook

Golford

High Tilt

Rogley
Farm

Crane Brook

Hemsted Forest

The
Freight

Chittenden
Farm

Droves and Settlements
in the Early Weald

Hemsted
(Benenden
School)

0   1   2 km   —— Droves

0   1 mile   ••••• Roman Road (course of)

▓▓▓ Present-day Woodlands

R Beult

mean there were animals in the Sissinghurst woods worth pursuing. How had they come? How did their life relate to this geography?

If you look at a map of the lowland that lies to the north-east of Sissinghurst, the 25,000 acres taken in by the view across the farmland of the Low Weald from the Tower, what you are looking at is the section of country that connects Sissinghurst to Canterbury and all the riches of the light, good soils in north-east Kent. Remove the villages and the farms, the railway and the Victorian toll road, and look for a moment only at the arrangement of the lanes. A pattern emerges. Quite consistently, over a front about seven miles wide, the country to the north-east of Sissinghurst is aligned around a set of long, sinuous but almost parallel lanes which snake across the Low Weald, each separated by about three-quarters of a mile from its neighbours. Sometimes the lanes visit the villages, but more often ignore them and slip onwards, across the clay lowlands. Farms are usually latched on to the lanes, but not always, and quite often little side routes diverge to a settlement, while the main drive moves on as if it had another motive beyond visiting the local and the immediate.

In the Dark Ages, 1500 years ago, these lanes undoubtedly became the drove roads of early English Kent, the routes by which settlements in the Weald were connected to the more established manors in the rich lands around Canterbury to the north-east, but there can be little doubt that they are far older than that. If you bicycle along them or even drive along them in the car, the sensation is quite different from driving along most lanes in England. They have an air of seamless continuity. There are no blind corners. You swerve across the miles with an extraordinary, liquid authority, gliding through Kent as if Kent were laid out for your pleasure. There are no obstructions. The lanes flow onwards, river roads, like the threads of a wide, braided stream making its way from north-east Kent to the woods of the High Weald. One French landscape historian, describing the lanes and paths of the Limousin, called them '*les lignes maîtresses du terroir*'. It is a phrase I have always loved, the mistress lines of the country, and that is what these subtle, unnoticed and slippery lanes of the Low Weald are like. They govern what they cross and predate the places they join. They are the matrix to which everything else in the end submits. Sometimes the old lane has not been taken up by the modern tarmac network but continues as a footpath across the fields or as a track used only by a farmer, and then, on foot, away from any traffic, you can feel as close to the beginnings of this place as in any other experience of the landscape.

This can only be a suggestion – it is neither provable nor disprovable – but it seems to me that these routes into the Weald are the oldest things here. And it is perfectly likely that they are not a human construct. They may be older than the presence of people here, the fossilisation and defining of routes into the great half-open, half-grassland forest, used by the early herds. This making of paths by the great herds into the wilderness is a universal fact. When men came to lay the first railways through the Appalachians in the mid-nineteenth century, the routes they chose were the tracks that had been made and kept open through the Virginian forests by the trampling and grazing of the bison. Our Kentish lanes may have the same beginnings.

Two of these herd-ways, both followable today, still come here. One makes its way down the greensand ridge at Grafty Green to the east of Ulcombe, getting that same dazzling, distant, forest-thick view, comes past Headcorn, strings its route across the clay, touching on a whole series of ancient farms and settlements, passes Frittenden, acquires a name, 'Sand Lane', and arrives at Sissinghurst as a long hedged track which we have always known as Blackberry

Lane, because when I was a boy it was a thick overgrown tunnel, on the outside of whose hedges the blackberries ripened in the sun. It was straightened by the improving George Neve in the 1860s, and so there is something of a restored, Victorian feeling to it, but whiffs of antiquity still hang about the track, never more than in the early summer, when the verges are lush, the thorns are in flower and it looks like the way to go. It doesn't come right up to Sissinghurst but characteristically swerves away, past Horse Race and on towards Cranbrook, where it merges with other routes coming in from the north and west.

The other Sissinghurst herd-way begins a little farther to the east. It crosses the North Downs at Charing, slides on to the green-sand at Little Chart, and then makes its way over the clay vale, through Pluckley and past a steady sequence of ancient farms, but not touching a village for more than ten miles, before again avoiding Sissinghurst itself, pushing instead on to the sandy ridge at the top of the wood (where it has been adopted as the main road from Biddenden) and moving on like the other towards Cranbrook.

Sissinghurst exists in the crook of these two tracks, as if it were the organ of a body held between its feeding arteries. There is nothing material about them. They are not made in any way. All they consist of is the earth and some transitory plants, some of which have been laid into hedges on either side. But the tracks have something, strangely, more lasting than a concrete, tangible existence: they are habits of use, a persistent pattern, a way in which things have been done. And if one is to think of this place in antiquity, one should not perhaps imagine it very different from the way these tracks are now. Sissinghurst then was not part of the solid, impenetrable and frighteningly dense forest, but threaded with these through-paths making their ways between the clearings and thickets, finding themselves sometimes in savannah-like parkland where the deer grazed and game was to be had, sometimes passing through patches where young oaks were sprouting up between the thorns and the hollies.

The deep past, then, was not, as we are so often encouraged to imagine it, some desperate and dreadful experience coloured only by threat and unkindness, but full of possibility, excitement and beauty in the empty half-open woodlands which were here then. Half-close your eyes one evening in Blackberry Lane and those four images from the Cranbrook bosses will come back to you: a relaxed beneficence among the fresh green hawthorns; some anxiety in the shadows; the bird half seen in the obscuring trees; and the big-mouthed grin of the goggle-eyed wood god. It is all here now and it was all here then.

There was one last object which if it had survived might have been the emblem of Sissinghurst two thousand years ago. It represents a little window on the distant past which opened in a Victorian summer and has since closed. George Neve, the distinguished tenant farmer here, a man of parts, contributor to the letter columns of national newspapers, was settled into the large and comfortable brick farmhouse at Sissinghurst which he had built almost twenty years before. The young cedars of Lebanon he had planted on his south lawn were eight years old and doing well. The laurels and rhododendrons in the dell next to his house were beginning to gloom over satisfactorily. It was time to show the county what sort of man he was.

George Neve invited the general meeting of the Kent Archaeological Society to spend part of its day at Sissinghurst. They came on 24 July 1873. Earl Amherst would be attending, as would Viscount Holmesdale, his son. There were about 140 people in all, including a general, an archdeacon and twenty-five vicars, many with their wives. After a preliminary meeting in the South Eastern Hotel in Staplehurst, they visited Staplehurst and Frittenden churches, and then came on to Sissinghurst in their carriages, where 'Mr George Neve, of Sissinghurst Castle, most hospitably invited the whole company to partake of luncheon in a shaded nook upon his lawn, where tables were laid with abundant refreshments'.

After lunch, the company re-entered their carriages and went on to Cranbrook church. Before they left, Neve would undoubtedly have shown them his treasure. It had been ploughed up five years before, at a depth of about eight inches, from a field near Bettenham, no more specific than that. A few years earlier, in another neighbouring field, the men on the farm had ploughed up an urn containing some bones. That, unfortunately, had been destroyed, but the treasure found in 1868 Neve had kept, and had even had photographed. An image of it would be reproduced in the volume of *Archaeologia Cantiana* that reported his lunch party. It was a gold ring, made of two gold wires, twisted together. One of the wires was thin and of the same diameter throughout; the other was three times as thick but tapered along its length to a point.

It was a piece of Celtic jewellery, belonging to someone about two thousand years ago who spoke a version of Welsh or Breton, the kind of ring that is found all over Europe, from Bohemia to the Hebrides. Its twistedness is the mark of a culture that liked complexity and the way in which things could turn inward and mix with their opposite. It was a beautiful thing: private not public, suggestive not assertive, symbolic not utilitarian. Perhaps it was a wedding ring, a binding of two lives, in gold because gold is everlasting. At some time in the last 130 years, this precious object has disappeared, but at least we have the image of it and the knowledge of its existence. I see in the Bettenham ring the culmination of this first phase of Sissinghurst's existence. It – and the fact of a burial being made here – confirms a certain view of the ancient Wealden past. This was not, at least by the time of Christ, some godforsaken, Tolkienian forest in which trees loomed and rivers dripped, where people trod rarely and fearfully. Far from it: people knew Bettenham and Sissinghurst as theirs. Stream, meadow, wood and track, long summer grasses, spring flowers, the spread of archangel, stitchwort, campion and bluebells on the edge of the wood, the flickering of light down on to the water, the flash of the kingfisher, the pike in the dark pools, the songs of the nightingales and the woodpeckers, the swallows and house martins dipping on to the ponds, the fluster of pigeons, the flicker of kestrel and sparrowhawk: they would have known it all – and more, not in some marginalised way, scraping a desperate, squatter existence from the woods, but with comfort, gold, elegance and the symbolising of love and mutuality in a ring. They would have farmed here. Even two thousand years ago, Sissinghurst was home.

FIVE

Testing

FROM OCTOBER 2005 ONWARDS, I slowly tried out the ideas I had for Sissinghurst. I started to think of them more publicly, not as desires but as facts, at least in embryo. Following my nose, asking my friends for hints and tips, I began to engage with the realities. I have nearly always worked alone and have loved that, the silence and privacy of it, the space which solitary work allows for ideas to accumulate and thicken like crystals dangling in a solution. On your own, understanding comes not by argument but accretion. It's quick. There is no need for persuasion or repetition on your own. I always knew this was going to be different: the meetings, the hierarchies, feeling my way past embedded difficulties, seeing my own ideas from other people's point of view. All of that was the price of getting something to happen for real, of pushing it beyond the limits of longing or regret, beyond the written. Real ambitions would mean real engagement. I knew from the start that any scheme here had to be commercially viable. This couldn't be a fantasy park. Any exercise in vanity farming, in aesthetics or window-dressing, would mean nothing and anyway would smell wrong. The fertility of the ground, if it meant anything at all, could not be subsidised. In modern terms, it had to survive in the market, providing something that people were actually prepared to buy. I felt sure they would; if we got it right, people would want to buy little else. But we needed, first, a feasibility study. It would cost, I discovered, between £15,000 and £20,000.

Jonathan Light, Sally Bushell, the property manager at Sissinghurst, Sarah and I had a meeting in our kitchen, the first of hundreds: Sally gentle, warm, organisational, consensus-conscious, increasingly investing in a hope and belief that this idea might work, always friendly to us; Jonathan a precisionist with a razored haircut and the straightest of backs, who in an earlier life was a chartered engineer with ICI, now married to a barrister, always working out his requirements beforehand, distinguishing between desires and needs, a careful, note-taking, systematic man, economical in what he said but with a sharp line in the sardonic remark, the embodiment of consistency and courtesy, precisely the calming and sustaining presence Sissinghurst needed; and Sarah and I both slightly anxious in meetings, not quite having the meeting language and so tending to look amateur and impetuous, the 'flaky creatives', as Sarah called us one day. But we four were calmly getting to know each other, daring a joke now and then, gathering a trust in each other's capabilities and good intentions. At the beginning, Jonathan asked whether I could get together an Outline Proposal for a Draft Project Brief for an Investigation of the Business Case to go out to Tender for a Consultative Exercise on the Ideas I had? Those were not quite his words but I said I could and it took a morning.

The ideal was of a kind of mixed farming that was traditional in the Weald until the 1960s, when the combination of an increasingly globalised market and the arrival of artificial fertilisers made it unviable. That kind of mixed farm was the frame in which the garden at Sissinghurst was originally set. The study needed to examine how far it was possible to reinvigorate the farming methods at Sissinghurst, with a view not to distant markets but to the value that its own restaurant and farm shop could create. The massive retail potential at Sissinghurst made the old landscape possible. The full polycultural variety should be the goal: soft fruit and top fruit, hops, dairy cattle, as well as cereals, beef cattle, pigs, sheep, chickens, pigeons and ducks.

There were a thousand questions. How would Sissinghurst sell the products of its landscape to its visitors? Could the farm really provide the restaurant with everything it offered its customers? What would the economics be of a farm shop at Sissinghurst? Could the restaurant and shop, at the beginning of the year, 'order' their requirements from the farm? Could Sissinghurst make its own ice cream, bread, cakes, scones and jams from the dairy cows, fruit fields, wheats and ryes grown in the fields? Could the woods produce pea sticks, hurdles, chestnut fencing and furniture to be bought by customers? Could people take hop bines away with them in their cars? Was pick-your-own a possibility, perhaps of flowers as well as fruit? Could a chicken-run provide the eggs for the omelettes the restaurant would make? Was there a place for a bakery with a takeaway counter? Bringing animals back to the farm, the repatriation of farm management to Sissinghurst, the growing of vegetables and the setting up of a farm shop would all need buildings and equipment. Where should they go? And how would they fit with the tourist business?

Alongside that was the question of a business structure. Were the profit margins to be set in advance? Or could the Trust tolerate a lower level of profit here in return for the landscape benefits? Was it necessary to stick with the idea of farmer as producer and restaurant as client? Or should a single enterprise become the tenant of the farm, the restaurant and the farm shop? How integrated, in other words, could the retail and production arms at Sissinghurst be? Could a loss on one be set against the profits on the other?

Driving blind – and not knowing the true situation – I guessed that the Trust would have little money to bring all this about. But I also knew that it had raised £360,000 in two years at Sheffield Park in Sussex from visitor contributions – with the same number of visitors per year as Sissinghurst. That money was for replanting trees which had been blown down in the great storm of 1987 rather than this more nebulous and commercial scheme, but still it was no more than one pound a visitor. Would the Sissinghurst visitors want to pay for the set-up costs of this?

There was also a question of land. The farmed area at Sissinghurst looked as if it might be too small at 259 acres. More land was probably needed, either rented or acquired. I knew, of course, of the neighbouring Bettenham and Brissenden farms, which once belonged to my grandmother and which now belonged to a ninety-two-year-old law professor, Professor James, who lived at Benenden. I rang him one evening. 'Ah yes,' he said, 'Nigel's son? You know he sold me those farms?' I did. 'A terrible price, terrible, really terrible.' For you? I asked. 'No, no,' he laughed. 'For him.' My poor father had sold those farms, now worth £3.5 million, for £15,000 in 1964. 'To do up his house, wasn't it?' Professor James asked. I didn't go into the details but instead risked my question. 'Do you think there is any chance, Professor, that when you die you might consider leaving those farms, or some of them anyway, to the National Trust, to reunite the estate as it was before the 1960s? We have great plans for the farm here.' A pause on the other end of the phone. 'If there is one organisation in England to which I would not leave my property, it is the National Trust.' He had been appalled, a few years earlier, when the Trust, which had accepted land on Exmoor on the condition, among others, that stag hunting would continue across it, had agreed under pressure from its own largely urban and anti-hunting membership to ban the hunt from its land. This was a question of honour, Professor James said, allied to one of uncertainty. How could he be sure that any agreement he made about these farms would be observed after he was dead? I said we would all do our best to see that agreements were honoured and how we had nothing but the best interests of the land in mind. 'No, no, no,' he said, swatting away a puppy. 'Anyway,

Robert Lewis, who has farmed it for many years for us, he's the man for that land.' So Bettenham and Brissenden were severed from Sissinghurst, perhaps for ever. We would have to live within our limits.

Sally, Jonathan, Sarah and I worked our way through the suggestions. I added a need for aesthetics. 'Whatever is done must both look and feel right for Sissinghurst, and enhance rather than detract from what is already here. Aesthetics cannot be a last-priority bolt-on.' Jonathan added the need for 'reversibility'. If it went wrong, nothing we had done should be undoable. The scheme 'must not land a white elephant on either the NT's or Sissinghurst's back'. And any scheme must be 'revenue-neutral'. Sissinghurst as a whole must earn as much after any changes we made as before.

Having looked at the leases of the four farming tenants, Jonathan also found some good news. There was a break clause in all of them which meant that if we had a coherent plan together by September 2006, the Trust could give them a year's notice to quit, which meant that by 26 September 2007, the land at Sissinghurst could be back in hand and the project could begin to work. The Trust had recently had some disastrous publicity when they had amalgamated two farm tenancies in the Lake District, and so they would have to tread with immense care around this issue. But this gave us a deadline and a timetable.

Fiona Reynolds had asked me to talk to the National Trust AGM that November in Brighton. 'Don't frighten the horses,' Jonathan said, and so I spoke to them after dinner in big generalities. What was the National Trust for? It came down, I told them, to a new understanding of what was meant by the word 'place'. That word is enshrined in the name of the Trust; it is a National Trust for Places. And what is a place? Not just a location.

The Trust does not own 'sites' in the way Asda or BP does. It doesn't plonk down its identity on a neutral spot. Nor is a place an idea or an image. It is intensely concrete, the opposite of anything virtual, something that is thick with its own reality. And, more than that, a place is somewhere with a quality you might call 'inner connectedness'. That is a subtle but powerful thing, which is related to a kind of self-sufficiency, a feeling in a place that its life is not borrowed or imposed from elsewhere, but is coming up out of its own soil.

The old debate, I told them, had always set commercialism and enterprise against poetry and conservation. But that was missing the point. People had a growing hunger for authenticity and the enriched place. The enormous proliferation in the modern world of slickly and thinly communicated meanings had generated a demand for the opposite, for the sense when you arrived somewhere that not only did this look wonderful but was wonderful, that it wasn't just a skin. Gertrude Stein had famously said of Oakland, California, that 'There is no *there* there'. For the Trust, and for all of us, *thereness* and turnover could be the same thing. All the NT had to do was make sure it was constantly cultivating and rejuvenating the thereness of the places it owned and its customers would flock in.

I did not feel in private quite as sanguine. I had underestimated the way in which these ideas would ruffle feathers at Sissinghurst. Anxiety was already raising its head. What people loved here was its 'tranquillity', and people were worried that my ideas would disturb it. Trucks, intensification, multiple demands: none of those felt very Sissinghursty. Nobody much liked the idea of chickens or pigs because of the smell. Already, just creaking open like a board splitting in the sunlight, the cracks were appearing between those who had the easy ideas and those who were expected to make them work.

In December, one freezing foggy Sunday, Sarah and I went to see Jacob Rothschild. The Rothschild house at Waddesdon belongs to the National Trust but the Rothschilds, because they are able to subsidise it to the tune of £1 million a year from a family trust, are able to decide pretty well everything that happens there. The garden writer and designer Mary Keen, who is a friend of the Rothschilds, had asked him to ask us to lunch. I wore a suit, which was a mistake as everyone else was in shirts and jerseys. A butler told us to park our dirty Land Rover next to a Swiss-number-plated Range Rover.

Lady Rothschild gave us champagne. 'Or would you prefer something else?' A classical pavilion of a house. Guardis on the wall. Lunch in a French rococo room. I felt like a suited prune amid such riches, but Lady Rothschild was warmth itself. 'Barbara Amiel said that Jacob marrying me was about as likely as the King of the Jews marrying a Hottentot,' she whispered at lunch.

Rothschild was a king, huge in his red jersey, loping, looking at the world from a great height but full of grace. Just audible beneath the surface a great deal of idling, ticking-over horsepower in reserve, but generous in his eyes, exuding interest. Sarah grows a bulb called *Gloriosa superba Rothschildiana*. I couldn't get the phrase out of my head. After lunch we talked about the Sissinghurst scheme. He thought the Sissinghurst Trust idea bad because it set up two power bases and an inbuilt tension. 'Why not take the whole thing over, including the garden?'

Impossible, I said.

'Why?'

For a million and one reasons. The great difference was that the Rothschilds had their huge fund hosing money into Waddesdon and the National Trust was happy to accept anything they were prepared to pour down its throat. We were not in that position. But he was also discouraging about the prospect of raising any money. 'It is much, much more difficult than you imagine.' There was a kind of shy directness to him, and he was funny. 'I couldn't sack a day-lily,' he said. But even talking to him about how to manage the relationship with the Trust was absurd. The idea that we could borrow any principles from Waddesdon was beyond a joke. In the car on the way home, Sarah said she didn't want to take on the burden of it all. 'Haven't we had enough burdens for the past few years? Haven't we got other things to do? What I want now is a rather unburdened existence. What exactly is the point of doing this now?'

So what was the point of doing it? That maybe we had some ideas of what might be good for Sissinghurst. That it was a place, which as a whole needed turning on to a better and richer course. That its current condition, as a whole, was a thin and singular version of what it might be – no one with any sense of a living reality could say it was a garden in a farm nowadays, which is what people imagined it was. That I felt a kind of bond with Sissinghurst which would not allow me to leave it like this. That I had in my mind a half-remembered, half-imagined state which, when set against the present, pained me. And, if I were honest with myself, I wanted to make my mark there. I did not simply want to be the receiving son. But I promised Sarah that if it did not work I would not continue to beat my head against this wall for ever. We would leave and do what we imagined was good elsewhere. We had long nurtured the idea of making a wild garden by a spring in the Amari valley in Crete, below Mount Ida, among the olives and the rocks. I promised her then that we wouldn't die without that dream becoming true.

At home at Sissinghurst a couple of days later we gave a drinks party for everyone living and working there. Sofas pushed back, hot mulled wine, a big fire. Some time into the party, a woman, flushed with the warmth, came up to me. 'You really think you're the lord of the manor now, don't you? Well, Adam, I can tell you something: you are not.' So here it was: the sunny visions of perfection exposed to a cold and withering wind. There were people at Sissinghurst who considered it theirs, who had devoted their lives to it, who loved it quite as much as I did, and who felt that Sarah and I were more interested in our own welfare than in Sissinghurst's. 'Are we helping you do what you want,' someone asked me, 'or are you helping us do what we want?' I thought even then that perhaps we should simply leave them to it and that they could make it in their own image.

We had a final meeting just before Christmas with Sue Saville. She said the Trust was happy to put some money into a feasibility study. A feasibility study! Have three words ever sounded quite so sweet? And how will it be paid for? I asked. 'Sissinghurst will pay for it,' Jonathan said. How, though? 'The clause your father inserted in the 1967 agreement has meant that Sissinghurst is what we call a Special Trust in Credit. It has a large reserve accumulated against a rainy day.' The disciplines exercised over the last fifteen years or so have meant that the size of the Sissinghurst financial cushion is astonishing. While the world has been borrowing, Sissinghurst has been saving, and the accumulated reserve now allows substantial annual expenditure with no diminution of the invested capital. People rarely applaud the National Trust for its financial management but this policy has been exemplary. Not a single aspect of the scheme this book describes would have been possible without it. As Jonathan said that afternoon, the farm project could not be allowed to lose money on its current account in the long term, but, within reason, it was not going to be constrained by shortage of capital.

Together, Jonathan, Sally, Sarah and I worked our way through the early part of the year. I made a list of target qualities for any scheme:

Authenticity

Richness

Rootedness

Connectedness

Vitality

Delight

Jonathan and Sally drew up a huge and careful tender document. Consultants came and made their bids for the work. We walked them around the place in the late winter, some in the rain, some on wonderful mornings when there was a frost on the moat, just a skin, not enough for a moorhen to walk on. The first spikes of the narcissus were up in the orchard and the aconites were out under the hedge between Delos and the White Garden, casually there like beautiful weeds. Against the light blue of the March mornings the consultants had ideas and questions. The old dairy and the barn next to it might be the farm shop and café. The Horse Race hedges would have to grow up if the fruit trees were to go back. Could the farm be enlarged? Could the restaurant expand into the barn? Did it have to be organic? There was a sense above all of potential in the air. Some of them were a bit highfalutin. 'I don't see why, when we know we've got our feet in the treacle,' Jonathan said after reading one report, 'we need to have our heads in it too.' Helen Browning from the Soil Association took a bit of the soil away in a napkin I gave her. It felt like a kind of spring, tentative, only half there but, still, half there.

I went for walks in the early woods. The colours were changing, the purple of the alder catkins now mixed with the hazel and then the goat willows coming on like lights, the 'palm trees', as my nanny Shirley Punnett always used to call them. The geese were clanging away across the farm, their voices a long, deep echoing you could hear a mile downwind. Sissinghurst was full of one of the miracles of spring: the light suddenly penetrating to the floor of the wood, for the first time since the previous year, reaching into its depths as if into an aquarium or an unfinished house.

It was a heady time for me. I had become used to the idea that changes would happen at Sissinghurst without my knowing about them in advance. My father as he got older had increasingly accepted the decisions being made around him. I remember finding him once almost in tears, sitting at the kitchen table, having come back from a walk down by the lake, where he had seen that the wood he had loved all his life, fringing the lake and the stream that runs beside it, had been cut down without anyone telling him. He did not like an argument and had said nothing. That silent acceptance of unannounced change had seemed like the prevailing reality. And so now, as I felt the National Trust responding to these ideas I had, seeing them under Jonathan's hands taking on a substance and a form, the experience was strange and unreal, almost vertigo-inducing. I realised I had never wielded influence before.

To my relief, the Soil Association, the champion of the organic idea, was awarded the contract, and their glamorous team turned up: Helen Browning, powerful, strong minded, clear voiced, a big farmer in Wiltshire, chair of a government committee on animal welfare, a partner in her own organic food business; alongside her, Katrin Hochberg, a cool, taut, courteous German in her twenties, with high cheekbones and eyes the colour of the North Sea in February. Both of them glowed with the kind of health that was a billboard for the organic idea. And Phil Stocker, a Bristol man, once a big-time chemical farmer who went to work for the RSPB, saw the organic light and now devotes every hour of his life to persuading the farmers of England to go the way he has gone. Every sentence he speaks delivers straight, persuasive idealism. When these three arrived, I felt as if I had bought a new car. With them we could go anywhere. No weariness and no viscosity, nor any sense that they were in service to some antiquated or inherited idea. They looked like ushers to the future.

We walked around the farm on a sunny day in April. Spring was coming on and the blackthorn was out in the hedges. An occasional wild cherry was a white flash in the wood. The higher trees had not yet leafed up but in the garden the magnolia petals were lying browned and scattered among the lungwort at their feet like the scales of a fish. There was colour in the world. The pigeons were sitting in the trees like fattened Christmas decorations. From out in the arable fields, where the soil was still as bare and brown as it had been at the end of August, the daffodils, the forsythia and the cherry blossom in the orchard blazed away. You could smell the soil drying in the sun as if it were some kind of vegetable mass.

With Helen and then again with Phil I walked across the empty arable fields. Nothing was growing in them. Nothing had been planted and the weeds had been sprayed off. Everywhere around us, the celandines were emerging in the hedge banks and the garlic along the stream, the anemones and the first of the bluebells were out in the wood. The cuckoo was cuckooing, there were yellow-hammers and blackcaps, and some larks were singing high above us, embroidering their song on the glowing air, but the earth beneath our feet was lifeless, a dusty and degraded place. Phil had a spade with him, and in one arable field after another he dug into the surface. Everywhere, in Frogmead and in Lodge and Large, even in Banky on the far side of the Hammer Brook, the spade went in an inch or two and stopped. That top couple of inches was loose and friable but below it the earth had compacted into solid and impenetrable clay. There were some wormcasts here and there on the surface, but when Phil dug deeper and revealed a section in the side of the small square hole, he showed me how nothing living was penetrating deeper than the surface inches. Here were the results of decade after decade of extractive agriculture. Some farmyard manure was still spread on these fields, and they were occasionally broken up with a subsoiling plough, but in essence they had been squeezed and compacted to within an inch or two of their lives. The Soil Association is called that for a reason: the basis of organic farming is attending to the well-being of the soil. It is the matrix in which life – bacterial, vegetable and animal – has its beginnings. Here the matrix was little better than a polystyrene block, the sterilised background into which artificial fertilisers could be injected and high-intensity grains grown. That pale, lifeless soil was a picture of everything that had gone wrong. You only had to look at it to see that an organic system here, one that rested the land from time to time in fertility-building leys, which restored organic matter to these lifeless soils, was the only way this scheme could go. Organic was the obvious and default option.

Only in one place did Phil's face light up. Just outside the restaurant, in the Cow Field, where the dairy herd had always been turned out after milking, I dug Phil's spade in. If you had been watching it in slow motion, you would have seen, with my first plunge, its worn and shiny leading edge slicing down into the green of the spring grass, slowly burying the full body of the blade in the earth and travelling on beyond it so that the spade came to rest with the ground level an inch up the shaft. Nothing wrong with that. I sliced out a square of turf and lifted it over. A delicious tweedy-brown crumbling soil appeared, a Bolognese sauce of a soil, rich and deep, smelling of life. Inside the small square trench, juicy beefsteak worms writhed in the sunlight. Here was James Stearns's 'best bit of dirt on the farm', the stuff in which he had said we could grow anything we liked. 'It's got to be the veg patch, hasn't it?' Phil said. Smiles all over his face. Peter Dear, the NT warden, came with his dog, and the three of us lay down on the grass there, looking across the Low Weald to the north-east, chatting about the birds, and how they loved the game crop in Lower Tassells. There were two larks making and remaking their song high over Large Field below us. How could we ensure the new farm was as friendly to birds as that?

It was a moment when I felt I could see something of the future, that slow, exploratory, otter-like feeling, which you recognise only as it rises to the surface inside you, that an idea might be one worth having.

It was clear from the beginning that the consultants' task was more than to provide a set of plans and figures. Anything new had to fit with the old. Helen said to me almost as soon as she arrived that none of it would work unless both Sissinghurst and the Trust subscribed to it. So we were to have meetings, partly to hear what Sissinghurst thought of the ideas and partly to tell Sissinghurst what the ideas were.

Late in April 2006, we all gathered in the lower part of the restaurant, the whole Sissinghurst community, which almost never gathered in one place. The anxiety was palpable in the room. I was nervous and I knew both Jonathan Light and Helen Browning were too. Helen had brought with her some facilitators, two glowingly beautiful, clear-eyed young women in plum and lime-green cardigans from the Soil Association. I told Helen afterwards how marvellous they were. 'I've got shedloads of those,' she said.

We split into groups and discussed what meant most to us about Sissinghurst. Jo Jones, one of the gardeners, summed the best of Sissinghurst up as 'established slowly over time; vulnerability; fragility; tenderness'. Claire Abery, another gardener, said she always liked seeing the visitors come but never minded seeing them go. People loved the sense that the place was full of its stories, that Sissinghurst somehow had an emotional existence beyond its bricks and lawns.

Then we came up with some ideas for the future. Several people said 'Do nothing' and 'Make no Change'. The anxiety had its origins, I think, in a fear that any changes could only be for the bad. For many years the people working at Sissinghurst had defended it against what they had seen as excessive commercialisation from NT Enterprises, the Trust's business arm, and thought of themselves as the guardians of Sissinghurst's soul. On top of that, the years of reduced spending had meant that the gardeners' eating and washing facilities had not been updated since the 1960s and were frankly disgraceful. The restaurant building had not been improved since the early 1990s. The offices and workshops were far below the standards expected in everyday commercial life. Many people working at Sissinghurst had been clamouring for these improvements for years and nothing had been done. Now here, apparently, as soon as Adam turns up, there was money à gogo for consultants, plans, changes. Why was that? And was it fair?

The head gardener, Alexis Datta, apologised to me later for the 'negativity' she had shown to these ideas over the months. Only slowly, I think, did we come to realise that we weren't as far apart as we thought. What I was suggesting had its roots deep in the historical soil of Sissinghurst, but no one here had ever seen any of it. They did not know what was missing. What I thought of as old and better they saw as new and suspect. Nor did they see any lack in the farm. 'What could be better than that?' Alexis asked me one day when pointing across the grass of the Cow Field and the big arable fields beyond it. 'I want it to be kept like that,' she said. We were told, as a kind of joke, that the way in which we were living here, with our rabbits and our bikes up against the hedges, was 'like having white trash move in'. It is not particularly easy to be told that, but I recognised well enough that we represented disruption, unneatness, a departure from the way it had been for the last ten or fifteen years.

I had not understood one crucial point. Everything I was suggesting drew its inspiration from what I had known and seen forty or forty-five years ago. My plans seemed to me like a regrounding of Sissinghurst, a return to the condition – or a version of it – in which it had existed for centuries. To almost everyone else, though – if not my sisters and not the Beales, Stearnses or Cliffords – it felt like a major disruption of something that, in their experience, up to seventeen years in one case, had 'always' been as it now was. My return to source was for them a destruction of perfection.

There was some recent history to this. Largely under my father's stimulus, and his unrelenting publicity campaign, visitor numbers had peaked at 197,000 in 1991. The whole place and everyone working in it were stretched beyond any sense of ease or comfort. It was felt that the 'spirit of the place' was being damaged by its tourist business and a new strategy was set up: stop all publicity, reduce visitor numbers, introduce timed tickets to the garden and cut expenditure so that Sissinghurst could begin to accumulate a financial reserve. The income from that reserve would mean in future that Sissinghurst no longer needed to rely on a huge visitor flow. By 1992 visitor numbers had dropped to 151,000, and went down to 135,000 in 2001. Meanwhile, the strategic reserve was steadily growing. The threat of crass commercialisation had been averted and the ideal of stillness and quiet, a steady state, had come to replace it.

What I was saying seemed to be overturning that, and it would continue to be difficult for months. At times it became personal. When I sat down opposite one of the gardeners at one meeting, she said, 'Oh God, do we really have to have you here?'

My head told me that it was a question of washing away the fears. And that there was also a perfectly hard set of constraints: Sissinghurst did not need any more visitors; nor too much of a drain on its running costs. Any plans had to be careful about not damaging what was already here. But in the face of all this it was difficult to maintain buoyancy and conviction. People higher up the Trust were prepared to countenance our plans; at Sissinghurst I felt increasingly besieged. I cherished tiny breakthroughs. Early one morning, Claire Abery told me that she had been given Sarah's book about growing vegetables, she was loving it and was planting up raised beds in her garden. 'Most of the time people don't join up the aesthetics with growing the veg but Sarah has done it,' she said. I said Sarah was keen to help in growing the vegetables here. 'Do you think I could do it with her?' Claire said. I could have kissed her.

At the end of April 2006, I asked Simon Fraser, a good and wise friend of mine, what we should do. He was sanity itself. I should put my ideas and energy into setting things up now in the way I thought they ought to be. Be patient. It takes time for ideas to become clear. Make sure the farm was combined with the farm shop and restaurant so that they were mutually supportive, not in some kind of market competition with each other. Don't get financially, managerially or practically involved, as that would end in grief and upset. Sarah and I should remain as members of the Sissinghurst Farm Board, to trim the direction it would take in the future. Eliminate risk, have no areas of conflict, give Sissinghurst what you can and then leave the National Trust to it. That was all we could do. It belonged to them and they would have to manage it. We shouldn't ever put ourselves in a position where we were claiming more than they could possibly give. Gauge that gap. Go where there is a door to be opened. Don't think of demolishing walls.

I realised, as Simon spoke, that this was an exercise in adulthood, in understanding the nature of organisations, and perhaps of places. It was unlike writing, where all you had to do was get the sentences and paragraphs in a clarifying and pleasing order. This was about having an idea, getting it in order, and only then creating a culture – in the sense of a laboratory culture, a growing environment – in which the ideas could take root and flourish. It was going to be slow and would never follow a straight line. And it needed the other side to speak. Nothing would happen unless everyone involved in the life of Sissinghurst made their claims on these ideas. It wasn't a question of recovering Sissinghurst but the opposite: allowing it a life, giving it what we could, gradually easing the concerns of people who worked here, understanding that we had to adapt our ideas to the sense of tranquillity that they cherished. The coexistence of vitality and tranquillity: that was the ideal, a kind of balanced health. And then confessing to ourselves that Sissinghurst had a life that stretched far beyond us.

I could feel myself being educated by this process. My previous experience of organisations had been either at the top or at the bottom. As a journalist, I merely did my best to provide what the paper wanted. A reporter is only a tool in the proprietor's hands; he certainly does not run the machine. And when I had run the small publishing company with my cousin Robert Sackville West or helped my wife Sarah run her Garden and Cookery School, we had made the simple decisions ourselves, with small staffs and with clear, single purposes to fulfil. Sissinghurst could not have been more different: viscous, anxious, convoluted, not entirely articulate about its needs, slow to respond, occasionally crabby. At other times warm, friendly, receptive, nurturing and generous. It was, in other words, rather old in the way it did things and that oldness and embeddedness, its maturity, had to be understood. New oldness: that was the goal.

SIX

Occupation

FROM OUT IN THE CLAY VALE, a mile or two away, Sissinghurst appears as a low, wooded ridge on the southern horizon. It looks, perhaps, like anywhere in the distance or on a map, full of promise and intrigue, a place, if you were given the chance, you might like to occupy. That is exactly how Sissinghurst first appears in a written record: as a ridge, with some slightly alien qualities to it, distant, not quite part of the homelands. This record, which is an Anglo-Saxon charter, takes its view from the north, from the world of property and government to which Sissinghurst has always been marginal. The charter is still in the archbishop's library in Canterbury Cathedral. Its clear and beautifully drawn Latin words were written by a Canterbury scribe on a large vellum sheet at the end of May 843. He was in a royal hunting lodge in Mereworth, with the king, near the great royal woods on the Greensand Hills, about twelve miles to the north-west of here. Æthelwulf, 'king of the West Saxons and also of the Men of Kent' – he was a Wessex warrior who had conquered Kent and was now distributing it among his favourites – was staying there, perhaps for some springtime hunting. While there, he gave several stretches of land to his 'faithful minister', Æthelmod, as autumn pastures for his pigs. One was called *Cadaca hrygc*: the second element of that name meaning back, spine or ridge; the first, in which every 'a' is pronounced long and thick – *Cardarker* – meaning 'of the jackdaws'.

Jackdaw Ridge: the name is perhaps three hundred years older than the charter that records it, and it marks the beginning of Sissinghurst – a stretch of mixed oak woodland on a long, lowish rise above the clays of the Low Weald, so far beyond the habits and knowledge of cultivated country that it could only be named after the small, pale-eyed crows to be found there. Their Saxon name – the *da* is the same as daw, the *ca* the same as caw – was an echo of their *kark-kark* call, and from that beginning over the centuries Cardarker Ridge drifted on men's lips through Karckeregge, Karkredge, Carkeregg, Harkeregge and Hokeregge to the Hawkridge, Hocker Edge and Hartridge of today, three rather swish and well-appointed country houses in the woods and dells a couple of miles to the west of Sissinghurst. But the name in the past, right up to the seventeenth century, was also attached to the land immediately to the west and south of Sissinghurst, covering much of modern Sissinghurst village, its neighbouring farmland and the house, garden and farm of Sissinghurst itself. It seems inescapable that *Cadaca hrygc* was the original and earliest English name of the whole block of country of which Sissinghurst is now a part.

It would be difficult to think of a set of syllables farther from the sibilance and ease of Sissinghurst, but Cardarker Ridget comes from the deepest levels of the knowable past here. It summons a distant world. The Roman road pushing south from Rochester to the Wealden ironworks would have continued in use even after the collapse of Roman administration and government in the fifth century AD. Little else, perhaps, was going on here. Angles, Saxons, Friesians and Jutes from different parts of Germanic Europe were crossing the narrow seas and taking control of the large, ex-Roman estates in northern Kent, many of them hinged to another Roman road, called Watling Street by the English, now the A2. But

Sissinghurst was well south of that zone of continuous occupation on the good soils. The Wealden ironworkings had been abandoned. All that was left at Lower Farningham Farm was cinders and cold slag. The gold-ring life of Celtic Bettenham might also have gone back for a while. Brambles and then trees would have recolonised abandoned fields. The meadows by the Hammer Brook would have reverted to marsh. Alder carr thickened over the bog. With the wild grazing herds now depleted by thousands of years of hunting, the great forest of the Weald might have begun to assume something of a dense and closed appearance.

There are places in the Sissinghurst woods which looked like that when I was a boy: huge oaks collapsed into dark, anoxic bogs where the streams had leaked outside their banks; if you walked into the wet, the mud would suck itself up over the top of your boots and fill the air with rot; streamers of green-leaved honeysuckle were the only sign of life in the decaying, mineralising wood; what had been living and vegetable was now falling apart, biology going back to its chemical constituents. The blackened and slimed timbers, whose fibres you could pull apart with your fingers, lay in the strangest and most exotic of pools, red, metal-stained, where groundwater seeping out through the nodules in the clay had taken on a rich, tomato-soup brilliance from the buried iron, but clearly poisonous, with swirls on the surface, slicked up and bleared, as if diesel had been dropped in the water.

That is how I think of the world of Cardarker Ridge 1500 years ago: damp, dark and disintegrating. There may be something in the name itself which hints at that marginality. The old English word *cadac* or *cadaw* and its equivalents throughout Europe were always used as a metaphor for a pilferer or petty thief. Jackdaws are little avian foxes. Like their cousins the magpies, they steal any bright, glittery thing. So perhaps this was the meaning of Cardarker Ridge. At the place where the crumbling Roman road began its climb into the wooded folds of the Weald – I pass it every day taking my daughters to the station on the way to school – there among the trees, in the fifth century, a band of outlaw, jackdaw pickpockets preyed on anyone who dared to come this way. Perhaps that was

Sissinghurst then, named like a place in a western: Thief Ridge?

Maybe. It would fit with the early days of the post-Roman Weald, when the officials and functionaries of the Roman fleet had withdrawn and the authority of any early English overlord in the north of the county scarcely stretched this far into the forest. But if it was a moment of disintegration and lawlessness, it was also the start of the great medieval movement which would transform the Weald. The end of Roman authority allowed a new, expansive and even entrepreneurial culture to flourish in Kent, nowhere more than in these woods and fields. An independent culture grew up here of men and women reliant on themselves, on their axes and ploughs, owing few duties to any feudal superior, able to own property and sell it, capable of leaving it to whoever they liked in their wills and looking for their well-being not to some lord but to their own struggles with the soils around them, a struggle that over many generations they succeeded in winning. It was a way of life that was called 'the custom of Kent'.

Beginning probably in the fifth century, the first of the English were coming to settle this part of the Weald. They walked or rode in from the north-east, down the sinuous droves, across the chalk and then over the Chart Hills, the routes that people and animals had already been using for thousands of years: down Sand Lane and Blackberry Lane, or along the track past Three Chimneys, which is still in part hedged well back from the road, wide enough to accommodate a driven herd or flock.

How did they arrive? Who were they? How did they establish themselves? How were these places made? In some ways the history of that settlement is particularly opaque. It seems that each drove led people from different parts of the periphery into the ancient forest. Around each drove, large, separate commons developed, a slice of Wealden lands, each common arranged to converge like the segments of a tangerine and each pushing in towards the centre of the Weald from a great manor on its northern boundary. To the north of Sissinghurst one large common led in from the manor of Hollingbourne through Sutton Valence and on to Staplehurst. To the east, another came in from the manor of Wye through Smarden and Biddenden. Converging on Sissinghurst itself from the north-east were two commons based on the manors of Faversham, coming down through Headcorn and Frittenden, and Sturry, following the line of the Hammer Brook from the direction of the Chart Hills, whose level brow is the horizon seen from Sissinghurst to the north-east.

That is the administrative picture – and it remains full of queries. How was it decided who should go where? Were people told to go? Or invited? On all of this there is nothing to say. But there is another level at which these questions can be asked, and here one is suddenly faced with a richness of detail, human and geographical, strange and immediate, which reveals the life here between 1500 and a thousand years ago. The place names become the key, and through them individual lives suddenly come up out of the landscape like bodies standing in their graves at the General Resurrection. Everywhere around Sissinghurst, as in most of Kent, the names of individual farms, woods, streams and hills portray the country just as it was first encountered by the colonising English.

There are a million acres in Kent. Scattered across them are more than eight thousand names marking places that have been occupied for more than a thousand years. No other part of England has anything equivalent to this density of ancient named settlement or this scattering of detailed continuity. It is a sign of the nature of Kentish individualism: no clustering; no early villages; little sense of community; a very early fragmentation into separate places, governed by the custom of gavelkind, by which a man divided his property between his children so that families spread into the corners of their holdings.

This detailed gazetteer of anonymous lives is distributed across Kent at a density of one to every 125 acres, in effect a name per farm. It makes for a country of private and secluded places, as if each place has a taproot diving into the past. The big villages are no older than the hamlets, the hamlets no older than the farms, the farms no older than the name of a wood or a stream. It is a landscape alive with detailed memory. Each tiny place is more significant to itself than to the parish or village of which it is a part. From the sandy hill between Sissinghurst and Bettenham, I can look across the neigh-bouring farms: Bettenham itself, Brissenden, Whitsunden and the manor farm at Frittenden. Just beyond the woods, obscured only by the trees, are Copden, Branden, a farm called High Tilt, others called Comenden and Camden, perhaps originally part of one place and divided by gavelkind. The far side of Hocker Edge, Hawk-ridge and Hartridge (three thirds of one holding?) are Tolehurst, Lovehurst and Snoad, Friezley, Buckhurst, Wilsley and Angley, Flishinghurst and Glassenbury.

These small places are the foundation of this landscape: I love them for the rounded angularity of their names, as Wealden as the timber-framed buildings still to be found on them, and as pure a litany of Wealden Kentishness as could ever be written. None is famous beyond itself. All have conducted their private lives across the centuries, wringing a living from difficult soils, all of them an interfolded mixture of wood and coppice, meadow and stream, all of them bedded into the sands and clays that underlie them.

Sissinghurst, despite its modern fame and the hundreds of thousands of visitors, is at root one of these places too. It is the landscape of its own privacy, continuous with its past, holding the secrets of what happened here in the marks and burrowings that cover its surface. It is a place, like everywhere else around it, that is worn and used, as Edward Thomas once described a stretch of country he knew and loved, 'like a schoolboy's desk that has blunted a hundred ingenious knives'.

Beyond that general understanding, though, and using the research done before the last war by J. K. Wallenberg, a Swedish etymologist from the University of Uppsala, one can start to read in these farm names the contours of a lived past. They record the phase after the bleakness of Cardarker Ridge, and represent a moment when once again the landscape became humanised and settled.

The twenty-five square miles around Sissinghurst cross the boundary between the clays to the north and east and the higher sandier ridges of the High Weald to the west and south. Within this little local province, five miles square, with nowhere more than three miles from Sissinghurst, there are, remarkably, seventy-four places that acquired their names at least a thousand years ago. What is here now, for all the roundabouts and golf clubs, the prison and crayfish lagoons, the public schools and the carpeted pubs, is in essence a depiction of what was here in the millennium before last.

The names of more than a third of Sissinghurst's neighbours (twenty-six of them in the twenty-five square miles) end in the suffix *–den*. Dens surround Sissinghurst on all sides. The name means 'a pasture for pigs', and so this, deep down, is swine country, which is one of the reasons I am so keen to have some pigs back at Sissinghurst. That does not mean that it was exclusively woodland. Pigs were and are the key ingredient of peasant farming throughout northern Europe. They breed quickly; they are omnivorous and, although certainly hungry for acorns and beechmast, cannot live

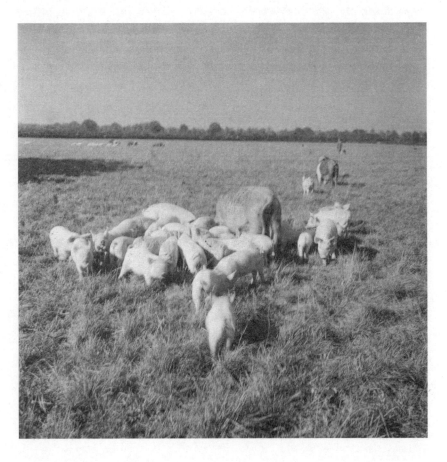

on them alone. Pigs fed only with that kind of tree-nut sicken and die. They need the worms and beetles and greenery they get from rootling around in a multiple and diverse environment if they are to thrive. They like the waste from kitchens. They are rather good to be with. Their meat can be preserved by smoking and salting (there were giant salt works on the north Kent marshes throughout the Middle Ages). They are the great generalists, relishing the acorns they would have got from the Wealden oaks but needing a mixed landscape. Of all farm animals, they are the natural companions for anyone deciding to make their way into new country.

Alongside the swine pastures are sixteen *–hursts* – from *hyrst*, meaning a wood, probably on a hill, perhaps enclosed. The hurst is the natural companion of the den, the surviving fragment of woodland, perhaps coppiced for firewood, alongside the open, treed pastures in which the pigs (cattle, horses, oxen, chickens, goats and sheep) are grazing. The existence of a place known as a wood can only mean that much of the landscape was not wooded around it. Most of the hursts are to the north and east of Sissinghurst, away from the great blocks of forest to the south, standing out in the largely cleared land of the Low Weald.

The third element, of which there are nine examples here, most of them concentrated to the south-west of Sissinghurst, on the high, light soils going towards Cranbrook, are places ending in *–ley*, a rubbed-down version of the Old English word *leah*. Its etymology is connected to 'light', a clearing, and the name is a sign of country made up of 'woodland with glades', perhaps the fragmentary edges of the forest, where corridors of pasture led into the thicker woods to the south.

Even at this most generalised level, it is an intriguing picture from the Dark Ages. These place names describe almost exactly what you would expect from the descendants of Frans Vera's open, browsed woodland: some pasture, perhaps cleared; knots of slightly denser wood; and passages of country, particularly on the lighter land to the south-west, that mark the transition between the two, the Kentish park-like savannah.

These names are the hyphen between now and then. Hurst, den

and ley make for a human landscape, one in which the atmosphere of Cardarker Ridge has been left far behind. A subtle, interfolded life was being lived here. Undoubtedly, the Germanic English coming into the Weald were expert carpenters. In the absence of many arable crops for thatching straw, they would have made oak shingles for the roofs of their large, rectangular timber houses, in which smoke rose from a central hearth to the height of an open hall. They could turn cups from blocks of applewood and field maple. Archaeologists have found Dark Age flutes made of hawthorn. The first Wealdsmen had hammers, adzes, drill-bits, gouges, planes, draw-knives, saws and wedges with which to transform timber into their houses and furniture – all of these have been found. But this was also the world of *Beowulf*, and in both landscape and poem it was the axe which was the instrument of destiny, for felling trees, lopping and topping the trunks and perhaps occasionally for imposing violence and asserting will. The axe was followed by the heavy plough, the team of oxen and the dogged ploughman behind it, described in one Old English poem as '*harholtes feond*' – the grey enemy of the wood. Here, on a kind of internal frontier, the expansive and acquisitive culture of the early Middle Ages was taking in the forest.

They would have hunted too, especially perhaps in the ley lands, the glades leading into the heart of the forest, some of which, around Angley near Cranbrook, were later in the Middle Ages to be converted by the archbishop into a park reserved for his hunting. In Saxon hunts, hounds were used to drive the wild boar on to the points of spears and javelins held by men standing in its path. Both roe and red deer were hunted through the English woods and wolves pursued, often into specially dug pits, where they could be killed and skinned, for the most glamorous coats known to Anglo-Saxon England. These perhaps were the higher-status hunts, of the sort Æthelwulf and Æthelmod were enjoying at Mereworth, but even here, you can be sure, foxes, beavers, otters, hares, wildcats and martens were all hunted through the valleys and over the ridges.

The place names are a guide to this landscape and one can chase them down to another level of detail. There are variations, flickerings of happiness and failure, of individual enterprise and fiercely staked identity, the cast of an ancient epic still distributed across the fields and woods. At their simplest, the names do no more than describe the places as the new arrivals found them. There is a Hartley the other side of Cranbrook, which means the glade of the deer. Two Buckhursts, one on either side of Sissinghurst, look as though they might also be deer woods, but they are in fact a corruption of *Boc–hyrst*, meaning beechwood. The modern owners of one of the Buckhursts have planted a beech avenue as an act of vegetable memory. There's a Maplehurst – a beautiful wood on a little hill which still does have maples in it – an Exhurst (ash – no wood at all there now), a Hazelden, an Iden (yew) and an Ibornden, which is a swine pasture by a stream with a yew. Others are simpler still. Hareplain near Bettenham is what it says it is. Rogley, on the edge of Hemsted Forest to the south, is a rough *leah*. Wadd, now a large and beautifully timbered fifteenth-century house on the way to Staplehurst, is the same word as Weald, meaning something like wood or perhaps wood-pasture, and it does indeed have a large hornbeam coppice next to it. Two Chittendens, one towards Benenden, the other near Staplehurst, were pastures where growth sprang up, the same word we now use for chitting potatoes, and The Freight, a luxurious house outside Cranbrook, where lawns spread and roses tumble between the yew hedges, comes from an Old English word that means the furzy growth on what had been cleared land.

This is the natural landscape, variegated and full of life in the margins of wood and pasture. The gaps between the old droveways were starting to fill, as if colour were flooding into the outlines of a drawing. Sewn into this natural world is a layer of places named after what people had done to them. These names, of great simplicity, are thought to be early, part of the first colonisation of the wood and its margins. So there is a place south of Sissinghurst which is simply called Hemsted, meaning homestead, the first place there that anyone had made their home. It became one of the great houses of Kent, and it was from Hemsted's Elizabethan halls that Lord Burghley wrote in 1573 complaining of the disgustingness of

Wealden roads. What is now called Sissinghurst village was until the nineteenth century known as Milkhouse or Milkhouse Street, a name older than it sounds, meaning a dairy settled around the old straight Roman road that ran through it. The farm called High Tilt, on the next ridge south from Sissinghurst, all tennis courts and gravel drives today, was originally called Tilgeseltha, which meant something like a collection of shacks by the tilled ground. (Tilt is the same as tilth.) And around High Tilt the soils are still good enough today for arable crops to be grown between the blocks of wood.

Among the natural riches of the forest and its margins, there was a scattering of modest human life: small buildings; a cow or two; sheds and a patch of cultivated ground. This was no Roman invasion but work was going on. Staplehurst was a woody hill where stakes or staples were grown, cut and made. Both Ayleswade (on the old drove towards Little Chart) and Snoad (near Staplehurst) were woods enclosed from the pasture, and Copton (now called Copden), Sissinghurst's nearest neighbour, which throughout the Middle Ages belonged to it, was a farm (a tun) where trees were pollarded or coppiced (copped – a word related to the French *couper*).

Then the individuals come up out of the ground: places named simply after the people that settled there. Bubhurst – now a beautiful house near Frittenden just off the old drove to Headcorn – is the wood of a man called Bubba. Frittenden itself and Friezley near Cranbrook were both settled by someone called Frithi. Branden, next to Copden, was originally called Berryingden, meaning the pasture of Berry's people. And at Bettenham there was a Betta or even a Betti, perhaps the first woman to own property here. The *–ham* element of the name – still pronounced as '*–hamm*' not '*–em*' – comes not from *–ham*, a farm, but from the Old Frisian for a flat meadow by a river, *hamme*. That is exactly where Bettenham is, on what are now arable fields but were until the nineteenth century a long string of lovely damp meadows by the Hammer Brook. The name of the stream itself may also be a memory, not of the much later ironworking hammers in Hammer Mill but of ancient meadows, the Hamme Brook, the name preserving almost uniquely the voiced second syllable of the Germanic –*hamme*. So Bettenham was Betty's Meadow on the Meadow Brook: could anything be more alluring than that?

A recognisable world seems to be ballooning up out of the names, as if a constancy and normality had survived the massive transformation of the intervening centuries. Already, in the very beginning, the generations were passing. Lovehurst down in the clay lands towards Staplehurst means 'the hurst that was left to someone in a will': Legacy Wood. Its near neighbour, Tolehurst, originally called Tunlafahirst, means something like Heir's Farm Wood. Inheritance and all the implications it carried of legality and order were already fully at work in what had become the highly legalised world of the Anglo-Saxons.

There is a final, surprising layer in this joint land-biography of a forgotten age: the place names around Sissinghurst are full of jokes and taunts, nicknames and insults thrown across the woods and fields by one set of neighbours at another. It is an element which brings the spark of life to this wood-margin-farming world. Out in the wet of the vale, where even now on a winter's day the water lies dead in the ditches, there are two neighbouring places called Sinkhurst and Hungerden. They are low in the damp ground, never where you would have gone if you had the choice, and their names clearly reflect what everyone else must originally have thought of them. (Hungerden did well in the hop boom of the nineteenth century and its ancient Wealden house was replaced then with a fine Victorian farmhouse. Sinkhurst still has nothing much to show for itself beyond a few cottages.) Both look like places in which it would be easy enough to sink into hunger and despair. Just as damp and not far away, until the nineteenth century, was a farm called Noah's Ark. By comparison, their near neighbours on slightly higher rising ground, Buckhurst and Maplehurst, glow with health and well-being.

The nicknames of individuals struggling to get on in this early landscape still survive. Lashenden, on the drove to Little Chart, is a pasture apparently belonging to 'a rival'; Biddenden belonged to a man who was always asking for things, a 'bidder'; Wilsley, just west of Sissinghurst, originally Wivelsleah, was the woodland glade of a man thought to be a weevil; Brissenden, the farm next to Bettenham once owned by my grandmother, was 'the den of a gadfly'; and its neighbour, now piously called Whitsunden, was originally Wichenden, the pasture farm of a witch or a wizard, now a lovely place, on a gentle rise above the lowest of the clays, divided between three families living in house, barn and oast.

And Sissinghurst's own place in this dense social network? Its name is among the most intriguing. It is a hurst, a wooded hill as seen from the open meadows along the Hammer Brook. Its second syllable *–ing* means 'the people of' or 'followers of'. And the first syllable, which had become 'Siss' by the late sixteenth century, had begun life in the Anglo-Saxon centuries as '*Seax*', which can mean any of three related things: a short sword, the *seaxa*, for which in Anglo-Saxon culture there was a reverence and cult, swords being handed down through the generations of a family; a man's nickname, *Seaxa*, his strength, flexibility and beauty reminding people of a sword; or the people themselves, the Saxons, who were named collectively after the battle weapon they had originally borrowed from the Franks. So what was Sissinghurst? The wood of the men of the knife? The place belonging to a blade-like hero and his followers? Or the Saxon place? You can't tell.

There is one hint in another place name, just to the west of here on the edge of the forest. It is possible that Angley near Cranbrook was the glade of the Angles. And so in the early English wood, it may be that two ethnically distinct settlements named themselves after the homelands they had left behind across the North Sea. This too is the world of *Beowulf*, an English poem, written and declaimed in England, to English men and women in English halls, but telling nostalgic stories, across the sea in the countries from which they all knew they had come. Perhaps Sissinghurst begins like that, as a colony, a planted place, whose inhabitants brought other memories and habits with them.

The name for me has always embraced the Dark Age world. It is not difficult, in the cold of an early winter evening, when the soil is cloddy and damp and the Hammer Brook is running thick and clotted with brown floodwater from rain on the hills to the south, to feel the presence of these people here: their timber hall, with the dark outside, a fire in the central hearth, the animals housed in the steading, shuffling in their straw or bracken beds, and in the light a tale being told, perhaps one of the great tales of Anglo-Saxon England, of our presence on earth being like the flight of a swallow through a winter hall, coming in from the night through one high window, spending a few airborne moments in the warmth and brilliance of the lit world, before flying out through the other end, back into the endless dark; or like the stories in *Beowulf*, of past heroes and blood, sea journeys and the monsters that stalk the night, in Seamus Heaney's time-shrinking phrase, 'as a kind of dog-breath in the dark'. That is what to imagine here: the Seaxingas drawn around their fires, alert to horror, held by stories which were intended to make their fears explicit, and to make more real their membership of the blood-band gathered beside them.

It would have been a good place. Seaxinghyrst was no Hungerden. It had some lightish, sandy-silty soils, which could be cultivated without too much labour. In the Park and in the Well Fields to the south of it, you can still see, in a low evening light, the shallow swellings and hollows of medieval strip cultivation on the light soils that modern agriculture no longer considers worth ploughing but which in the Dark Ages and the centuries that followed would have been invaluable. Even in what is now the wood, in the winter when the place is bare, you can see the rise and fall of what were clearly the boundaries of medieval fields. Sissinghurst was workable from the start, and it may be that these light soils were open and treeless then. But Sissinghurst also had its woods, for heating and buildings. It had streams of sweet fresh water coming down through those woods and many springs emerging in the hillside to the south. Even in the 1920s, the gentlemen farmers who then owned Sissinghurst, the Cheesemans, used to bottle up the water and take it to families living out in the clay vale, where the people would fall on it as something more drinkable than the murky water from their own wells. And Sissinghurst had, above all, the meadows by the Hammer Brook, well-watered land that would grow grass early in the year, might even produce two hay crops in one summer and which, until the coming of modern agriculture, was the most valuable land you could have.

The sequence by which the Kentish Weald was settled remains obscure. It is a story filled with conjecture and speculation, but in broad outline you can say that in the early centuries after the Romans left and the English arrived from Europe, people made their way down the old droveways into the relatively empty land of the Weald. That word itself is traditionally translated as 'Wood', but in medieval Europe it meant something more. A Weald, as understood by Angles, Saxons, Jutes, Franks and Friesians, was very nearly the same as a wood-pasture, a place where animals would come to feed, not only on the acorns and beechmast but on the leaves themselves and on the grazing within the glades and margins

of a wood. Throughout much of Germanic Europe, the word *Wald*
still means not only the wood but the leaves of the trees in the wood.
In medieval Kent, it meant above all a place that was not cultivated,
in the way that the fertile loams at the foot of the Downs always
had been. A Weald was not a closed oaken wilderness but a half-
open woodland, with dens, hursts and leahs, where your animals
could thrive.

By the time there are any documents describing this place,
though, that first folk-settlement phase was over and parts of this
wood-pasture world were being explicitly granted to the manors on
the good land lying beyond it. That is the moment at which this
chapter began. In 843 the King of Kent gave this whole stretch
of country to his 'faithful minister' as an autumn pasture for his
pigs. The king ordained that every year, for ever, Æthelmod's pigs
were to be driven up here from Little Chart (along the drove coming south-west to Sissinghurst) to fatten on the acorns from the

Wealden oaks. Anyone who interfered with the pigs, the charter makes clear, would suffer 'everlasting damnation'. The pigs were to stay for seven delicious and terminal weeks, from the equinox on 21 September, when by tradition the acorns begin to fall, until Martinmas on 11 November, the feast of St Martin, the patron saint of butchers, when they would be driven back to Æthelmod's manor in Little Chart to be slaughtered and salted for the winter. Sissinghurst had become a Saxon grandee's pig-fattening ground.

Nobody quite knows how all this worked. Pigs don't like being driven and tend to wander off at will. Would they really have been driven the fourteen miles from Little Chart and back again? Surely, the journey to Sissinghurst and back was likely to slim them down quite as much as they would have fattened up on the fruits of Sissinghurst's forest? Nor is the situation on the ground at all clear. By the ninth century, the large early pieces of common, such as the original *Cadaca hrygc*, were being divided up into much smaller dens, each of them allocated to different manors. The ownership map of Sissinghurst and its neighbouring lands, along with almost everywhere else in the Weald, soon became intensely complicated and has yet to be unravelled. Sissinghurst became a mosaic of wood, field, pasture and meadow, but of many different landlords' holdings. The manor of Little Chart, the archbishop's manor of Westgate just outside Canterbury, the manors of Wye and Charing and the abbey at Battle in Sussex all had separate little dens of two or three hundred acres each within a mile or two of here. Some land, in what is still called Cranbrook Common, remained unallocated to any of the surrounding manors.

Because of this dispersal of the ownership of the Weald, almost none of it appears in the Domesday Book. Whatever was at Sissing-hurst in 1086 was counted, invisibly, as part of the archbishop's manor of Westgate. So Sissinghurst enters the Middle Ages in a fog, unseen and unknowable. What was here? Surely more than a seasonal pig-camp. People must have been here all year round. This was not merely autumn swine-grazing. There must have been a cluster of small buildings, houses, cow sheds, stables, barns. By the eleventh century, Saxons had been at Sissinghurst for five hundred years. The practice of gavelkind meant that the original holding must have been divided many times over. There may have been a hamlet of small farms here, but of that there is no evidence, nothing written and nothing on the ground. There remains, in fact, very little evidence for anything for several centuries to come. One can guess at and feel one's way towards the general condition of life in medieval Sissinghurst but it is difficult to pin down. Until the beginning of the sixteenth century, no more than tiny fragments hint at what happened here.

Kent was certainly an increasingly busy place in the centuries before the Black Death in the mid-fourteenth century. The skeletal structure of the late Dark Age Weald was filling up. Many of the farms and hamlets surrounding Sissinghurst were occupied by incomers from the north of the county, squatting in the manorial waste or encouraged by the lords of those manors to bring the Weald into cultivation. The whole of the Weald had already been shared out, about five hundred dens belonging to 130 manors, with few fragments of common lying between them. Now, though, from the twelfth century onwards, slowly and piecemeal, the third phase began: the emergence of separate manors within the Weald itself, not dependent on lordships in north Kent, but acting as the centre of their own worlds. It is the point at which a visible identity for Sissinghurst begins at last to surface.

The name of the place, which until the nineteenth century was always part of the parish of Cranbrook, first appears attached to a man, Stephen. He is called 'Stephen de Saxingherste'. Fifty years later, his relation John de Saxenhurst is taxed for some lands in the parish of Cranbrook. These lands must have been the manor at Sissinghurst itself, and this John built himself a chapel here, dedicated to John the Baptist. A few years later, in 1242, a man who was perhaps John's son, Galfridus de Saxinherst, appears in a document named as the friend of the head of a priory at Combewell, a few miles away near Goudhurst.

It isn't much to go on, but it is possible – just – to construct a world from these fragments: a manor, pious, refined, just starting to materialise out of the blurred background of wood and stream.

Sissinghurst has come onstage occupied by its own family: the de Saxinghersts. If there had ever been a scattered hamlet of Seaxinga descendants, that moment was now over. This one family owned and dominated the place. It was a manor with its own 'rents, services, escheats and heriots' – in other words a place where these lords could charge others to live and farm, demand work from them, reclaim property if a tenant misbehaved or died without heirs, and charge death duties on the death of any tenant. The hierarchies and expectations of feudal Europe had arrived. The de Saxinghersts sat at the top of their own small pyramid, friends of the higher clergy, with their own chapel and lands elsewhere in the county.

The family held an estate that had a central core at Sissinghurst itself, Copton, now called Copden, just over the ridge to the south, and a place called Stone, which has disappeared, but may be remembered either in Milestone Wood, which is just to the south of Copden, or may be the place near Cranbrook Common, recorded in the early eighteenth century when Sissinghurst still owned some-where called 'Milestone Fields in the manor of Stone'. Beyond that central clump, the de Saxinghersts also had some properties in 'Melkhous' – the old name for Sissinghurst village – and were the tenants in 1283 of two of the archbishop's dens, Haselden just to the north of Milkhouse and Bletchenden in Headcorn, which their ancestor may have owned a hundred years before. 'The heirs of Sissinghurst' were also in possession of a place called Holred. They paid five shillings a year for the 'game they take there', easily the most rent paid to the archbishop by anyone in the Weald. Among the archbishop's papers, there are records of Kentish partridges caught by hawks, only a few pheasants, and some rabbits, as well as geese and swans, with woodcock in the winter woods, where they still come today, lurking in the thorns of the hedges, seen in the headlights when you come back late.

So the picture thickens: a small but high-quality estate distrib-uted along the old grain of the country, the ancient droveways into the Weald from the north-east, with some good hunting attached, in what might perhaps have been a park near the house. Today, if I walk out of the door at Sissinghurst, the possible site of Holred (a wood) is seven minutes away; it takes me about a quarter of an hour to get to Copden (a house in a wood to the south); the same to the village; ten minutes beyond that to the site of Stone (many modern houses on small plots), which is next to Haselden (a medieval house). Bletchenden (now a wonderful half-moated medieval house and barns) is an hour and a half's walk in the other direction, up the old drove towards Canterbury, past Brissenden and Bubhurst, on a track which for part of the way is now no more than sheep-mown grass between ancient hedges.

It is one coherent world, a country of lands and manors cut out of the Weald. But what was it like? That is the repeated question. What did it feel like then? It does at least become possible in the fourteenth century to hear the people of Kent for the first time. It seems as if the Kentish men spoke something like a kind of old Frisian, halfway between English and Dutch, the consonants heavily voiced, with 'v' for 'f' and 'z' for 's'. Their vowels still smelled of the Low Countries: hond for hand, hong for hang, plont for plant and thonke for thank, bocle for buckle, trost for trust, bres for brass, threll for thrall, melk for milk and pet for pit, keaf for calf, be-am for beam, dyad for dead, zennes for sins. Englishmen from the other end of the kingdom had no chance of understanding them, nor the people of Kent their visitors. A Yorkshireman landing on the north Kent coast in the late 1300s asked a farmer's wife for some eggs. 'I don't speak French,' she told him, and shut the door. Even as late as 1611, by now a joke, this was *A wooing song of a yeomen of Kent's sonne* printed and sold in London.

> Ich am my vathers eldest zonne,
> My mother eke doth love me well,
> For ich can bravely clout my shoone
> And ich full well can ring a bell.

Across the centuries, you can hear them like long-lost cousins, deeply foreign, Germanic but, what is miraculous to me, knowing this place better than I do.

In return for protection and as a means of dominance, the de Saxinghersts would have imposed duties on the peasants who worked the land for them. It was a life of unremitting labour for the poor. They had to thresh the corn and cart the manure to the fields, maintain the lord's buildings, collect the straw, deliver wood, provide men for the bakehouse, the kitchens and the brewhouse, make hazel hurdles for the sheepfold and then supervise the sheep when in it, fence off the young coppice woods from any marauding animals, mow, spread and lift the hay in the lord's meadows, carry his letters, drive animals to other manors if required, drive pigs to the autumn pannage, collect the hens due from tenants, collect and carry the eggs, put their sheep into the lord's fold by which the sheep manured the arable ground in the lord's demesne, from which of course the lord would derive the benefit in the years to come.

The woods had shifted in purpose. In an increasingly populated world, the acorns and beechmast for pigs had become less valuable than timber and wood for people. The long story of coppice-with-standards, which came to dominate the Weald and the Sissinghurst woods, was in operation by the fourteenth century. The long-growing standard oaks provided the structural timber for buildings; the coppiced underwood the heating and fencing, faggots and tool handles, reinforcements for river banks and even beds for the poor. Woodland was worth about the same per acre as good arable ground, not as much as meadow, and over a coppice cycle, the value was not in the standard trees but in the repeated cropping of the underwood. It was a wood world: wooden shoes, wooden tools and instruments, wooden wheels and cogs for mills, wooden vehicles, wooden furniture, wooden houses, wooden heat, wooden shutters, wooden fencing, wooden hurdles. As late as the 1950s, the families who came from London to pick the Sissinghurst hops were given beds in their huts made of straw palliasses placed on an underlayer of hazel faggots from the wood. Mary Stearns has a wonderful photograph of her son James driving a trailer-load of them up the lane.

The great trees, which had originally been the source of the acorns and were often pollarded when young to produce a big head of acorn-bearing boughs, continued to belong to the landlords as a source of timber, even when the ground below the trees had been let to the tenants. The archbishop's bailiffs were fiercely defensive of the trees their master owned, prosecuting the tenants of Bettenham and seven other dens in the early fourteenth century for cutting down an extraordinary six hundred oaks and beeches, forty of them at Bettenham. This was one of the longest-lasting customs of the Weald. Even in the leases drawn up for my grandmother in the twentieth century, that ancient practice continued. When the farm was let to Captain Beale in 1936, he agreed 'to keep all hedges properly slashed laid and trimmed in a workmanlike manner according to the best practice known in the district and to use no wire or dead thorns for repairing any quick hedges'. All 'timber and timber-like trees sellers and saplings' were to remain Vita's property and Captain Beale was to pay her five pounds for every tree or sapling he cut down.

In case this was still unclear, he agreed 'to preserve all timber and other trees pollards and saplings underwood and live fences from injury and not to lop top or crop any of the timber timberlike trees or saplings likely to become timber'. Unknown to either of them, it was a form of agreement that was at least seven hundred years old when they made it.

Among the woods, in the fields, or at least on the drier ground at the top of the farm, the Kentish men and women living here, speaking in their strange half-Dutch, would have striven for survival. Medieval England had no root crops. It was a world without potatoes, turnips, swedes or parsnips. Instead, on the light land, they might have grown barley for brewing and as the staple for bread. On the best demesne lands wheat was grown for sale in markets (Cranbrook had one from 1289), but it is unlikely they would have grown it here. Instead, on the damp and heavy land they could have grown rye, which is drought-resistant and survives in dry years, and oats for animal fodder, which can tolerate wet and heavy soils. By the mid-thirteenth century, even here, legumes were being introduced: peas, beans and vetches to renew and refresh the soil, fixing nitrogen from the atmosphere as we now know, but then thought at least to be an improved version of a fallow, with the added benefit that stock could be turned into the pea or bean fields when they were ready. The yields were pitiful: for wheat you might harvest three grains for every one sown, spring barley 2.5 to one, oats maybe 3.5 to one. These figures meant that hunger stalked them. As the population grew and the poor soils were driven harder, they sank ever deeper into a fertility trap: not enough goodness going back into the soil, too much land going into feeding the draught animals on whose muscle power they depended, declining yields, more people, fewer nutrients per person. By the early fourteenth century, famine and chronic malnutrition prevailed across the whole of Europe. The Black Death arrived in the 1340s at a landscape and a population that were ready to welcome it.

In this system, nothing would have been more important than the draught animals. On the archbishop's manor at Bexley in north Kent, there were 312 farmed acres, a little bigger than Sissinghurst, and on better land, but broadly comparable. There were two hundred ewes, all-purpose animals, from which milk, lambs, wool and skins for parchment could all be had. The sheep was the mainstay of mixed farming. Bexley also had twelve cows and a bull, but what is most surprising is the number of working animals, the tractors of the medieval enterprise: twenty plough animals, both oxen and horses, driven in teams of eight, often mixed, with one or two horses leading the ranks of oxen behind them, and sixteen draught oxen on top of that. They needed feeding, and of Bexley's farmed area, very nearly a third, ninety-six acres, was devoted to meadow, to the grass on which these animals could survive.

Oxen were valuable: in 1264 four were sold at Bethersden for 7s 6d each. But meadows were more valuable still. They were richly treasured by the archbishop's estate managers, and it seems as if archiepiscopal farms were focused entirely on the availability of meadowland. On the archbishop's riverside estates at Westgate itself, outside Canterbury, at Otford, Maidstone and Charing, and even at the outlying den of Bettenham, which was still attached to Westgate, meadow looms large in the accounts. Rent for a well-watered meadow per acre was double the rent on arable land and perhaps three or four times as much as on ordinary pasture. Meadows meant riches: more hay, which allowed you to keep more stock, including more oxen and so more animal power to plough and harrow the land, more manure with which to enrich it, more cereal crops, more grains and more food. The meadow was the route to well-being.

The meadows at Sissinghurst have gone now but they continue to have a flickering ghost existence near by. The neighbouring meadows upstream have belonged to the Halls at Hammer Mill since the early twentieth century, but they certainly belonged to Sissinghurst in the Middle Ages and right up until 1903, or at least to its subsidiary manor of Copden in the wood beside them. They are there as a kind of reproach, still grassy, damp, alluring on a morning heavy with summer wetness, or in the dank and dusk of a winter evening when the mist drifts up out of them and the smell of the wind-blown apples in Mrs Hall's orchard comes into your nostrils, musty and sweet. I have often been for late walks there, secretly, while the owls hoot in Floodgate Wood, beyond the banked leat that fringes the grass, and the lights in Hammer Mill Farm glow as yellow as apricots. If you can feel a lust for a kind of land, I feel it for those meadows, wanting more than anything else to return the Sissinghurst margins of the Hammer Brook to that condition. Instead, where our meadows once were, we have, at the moment, a dead and dreary arable field, which has suffered one cereal crop after another without break for years, where the soil itself is heavily compacted, and where in the winter the rain doesn't soak into a delicious, light, open soil structure but lies on its surface in sad-eyed pools. Only the name of the field recalls what it once was: Frogmead, a damp and froggy place, along the banks of the meadow brook, a name redolent of everything a Wealden John Clare would have loved here, a kind of thick-pelted richness, with secrets buried inside it.

Frogmead is something of a test of Sissinghurst's condition. It was once a marshland, a wet willow and alder wood. There are some heavy willow pollards and giant alder stools here by the stream, eight or nine feet across. The alders must be centuries old. Every year, they throw out vigorous, purple-budded seedlings into the edges of the arable crops, which survive until the summer when the combine shears them off an inch or two above the soil and the power harrow mashes their roots. Without that annual destruction, this would be a wet wood within a decade. The first settlers would have loved the prospect of lush meadowland and would have cleared the alder wood for the grass as soon as they arrived. Alder scarcely burns (I have tried: even after a year in the shed it moulders and hisses in the fireplace, giving out more damp smoke than any heat) but it looks good as furniture, and they could have turned cups and plates from it. Frogmead would then have remained an endlessly self-renewing meadow for centuries, perhaps even for thousands of years. It may have gone back to wet woodland at the end of the Roman period but the early English would have cleared it again, and hay crops would have been taken here throughout the Middle Ages and on until the nineteenth century. The hay for the great brick barns built at Sissinghurst in the sixteenth century would have come from these meadows, but in the 1860s the feeder channels bringing water into the meadowland were bridged over and filled in and a hop garden planted here. When the hops were abandoned in 1968, Frogmead became an arable field, which it has remained ever since. No hay comes off it any more and the barns remain empty from one year to the next. Frogmead's story is Sissinghurst's biography in miniature: after the Ice Age about eighty centuries of wild marsh, twenty of meadow to sustain this place, one of hops for the London thirst, and approaching half a century of subsidised cereals for a global market. Only in the wettest depths of the winter, when the Hammer Brook floods, and brown rivers of clay-thick water leak out over the fields, do you see again the old multiple beds of the meadow watercourses very lightly creased into the land, invisible when dry, but made apparent when the Hammer Brook once again reclaims its own. Knowing this and seeing this, on the maps and in the floods, I determined to persuade the Trust to restore the meadows that had been here for so long.

At the centre of the interlocked medieval world was the manor house and the high-gentry family to whom it all belonged. At some time towards the end of the thirteenth century, the line of the de Saxinghersts failed and they disappear from history. Their place was taken by the de Berhams, a family with other holdings in Kent, perhaps related to the de Saxinghersts by marriage and of great distinction. With them Sissinghurst achieved its late medieval flowering. They made this their principal seat and through them something of the quality of late medieval life can be felt here. It was still as remote a place as England knew. In 1260, Cranbrook church was described as being 'in a wooded and desert part of the diocese through which the Archbishop has to pass and where no lodging can be found during a long day's journey'. Even in midsummer, the roads were not clear. When the great warrior king Edward I came through the Weald in June 1299 (as he had two years before and would again almost at the end of his life in 1305), the royal exchequer issued 'money paid by order of the King to seventeen guides leading the King when going on his journey'. He had been at Canterbury, had gone down to Dover, come back up to the great manor house at Wye and from there went on to the archbishop's palace at Charing. He had with him his son, the fifteen-year-old Edward, soon to be Prince of Wales, and his grandson, the eight-year-old Gilbert de Clare, as well as the knights William de Bromfield and Nicholas de Chilham. It was a busy royal cavalcade, distributing four shillings a day in alms to the poor, accompanied by messengers sent off each evening on royal business. Edward had his cook and sauce-maker with him, as well as William de Rude, the King's Foxhunter, and two helpers, all dressed in English russet, along with John de Bikenorre, keeper of the king's hawks. Greyhounds, deerhounds, harriers and beagles accompanied the horsemen. It was a court on the road, all conducted in Norman French, buying parchments at twelve pence a dozen on which to draw up official documents, and paying wherever they went for horse fodder and harness, faggots and charcoal, as well as mountains of oxen, pigs, sheep, wine, swans, peacocks and 'little trout'. In the middle of June, this busy and impressive party came down the old drove road from Charing, through Little Chart, past Smarden, and on the evening of 19 June 1299 arrived to spend the night at Sissinghurst.

Can one say what the king and his companions found there? Certainly a pious family of high status. The name of the bailiff employed by the de Berhams has survived: a man called Manger, the son of Elie Monmatre de Petham, whose high-class Norman-French name stands out from the Jutish-Friesian world in which they moved. One of the de Berhams was a major official of the archbishop's office in Canterbury. Another was knighted. A third, Richard, became sheriff of Kent, the county's chief law enforcement officer, married a Cranbrook girl, Constance Gibbon, and was one of the knights charged with command of the local militia. As well as Sissinghurst, he gathered estates on the Chart Hills, up the drove-ways in Charing and Pluckley, and was worth forty pounds a year.

A higher, finer version of the medieval world begins to emerge among the woods and fields. Among the de Berhams' neighbours are people called Nicolas and Petronilla, Bertram and Benedicta. From the tiny Trinitarian friary at Mottenden near Headcorn (now a farm called Moatenden) they had two friars to celebrate mass in the Sissinghurst chapel, an arrangement made decades earlier by the de Saxinghersts. One or two manuscript books survive in the Bodleian in Oxford from the Mottenden Priory library – works on medieval logic and grammar – and it is not unreasonable to imagine that the visiting friars may have brought them here too. The friars assisted the chaplain, an employee of the family's.

There is one document above all which for the first time brings to Sissinghurst a sense of the interiors and even of interior life. It is a will made by Elisia de Berham in April 1381, now in the National Archives. She was the mother of Richard, who was to become sheriff of Kent, and was clearly a cultivated woman of fine sensibilities and deep piety. She asked to be buried in Cranbrook church and left money for prayers to be said for her soul. The vicars of other churches on the edges of Romney Marsh received legacies from her, as did her chaplain at Sissinghurst, Robert Couert, the friars in Canterbury, and the Carmelite friars at a small friary at Lossenham near Newenden, which is now a farm. The friars and master at Mottenden, who would have known her well, all received money.

Once she had catered for her soul, Elisia Berham attended to those near her, perhaps those who had looked after her. For the first time, ordinary people living at Sissinghurst acquire their names. Robert Goldyng, Simon Addcock, Thomas Herth, Alice Addcok: small legacies of 6s 8d to each of them. Then the precious objects in her life:

> To Johan Herst my daughter 10 marcs one of the best towels and a napkin. To Alice Creyse a blue bed and a saddle. To the wife of Thomas Hardregh a towel with napkin. To Elisia Addcok 10 marcs and a bed in which I lye with one 'curtyn' and over-cover and a casket with little garments (*parvis velaminibus*) within.

This is not a world of high luxury but one in which the lady of the house gives something she cherishes to the women with whom she has lived. Finally, and poignantly, to her son:

> To Richard my son 10 marcs and a white bed complete and my Matins book and six silver spoons and one broken piece of silver, a good towel and napkin.

Here, then, is medieval Sissinghurst, a place not of riches but of great dignity, with precious beds in various rooms, some silver objects but not so many that a broken piece is not valued. This is a place both deeply engaged with the sanctified life of pre-Reformation England and somewhere that exudes its own kind of gracefulness and clarity. 'A casket with little garments' is a measure of its delicacy; 'a white bed complete' – with all its white hangings and white linen – a symbol of its virtue. Most striking of all is the phrase 'my Matins book'. It means a Book of Hours, and a whole culture-world pours into Sissinghurst in the wake of those words.

The Book of Hours, also called 'Our Lady's Matins', a primer or, as Elisia Berham terms it in her will, a matins book, was a selection of psalms, hymns and prayers, many dedicated to the Virgin, designed for intense and highly personal, often private, devotion. These books were precious objects, often the most valuable thing a person owned, finely bound, with illuminations painted in, closed with gold or silver clasps, sometimes enamelled, sometimes with their own protective 'chemise', to be handed down through the generations of a family, as here. They could be carried in a sleeve or tucked into a belt and were used most often in the privacy of a closet, or even a curtained bed. They were an aspect of what Eamon Duffy has called 'the devout interiority' of medieval religion, not in rivalry to the public devotions of the church, but complementary to them. The matins book is the religious equivalent of the lay world brought to mind by Elisia's 'white bed complete' and 'casket with little garments', objects from a Sissinghurst suddenly awash with medieval purity.

The de Berhams certainly contributed to the beautification of Cranbrook church. Their arms, along with those of the archbishop and the de Bettenhams, are on the west face of the church tower. What this means, intriguingly, is that the wonderful distilled lucidity and simplicity of Elisia Berham's will, its delicacy and distance, are almost exactly contemporary with the wild-green-men bosses in that church, which the de Berhams almost certainly helped pay for. But does that grinning, snake-mouthed wood god, and the dense mystery of the half-hidden wood bird, connect with 'the white bed complete' and Elisia's treasured Book of Hours? Is that the combination which reveals the nature of medieval Sissinghurst, a refined world richly and deeply connected to the earlier and earthier presence which surrounded and enveloped it? I like to think so.

Nothing much survived from that moment. The two friaries were dissolved, Mottenden in 1536 and Lossenham in 1538. Their vestments, a chalice or two, the bells, the kitchen equipment and some of the friars' hay was sold off and the land leased out. At Sissinghurst itself, the de Berhams lasted probably until the 1530s, when they sold up, no one knows why. It has often been written that they sold Sissinghurst in the 1490s but I can find no evidence of that. Only in 1533 did a newly rich family, the Bakers of Cranbrook, buy from them the manor of Sissinghurst and its lands, and with the Bakers Sissinghurst entered a new and dramatically different phase of its existence.

Almost nothing remains from the de Saxingherst–de Berham years beyond their beautiful memory. The moat, which now defines two sides of the orchard, is likely to be medieval in origin, even if adapted later. On an autumn day, its 'black mirror of quiet water', as Vita described it, is another of the places into which the acorns steadily fall. There is nothing to be seen above ground of the medieval house. The stone lip of a drain possibly connected to the well in the court of that house can still be found in the wall of the Moat Walk. That well, just outside the South Cottage, was excavated by George Neve, the farmer and amateur antiquarian, to a depth of thirty-five feet in the nineteenth century, when human remains were found in it. It has now disappeared, but instead Peter Rumley, a Kent archaeologist and building historian, has made a new suggestion: the timbered buildings visible in a drawing made by one of the officers guarding French prisoners here in the 1760s might in fact be the de Berhams' medieval house, or at least an Elizabethan adaptation of it.

Big brick Elizabethan chimneys have been added to the timber frame, but the fretted bargeboards on the gables, the jettied-out upper storeys and the sense of accretion, of parts being added and adapted, as well as the close-studded oak timbers in the façades, all hint at this being a medieval building. In the washy pen and ink of a certain Captain Francis Grose, with the sentry boxes of the Hampshire militia in the foreground, this is probably as near as we can ever get to Sissinghurst before the Renaissance and its money changed it.

SEVEN

Rejection

EACH SPRING, Sissinghurst clicks back into its public life. Before it opens to the public in March, there is a flurry of preparation. The garden beds are forked over, the lawns are given their first mow of the year. Paths are swept, the sign asking people not to tread on the flowers is wiped down and put out under the arch. The shop is re-stocked, the new restaurant staff are trained up in the arcane and complex systems of the kitchen and self-service counter, the warden has ensured that no tree is about to fall on any visitor, the stewards are asked to learn or re-learn about the contents of the rooms where they stand guard and the volunteers in the car park are trained in asking for the £2 parking fee. There is a sort of pre-party buzz, a place reawakening from its winter ease and privacy. It is a highly evolved and interlocking system, with over 200 people working here as permanent staff, seasonal staff or volunteers. You only have to walk around this preoccupied, busy place to see that changing it was never going to be a question of simply having an idea.

Throughout the spring of 2006, the meetings on the farm project rolled on as before. Meetings! I have never sat around so many tables in my life. Jonathan said he had never taken part in anything that had involved so much consultation since closing down a factory with a workforce of four hundred. From time to time, someone would voice the idealism of it all. Caroline Thackray, the Trust's regional archaeologist, said that 'The garden is there because the landscape is there. The setting is what lit up Vita's mind.' Sarah Roots, the Trust's head of marketing in the south-east, told us all one day that 'people should be walking through cowpats to get to the garden. They need to smell the farm as they go into the garden.'

Katrin Hochberg from the Soil Association said we should be 'steered by a sense of community', and Sally Bushell that we should try to feel we had 'the freedom to experiment'.

The anxiety about change was never far away. I often felt I was trying to push a fat clay-mucky lump of otherness into the neat and productive workings of a clock. Ginny Coombes, the restaurant manager, was at full stretch, with 115,000 people coming through the restaurant over six months, a third of them in the six weeks between the Chelsea Flower Show and mid-July. The head gardener, Alexis Datta, although she said she was keen on the project overall, didn't like the idea of vegetable-growing. 'Commercial horticulture is not as pretty as what we've got now,' she said at one meeting. 'I would prefer grass. Horticulture won't enhance the farm. I don't like the idea of polytunnels. But I don't want it looking deliberately old fashioned either. I don't want to attract more people.' She made a careful list of her worries: visitor numbers, housing the people who were coming to work here, buildings, where they were going to be built, water supply, car parking, the capacity of the lane, what it was all going to look like, the effect on the surroundings. 'I feel we are rushing into it,' she said. 'I don't want to sound negative. I don't really mind veg but I do mind the view from the top of the tower. And we don't need any more people. When we had two hundred thousand people here every year at the beginning of the nineties it was wrecking the place. I just wish this was a smaller, less high-profile property.' Had we, she asked, thought about squirrels in the new orchards? We were going to need netting, and what would that look like? There were lots of cherry growers around here anyway, so why grow more? Later she told me she was worried that some of the smaller fields I was advocating were going to look like 'one of those privately owned stately homes where the owner is trying to get the punters in by having a few rare breeds in a little paddock'.

Difficulties clustered around the business questions. The NT likes to see a 40 per cent return on its restaurant turnover, the source of much of the money that funds their properties. Anything like that was looking very difficult under the new scheme. Could

Sissinghurst be allowed, within the National Trust system, a special derogation so that it did not, at least for a year or two, have to generate quite such a high percentage of profit? That might be difficult, it was said, because other properties would complain.

Phil Stocker of the Soil Association produced some figures which laid out precisely what sort of farm resource the restaurant would need. The surprising fact to emerge was just how productive the land, even when managed on a low-intensity, organic basis, could actually be. The restaurant, with 115,000 customers a year, could be supplied from:

> 86 chickens laying eggs
>
> 2 dairy cows in milk at any one time
>
> 25 beef cattle
>
> 3 sows
>
> a tenth of an acre of lettuce
>
> half an acre of potatoes
>
> a fifth of an acre of carrots
>
> 3 acres of wheat

The problem was not that Sissinghurst was too small; it was too big. But the economies of scale meant that a farm working with the quantities needed by a single restaurant would never be viable. A single sausage would cost ten pounds. The farm had to sell more elsewhere in order to reduce the cost of the produce sold to the restaurant to a reasonable price. To make the farm viable, it would also need to sell 48,000 eggs, 3400 kilograms of beef and 170 tons of grain. We all thought that much of this could go through a farm shop. But a farm shop with nothing but eggs, beef and flour would be a sorry thing. So most of the farm shop would have to be stocked from elsewhere, which would mean that the village shop in Sissinghurst would have a competitor on its doorstep, tails would be wagging dogs and a local crisis would erupt. I may have thought that what was needed at Sissinghurst was a little more connectedness. What each of these exercises revealed was the intricately knotted and knitted condition of life as it was.

We were confronting head on precisely the problems which had produced the sort of landscape from which small farms, and even mixed farms of any size, had largely disappeared. These intractable difficulties were what lay behind the erosion of the world I had known as a boy. On top of all this, there were deep suspicions from some parts of the Trust about the viability of an organic system. Some people thought organic farming was worse for the environment. The commercial arm said their customers were not interested in organic produce. In 2005 the Trust had sold a million pots of local jams and honey and it was clear from market research that most people thought the Trust was organic anyway. Wasn't going organic in danger of putting the whole Sissinghurst scheme at risk? What was the point in upping the ante when so much else was uncertain? One member of the NT Regional Committee, an agricultural finance specialist, said ominously at one meeting that 'The loss-making potential in horticulture and top fruit are both huge'. She spoke about 'volatility in the markets' and 'hyper-wobbly figures for organic top fruit'. Her conclusion was that we needed 'to interrogate the numbers'.

I was driven into paroxysms of frustration by all of this, but on the whole kept them to myself. My ideas would be no good if they did not fit real-world conditions. It was all very well recovering the atmosphere of medieval Sissinghurst, but what good was that if the modern world could not accommodate those ideals? These were real objections, not mere anxieties or neuroses. The Trust understood the virtues of what I was suggesting, but they didn't want to end up looking stupid, and I had to understand that myself.

Early in June I went to a meeting held in London by the National Trust for all its donor families. It was a beautiful early summer morning when the sunlight stuck out from the side-streets in diagonal mote-filled slabs. We were to meet in Spencer House, the great eighteenth-century private palace in St James's, restored by

Jacob Rothschild. I walked there from the station through the richest streets in Europe. Swallows cruised the length of the tarmac and early white roses were in flower on the edge of the park.

Spencer House is in the part of London where in the eighteenth and nineteenth centuries every great family used to live, in a narrow street but with a façade looking over Green Park. It is like a palace in eighteenth-century Rome. A stone hallway. Upper-class men in soft, well-cut suits, their skin as pampered as the wool. Ties that start out at the horizontal buckle beyond the knot and dive for gold pins. Cufflinked cuffs, tugged and adjusted. Burnished, pointy, black lace-ups. The deepest level of the English establishment which, for all the changes of the last century, seems to be as established as it ever was. Some women in their own wool suits, sub-Chanel. Giant diamonds. A gathering of the most ancient of England. I talked to an old friend of my father's, the woman with the most wonderful name in England: Mrs Horneyold Strickland. She had been having trouble with the Trust over the flag at Sizergh Castle in Cumbria. On a table were badges for everyone, a catalogue of the peerage and its wives, ranks of earls and viscounts, with their properties named beneath them, or to be exact their ex-properties, their ancestral places, which now belonged to the Trust. I had never seen so many titles gathered together. It looked like the Congress of Vienna or Agincourt. I pinned my badge on: 'Adam Nicolson – Sissinghurst'.

The NT high-ups were there: Fiona Reynolds, the director-general; Sir William Proby, the chairman; Simon Murray, the director of operations; Sue Saville, our regional director. 'I always introduce people at this thing,' Sue said to me, 'but they always know each other already. Freddy? He's my mother's second cousin. None of them have the faintest idea who we are.' So, indeed, I met my first cousin once removed, John St Levan, who lives on St Michael's Mount, a National Trust house in Cornwall. And my second cousin once removed, Robert Sackville West, my oldest friend, who lives at Knole, a National Trust house in Kent. A colonel of the Grenadiers asked me, 'How long have you put up with the Trust?' A couple of years, I said. 'You wait,' he said. 'It won't be long before you're not quite as cheery.' Coffee came round.

Jacob Rothschild saw me. 'How's the scheme?' Fine, I said. Paintings from the Italian Renaissance on the walls, a perfect private palace, like a hotel that wasn't scuffed in the way of hotels. We sat on rows of little chairs in the great dining room. Robert and I were together in the front row, a wonderful team feeling to have him there. Simon Murray said the Trust wanted to delegate, to push decision-making down to the regions. Then the grumbling began.

The only reason these people were there is that they had been taxed into these chairs. The NT mechanism had provided them, or their fathers, with a way of continuing to stay in their houses, to pretend that the world remained as it was before 1911, before modern tax laws began to redistribute the extraordinary wealth this room had once represented. Now these dinosaur donors had the illusion of significance but not the substance or the power. The low whine of impotence came from the ranks behind me. The NT staff were hopeless because they were poorly paid. The NT was taking a purely commercial attitude with its estates and should understand something about communal coexistence. One famously cantankerous lady could barely contain her rage, about what was not clear. Someone asked how the Trust could think of buying new properties such as Tyntesfield, the huge Victorian country house near Bristol, when they couldn't pay their property managers enough. Murray explained the difference between grant-funded capital expenditure and daily running costs.

It was a pitiable scene. What was intended, I suppose, as an airing of views, even a gesture by the Trust to show that the dinosaurs mattered, felt in the event like a demonstration of their irrelevance. The very meeting in this glamorous London palace set up the Trust as a large, powerful, centralised body, and the lords and ladies assembled in the room as an old, nostalgic and emasculated audience, saturated in self-pity. I thought, first, as I sat there, how much I would prefer to be at the National Trust table looking at us than in one of our little chairs looking up at them. But then I remembered that every occupant of every chair in that room had their own Sissinghurst, their own book like this one bundled up inside them, written or unwritten, thought or unthought, and that these thin, wheedling complaints were only the voices of attachment and the love of place somehow translated into the wrong tone and the wrong language. I wondered then whether the Trust's relationship to its donors was correctly framed. There was so much buried passion in this room, but apparently so little engagement. It was framed as an opposition, but could it not be framed as a partnership? Perhaps these crusty men and women could become in effect 'inheritance consultants', the experts in buried meaning, in the folding of the past into the management of the future? If the Trust didn't do that, the result was this: complaint, a jangled joylessness, the old, long-repeated idea that things weren't what they used to be.

At lunch, on one side, I was next to a high-coloured lady with angry opinions and antediluvian views, loathing the Trust on class grounds, making no pretence that she didn't, as she ate their lunch, and describing at length the 'agonies' of building an extension to her house. On the other side was Sarah Staniforth, the Trust's Historic Properties director, wife of Jonathon Porritt. She talked about how houses had to be slept in if they were to be known. I talked to her about Gaston Bachelard and his idea that the purpose of a house was that it allowed one to dream in peace. If you got that right, everything else would be right. Maybe the tenancy of the Priest's House at Sissinghurst, I said, might become the prize for an arts competition? A year's tenancy with a poem or a painting as the rent? She wasn't completely averse.

After lunch I talk to the Cornish colonel again. He and his brother had twinned estates. They were too rich to feel comfortable in the position they were in but not rich enough to do anything about it. It was clearly best either to be a Rothschild – with enough money to call the shots – or a Nicolson, with no money and happy in the end to receive whatever might be on offer.

Later that week, Sarah and I had what Claire Abery, the gardener, called our 'famous day'. We invited a cluster of people to come to Sissinghurst to discuss the ideas we had been chewing over: garden designers, chefs, experts in retailing and restaurants, journalists interested in the new food culture, organic growers, people with a passion for the meaning of the landscape. It was in effect a company strategy day, an attempt to enthuse Sissinghurst and the people who work there with the sort of thinking which all these outsiders were dedicated to, and who in their different ways represented new attitudes to land, food, people and the connections between them. Was it naïve to think that Sissinghurst might take to their suggestions with alacrity? In retrospect, I think it might have been. People really don't want to be told to do things differently, whoever is doing the telling.

The outsiders all gathered at Sissinghurst on a beautiful evening early in June to spend the night here and talk the following day. It was a strange summer. The irises and the roses were out at the same time, which was rare, playing havoc with the colour system in the garden. But the southern end of the White Garden was in full fiesta, the lovely white Sibirica irises, the white poppies, the little white rose like something from a Persian miniature all covered in bees. The orchard was thick with sorrel and buttercup-sprinkled grass.

Sarah had filled the house with flowers from Perch Hill, sweet-smelling stocks, the firework alliums called *Schubertii*, creamy speck-led foxgloves, some crinkled Iceland poppies and dark purple columbines. The doors of the house were all open and the light came flooding into spaces that all winter and spring had been dark. Just to look at it filled my balloon of optimism. Surely, here, from this, people could find their way to a better future.

But Sissinghurst seems inseparable from anxiety. We had first the worries over the seating plan at dinner. The scheme was to surround each of the people who work here with the people who had come from outside, hopefully with inspiring ideas. Katrin Hochberg from the Soil Association was convinced that this was going to backfire. The people who work at Sissinghurst, she told me over the phone, were going to think, 'What the hell is going on? Who are these people swinging in here telling us what to do?' There was the danger that after so much careful build-up and so much consultation the thing would explode in acrimony and resent-ment. Then we heard that afternoon that one Sissinghurst employee had refused to come to dinner with us, in a tent we had put up in the garden, because her partner had not been asked. We reshuffled the places and waited for the others to arrive.

There were drinks under and on top of the Tower. Kent was looking as beautiful as the day my father had showed it all to the secretary of the National Trust forty years before. The Italian chef Antonio Carluccio and his wife Priscilla Conran were warmth and encouragement. Jo Fairley, who invented Green & Black chocolate, said I should have courage. I said I was overbrimming with it. Guy Watson, who runs the Riverford organic box scheme in Dorset, and Will Kendall, who made a national success of the Covent Garden Soup Company, both said, 'It's just so obvious. None of us can work out why we are even here. Why don't they just do it?' I told my old university friend, the writer and gardener Montagu Don, what they had said. He said everybody thought the same. Here was one of the central aspects of this story. An individual entrepreneur would feel in his bones that he should just do it. But somehow institutions can't behave like that. They have to commission studies, articulate the opportunities and risks, weigh the strengths of an idea against its weaknesses and bring every aspect of a scheme into fully examined light. That, to me, and these friends of mine looked very like sclerosis, a furred and clogged decision-making system, when what was needed was simple, quick decisiveness. But I couldn't avoid a disturbing thought: institutions may be unable just to do it, but institutions, mysteriously, are what do it more than anything else *in the end*. None of these famous media and business entrepreneurs had 3.5 million members behind them, but the National Trust did. What was the relationship between these things? Was the Trust slow to decide because it was big and old? Or was it big because it was slow? Had it lasted because it was slow and careful? Was there a relationship between the viscosity of institutions and the power they wield? And was this lack of spontaneity the reason they survived? Or was it just big-organisation small-c conservatism: we've always done it like this, so there is no reason to change?

I sat next to Fiona Reynolds and for the first time had a talk with her about the deeper motivation for these ideas. She told me how when she was at Cambridge she had been entranced by *The Making of the English Landscape*, the book by W. G. Hoskins that had invented the idea of landscape history. It was a book I had fallen in love with at exactly the same time. And then I talked to her about Sissinghurst, what we were trying to do. It was a chance to encourage people into a new way of seeing things, I said. She undoubtedly saw the Trust as an organisation for leading people a bit farther, for providing the enrichment that comes from beautiful places. She had spent four years sorting out the Trust's finances and governance. Now, maybe, I said, was the point when something else could come to the front, when the Trust could be renewed as something that reconnected itself to other, newer, older, more inspiring ideas, where it wasn't just a middle-class comfort zone. Meaning? she asked. Would she consider, for example, experimenting with Sissinghurst as a place in which financial targets set from elsewhere in the Trust might be suspended? Where we could look to set up a garden-farm-shop-restaurant system that focused more on the place's own well-being than on the straightforward bottom line? Where a glowing ideal of a landscape and a life wasn't hung up on gross profit margins? Her reaction to that was an 'Mmm', but with a rising inflection . . .

An unlikely analogy came to my mind. I had been sent to Hawaii by a magazine a few months before and seen there the wreck of the USS *Arizona*, one of the battleships sunk by the Japanese in Pearl Harbor, on which nearly 1200 sailors had died. You can stand on a kind of bridge built over the huge ghost presence of the ship lying just beneath the waters of the harbour. Every now and then a spot of oil floats up from the *Arizona*'s drowned engines and spreads in a rainbow disc across the surface of the harbour waters. It is like a soul welling up from the drowned depths, every minute or so, a slow breathing, the release of hidden memories. That, I said to Fiona, is exactly what these places should have too: a steady, present flowering from the depths, a gentle and profound emergence of the sort of meanings we all need to remember. How far is that from people's usual idea of the National Trust? But I think she heard every word.

'Would you mind if I said something?' she said to me quietly, and stood up to make a speech about fertility and fecundity, how *The Making of the English Landscape* had meant so much to her, and how this here now was that landscape in the making, a reinfusion of life and purpose into an ancient frame. Everyone had always known that Sissinghurst had 'an iconic status as a garden'. But this new idea had rediscovered its wholeness as a wider estate. There were clearly mechanical things to be done in the way it was farmed, 'but what's so exciting', she said, 'is the positive vision, for reuniting the estate in a way that is not only historically resonant but deeply contemporary – feeding into all our modern search for the local, for slow food and so on, all of which is part of tomorrow as well as our past'.

We had our long, enjoyable and sometimes slightly angry talking-shops in the sunshine the next day. Everyone agreed that there should be no hint of the farm being a demonstration farm, with signboards or the rest of it. It should simply function and be, remaining subsidiary to the garden. Its new fields and buildings should have understood the historic form here but not be a slavish copy of them. It needed to work. Tom Oliver of the Campaign to Protect Rural England argued for the landscape as a place of life and mobility, nothing should be tarted up, and the landscape designer Kim Wilkie said that 'The aesthetic framework should be poetry not painting – not just a seen picture but a whole-body, all-senses experience'. Decisions about Sissinghurst should be made at Sissinghurst; the landscape identity would then emerge from the place itself. The farm should be brought in 'peninsulas' – Kim's word – close up to the garden boundaries. The connection should be visceral and felt. The garden should never be brought into the farm. The farm should always be its own self-motivated place.

That was the easiest of the groups. Others, talking about the restaurant, found it more difficult to reach common ground. The real-food champion Hugh Fearnley-Whittingstall made an impassioned speech on behalf of authenticity and freshness. How do you really bring the landscape into the restaurant? How can you make it feel as if the food comes from here? But the task was to accommodate 115,000 visitors a year inside that real-food ideal. It could never be a River Café-style experience. You couldn't have waitress service with such numbers. Food had to be collected from a counter and food sitting on a counter had to be different from food served on a plate. But lots could be done about the ambience. Herbs could be grown in pots outside the door. The veg garden should be beautiful and visitable. There could be outside seating in the summer. In winter there could be special game evenings. The chefs could be trained up to relish this river of produce streaming in from outside. Ginny Coombes said the excitement in the team outweighed the anxiety. 'But *please* let's have some support.' Stuart Richards, the big wheel in National Trust Enterprises, confirmed that Sissinghurst no longer needed to turn in a 40 per cent net margin as profit. Fiona Reynolds had told him that. The Trust had decided in other words that the landscape benefits of the idea were worth buying.

The Soil Association now had to pull together a model for the farm/restaurant/shop. In one version, the capital cost would be £330,000 but even after five years it would be still be losing £50,000 a year. In another, the investment required was £650,000 and was projected after five years to end up a mere £6000 in annual profit. Neither was ideal, but the Soil Association had been working to some exceptionally tough NT ceilings. No increase in revenue was to be allowed from an increase in the number of people who might want to visit this new farm. And because of the demands imposed by a National Trust environment – beautiful materials, elaborate approvals, sensitive surroundings – a cow shed that might have cost £100,000 on an ordinary farm would cost £200,000 here. Overall, the total investment, if you included the use of working capital, came to £1.2 million. I couldn't quite tell if we were in cloud cuckoo land.

I went for magical walks that summer with the National Trust warden Peter Dear, a man still in his thirties, with whom I felt the closest possible identity of purpose and mind, and who knew more about the wild life of Sissinghurst than anyone else alive. He had made new ponds in which beetles and bugs proliferated. We scooped them out with nets. He guided me to a knowledge of the damselflies and dragonflies on a level I had never guessed at before: the Cinnabar moths and the four-spotted chaser, the black-tailed skimmer and the Beautiful Demoiselle, whose dazzling body Peter called 'emerald blue'. He found a White Admiral on the marsh thistles, whose underwing was a rare and delicious creamy orange. He knew there were Purple Emperors in the wood, but they lived in the upper canopy of the oaks and so we never saw one. But he showed me where the trout were still hanging in sunlit pools in the Hammer Brook. He planned out, and would later plant, stake and fence with my whole family, a ring of twelve oaks in the field across the moat, as a memorial to my father. He wrangled with me as we walked through the shadowy thickness of the summer wood over the benefits and drawbacks of organic farming. He rigged up for me one evening a net of ropes – he climbs rocks in his spare time – in the oldest tree at Sissinghurst, a four-hundred-year-old oak pollard buried in the chestnut coppice, and I spent a day in that tree from dawn onwards, clipped to Peter's webbing slings, enveloped first in the barrage of summer song, then drifting in the midge- and spider-thick world of a great silent tree, its skin of leaves a globe above me, while the pigeons walked about like beadles on the wood floor and treecreepers ran up the trunks, corkscrewing their way along one beetle-rich line after another. Black-and-white woodpeckers hammered crazily into the dry dead branches, unable to settle or decide. Squirrels skittered past without the first idea I was there, but still taut, quivering, looking over their shoulder. Rabbits

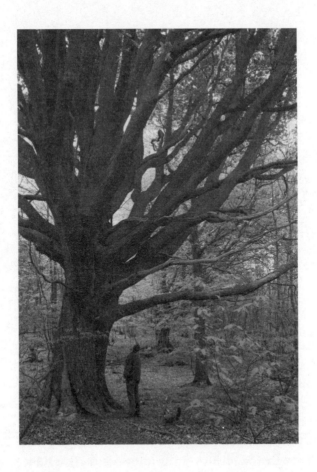

played anxiously in the grassy open rides below: a second or two in one spot, a skip to the next. There was no ease in the wood. All life here flickered and jumped. I lay stretched out on the sloping branches of the oak in a world that knew nothing but tension. The great patience of the tree stood there in silence, an ideal nothing else could seem to manage.

I thought about what we had done in all our year of meetings and I knew that our solutions and suggestions only restated the problem: the beautiful idea looked as if it was too expensive. The application of real costings meant the world of Sissinghurst would remain diminished. The circle wasn't square, and my instinct that we could do something new and good here was looking like an empty hope.

I was in Scotland when the answer came. It was towards the end of July. My mobile rang. Jonathan Light: 'I just wanted to tell you the outcome of the Regional Planning Group's meeting,' he said.

Yes, I said.

'The top and the bottom of it is that the Group are not going to recommend either of the schemes to the Regional Committee on the third of August.' Sinking. 'Yes,' I said to him. 'I thought that might be the direction you'd take. When I saw the £1.2 million low point.' 'Of course,' he said, 'we might be able to salvage something – an orchard, some sheep and some new hedges, maybe some veg and chickens, and that would push Sissinghurst in the right direction, wouldn't it?'

I put the phone down, devastated by the point we had reached. The idea I had floated a year before was straightforward enough: the landscape surrounding the garden at Sissinghurst could be made beautiful and more appropriate to the spirit of the place by using the farmland there to grow food for the tens of thousands of visitors who come to Sissinghurst each year. Mass-produced wheat and oilseed rape in a degraded farm landscape would be replaced by a detailed, various, mixed farm producing delicious, good food for 115,000 visitors each year.

Intuitively, viscerally, this felt right. It attended to the appetite for local food and real food, for a sense of authenticity in the landscape and the feeling that the best places are deeply fuelled by their own agendas, that they are richly themselves. The idea in its development had generated a great deal of tension but also some excitement and enthusiasm at Sissinghurst. It had become, to an extent, a shared view of how the future there might look. There was a lustre to it.

Now, at the end of all this, we had arrived at a rejection. Risk was the problem. The questions asked had defined the answers. It was as if the pilot of a plane, anxious about arriving at his destination, had loaded up with so much spare fuel that the plane had become too heavy to take off.

What it meant, though, was that the heart of the idea had been stripped out. Maybe there still would be some apple trees grown and chickens raised at Sissinghurst. But it felt as if a mediocrity filter had been applied. That it would be safer to supply food in vans from elsewhere. That the visitors could continue to be patronised, and that other unvisited farms could continue to provide the revenue on which the place relied. It was a victory of safety over imagination. That is why it was disappointing, because it set a frame of ordinariness for Sissinghurst. It didn't feel like a missed opportunity; more like an opportunity carefully presented and wilfully denied.

I wrote an email to Jonathan, who was caught between fires and I knew was already looking for other ways forward.

> There is a point at which carefulness becomes a figleaf for lack of enterprise. The greatest spur to success – and I mean success on a wider level than the financial bottom line – is the risk having been taken. Sue Saville has talked about the triple bottom line: money, conservation, social benefit. The planning group's recommendation attends only to the first of these and even to that in a highly pre-defined way. A good idea has been skewered on a lack of entrepreneurial spirit.

In August 2006 the whole project looked like it was lying dead on the floor.

EIGHT

Glory

I PLUNGED BACK into Sissinghurst's past, to look for the aspects of Sissinghurst that stretched beyond modern tensions and difficulties. I hoped to find Sissinghurst in its glory, in the sixteenth century, when it leaped up out of its rooted and Kentish condition and became for a moment a place of power and glamour. Intriguingly it turned out that Sissinghurst was never a more troubled place than then.

In the decades before 1500, the Wealden villages around Sissinghurst boomed. Money surged into them. The Weald was not part of the strictly regulated, seigneurial world of the good lands in the north of the county, and so the people here had long nurtured their liberties. The ability to rent and buy land; small dues owed to distant overlords; a habit of dividing property between all children; a poverty in the soils which created the need for a mixed system of farming: all of this made for a radical independence of spirit and a competitive, entrepreneurial world. There was a long history here of rebellion and resistance to authority, stretching back to the Peasants' Revolt in 1381. Nowhere else in England did the new Protestant ideas take such quick and vivid root. William Tyndale, the great early translator of the Bible, in exile in the Low Countries, had contacts in Cranbrook, had his works smuggled into England by Cranbrook clothiers and for a while was living in the Antwerp house of Richard Harman, a Cranbrook man, dissenter and merchant. When Thomas Wyatt led a rebellion against Bloody Mary in 1554, no parish contributed more men than Cranbrook to his fiercely

Protestant following. And this was one of the parishes in the next century from which a steady stream of Puritans would leave for the freedoms of Massachusetts.

A modern land market was fully operating by the fifteenth century. Estate agents, auctions, gazumping, short-term rentals, buying to let, speculation and mortgages were all at work in the Kent Weald, embedded in a rapidly modernising and commercialising world. Business and farming were deeply intertwined here. Cranbrook was the largest town in Kent (with over two thousand inhabitants) and the parishes around it were one of the busiest parts of England. Most of it was occupied by a free peasantry, who farmed holdings made up of small fields or closes, almost never in single blocks but scattered across parishes and between them. It was cattle country, with few sheep and only a little arable. Wheat and oats were grown but no barley and no hops. Beef cattle were the source of cash. A trade was maintained with north Kent, along the old droveways, by which beef walked north and barley came south. No records survive for the farm at sixteenth-century Sissinghurst, but they do for another gentry estate belonging to the Culpepers at Bedgbury in the neighbouring parish of Goudhurst. There in 1542 they planted 14 acres of wheat and 34 acres of oats, about 20 acres lay fallow and there were about 160 acres of grassland – some pasture for grazing, some meadow from which hay was taken – on which about thirty breeding cows and their followers and forty ewes and their lambs were raised. Gradually I came to realise that if we were ever to introduce a system to Sissinghurst which would work, it would be not unlike this. The land itself would dictate our use of it.

In the early sixteenth century, the parishes around Sissinghurst were doing exceptionally well, the population rising decade after decade. By the 1550s, this was the most densely occupied part of Kent, with the families and immigrants afloat on an extraordinary industry: the manufacture of about twelve thousand luxury woollen broadcloths each year. The wool did not come from here and the cloths were not sold here. A group of large, proto-capitalist clothiers bought the wool (usually in London markets), had it shipped down the Thames and then up the Medway to Maidstone and from there carted it south on the old Roman road. Unlikely as it might sound, this amphibious route remained the recommended way to come to Sissinghurst from London, particularly for goods, at least until the end of the seventeenth century. Shiploads of wool, 30,000 pounds at a time, 450 tons of wool a year, were brought down to these parishes and converted into cloth, which was shipped back out to London, Antwerp and the markets in France, Spain and the Mediterranean. Dyes came from Brazil and Africa, indigo and cochineal, woad from France, Seville oil from Spain, much of it shipped in via Rye.

A fuzzy boundary existed between smallholder, labourer and artisan. There were dozens of holdings no bigger than seven acres. Little orchards were planted next to modest one-up, one-down houses. Chickens and pigs were everywhere. There were yeoman farms of some thirty acres – not many and rarely in a single block – and only one or two per parish that were bigger than that. Almost everyone who worked on the land also had a trade. This landscape was almost suburban in character, the cloth business sewn into every corner of the country. Nor was it a place of great rootedness. Although most people living here came from Kent, most of them, according to their wills, did not die in the village where they had been born. It was, in other words, a surprisingly modern world. Elizabethan Cranbrook had shoemakers, carpenters, tailors, glovers, masons, butchers, truggers, eight shopkeepers, a copper and smith, three barber-surgeons, a haberdasher and a milliner.

The town and the surrounding villages were animated with the trades associated with cloth-making. At least thirty or forty people were involved in the making of each cloth: carding, dyeing and spinning the wool, weaving the cloths, fulling them, raising the nap, shearing them. A finished cloth, twenty-eight yards long, weighing ninety pounds, was worth as much as fifteen deer. 'Clothing in the Wylde of Kent', according to one petition from the clothiers to the queen, 'is the nurse of the people.'

A tenth of all English cloth manufacture came from six parishes around Sissinghurst. These Wealden cloths were famous for their colours: scarlet, russet, damson, ginger, blue medley, grey, orange tawney and 'rattescolour', pheasant, pepper and mallard. The boys at

Eton were dressed in 'sad Kent' from Cranbrook, and there were undoubtedly quantities of money around. No one should imagine it as a world of delight. It was rough, raw and exploitative. The large clothiers' houses had apprentices sleeping in the attics at night, working by day in the filthy, hot, wet dye houses at the back. In outhouses and those attics, vast piles of wool, wood and finished cloth were stored. One person in five was a spinner, at the poverty pay of twopence or threepence a day, often paid many months late. Whenever clothiers died, they owed money to the spinsters, the poorest of the poor who had nowhere else to turn for work or sustenance in an overpopulated country. The soils were not good enough and most of the people were dependent on the clothiers, who acted as bankers, entrepreneurs, employers, controllers, landlords and magistrates. Life expectancy was still low; most deaths still occurred in the 'hungry gap' of March and April. Across the sixteenth century as a whole in the parish of Cranbrook, for every 80 people that died in August, 130 died in April, twice the modern seasonal difference. People in the sixteenth century were still as vulnerable to the turning of the year as a population of weasels or rabbits.

This hard-driven, commercialising world is the one from which Renaissance Sissinghurst, in the hands of the next Sissinghurst family, now emerges. The Bakers, like their fellow townsmen, were men on the make. One of their ancestors, a Thomas Baker, had been taken to court in 1371 for illegally cutting down the archbishop's trees. A hundred years later, it had become a pious and well-established family. In the late fifteenth century, another Thomas Baker owned lands in several parishes running south into Sussex, and when he died left money for masses to be said and the churches to be repaired in all of them. The little friaries at Moatenden and Lossenham had legacies and his daughters had some silver, feather beds and cushions. He left his best cow to his wife and to all his sons small pieces of land. Although Edward Hasted, the great eighteenth-century historian of Kent, wrote, and it has often been repeated, that this Thomas Baker first acquired at least part of Sissinghurst, there is no evidence that either he or his son Richard did so, and Sissinghurst appears in neither of their detailed wills.

The surge begins with Thomas's grandson, John Baker, Richard's son, born in about 1488. When he was about fifteen, he was sent to London, with ten pounds a year to keep him at Lincoln's Inn, where he was trained as a lawyer. It was the moment when the Bakers began to lift away from the Wealden entrepreneurial society and enter the boom conditions of Tudor London. John Baker thrived, becoming a leading barrister, an under-sheriff, recorder and Member of Parliament for London. It was a familiar track for a clever and ambitious man, and everything that is now at Sissinghurst, all the grandeur and riches that were once here, even if now worn and crumbled, had their origins in this man's enterprise.

In the early 1520s he married Catherine Sackville, the daughter of a Sussex knight. One of her brothers, Thomas, was married to Anne Boleyn's aunt. It was the kind of invaluable connection that pushed John Baker into the mainstream of the English court and Reformation. That four-hundred-year-old Sackville relationship to Sissinghurst was one of the factors playing in Vita's mind when she decided to come here in 1930. At Anne Boleyn's coronation in 1533, Baker made a speech to the young queen on behalf of the merchants and financiers of the City of London, where he was still the Recorder. Within a couple of years he had begun to make his way into the coils of government and power. In 1535 he had become an attorney in the pay of the Crown. A year later he was attorney general, pursuing papists on behalf of the reforming king, executing instructions prepared by Thomas Cromwell, the king's first minister, who was in full, self-enriching career. When Cromwell fell in 1540, finally destroyed by the enmity and jealousy of those around him, Baker was there to benefit. He became Chancellor of the Exchequer, was appointed to the Privy Council, knighted and, most important of all, became Chancellor of the Court of First Fruits and Tenths, the court through which taxes that had previously gone to the pope now came to the Crown. Baker stood at the sluice gate through which the new money-river flowed into the royal exchequer, a flow into which Baker could dip his cup whenever he liked. He became Speaker of the House of Commons, a royal appointment. The electors of Kent refused to have him for one election in the 1540s but the royal officials found him another seat. He slid on in these jobs through the reigns of Edward VI and his sister Mary, and at every turn the lands and riches on which Sissinghurst would come to float steadily accrued around him.

He already had his grandfather's lands in Sussex and Kent. His first acquisition, bought from the de Berhams in 1533, was Sissinghurst itself, with its subsidiary manors of Copton and Stone. Five years later, when the Priory of Hastings was dissolved, the king gave his loyal attorney slabs of Sussex 'to have to him and his heirs for ever'. Two years later, when Cromwell was dismissed and bloodily executed, Baker gratefully received lands all over the Kent and Sussex Weald which had previously belonged to his chief. On through the 1540s, scarcely a year passed without Sir John acquiring another manor or two. When Catholic rebels against Edward VI were condemned to death, Baker had some of their lands; and when Protestant rebels against Queen Mary fell and were executed, he had some of their lands too. Many places he bought with the money that came his way from his chancellorship of the Court of First Fruits.

The result was that by the 1550s the Baker estate was one of the largest in Kent and Sussex, its archipelago of lands and manors stretching from beyond Eastbourne up to Maidstone and from Winchelsea to Pluckley. There were other manors in Hampshire, Oxfordshire, Gloucestershire and Essex, houses in Southwark and in the City of London, but the core was in the central Wealden parishes around Sissinghurst. It may, in all, have stretched to something approaching 15,000 acres, a spread of land that would be worth £75 million today.

Those are the economic and political facts of his life, but there are further elements which add depth and colour to Baker's story. The first is what he did at Sissinghurst after he had bought it from the de Berhams in 1533. In the 1930s my grandmother thought that Sir John had built himself an enormous brick house here, with an entrance range, a tower and a large courtyard beyond it. It seemed to make sense that the acquirer of the lands had created the monument at its heart. But in the 1960s my father looked into it more carefully and it became clear, first of all, that Sissinghurst was not all of one phase. He consulted various architectural luminaries, including Sir Nikolaus Pevsner, Jim Lees-Milne and Sir John Summerson, and came up with a building history that has been the orthodoxy ever since. According to my father, in the late fifteenth century the de Berhams abandoned a stone medieval house by the moat (said to have resembled Ightham Mote, a romantic building near Sevenoaks) and built themselves a brick house to the west of it, around a courtyard, and resembling instead Compton Wynyates, the great medieval brick house in Warwickshire. When John Baker bought this house in 1533, he is said to have inserted a modern Tudor gateway into the late-fifteenth-century entrance range. And when John Baker's son Richard inherited the house in 1558, he was said to have knocked down all except that earlier entrance range and built a huge Renaissance palace in the place of the demolished Compton Wynyates, with a tower in its centre and its further reaches stretching out into the orchard.

I, in my turn, with help from architectural historians and archaeologists, have now had another look at this story. There seems to be, first, no evidence of any Ightham Mote-like house. The medieval house almost certainly occupied only the south-west corner of the orchard, not the whole of it, and was almost certainly timber framed, perhaps with some stone footings. Its tall barge-boarded gables are probably shown in the drawing of the back of the house made by Francis Grose in 1760. Nor is there any evidence of a house resembling Compton Wynyates built to replace it. These were the two great early English houses my father was most in love with, and he seems simply to have imported them into Sissinghurst because he liked the idea.

The entrance gateway, from the style of its chimneys and their playing with geometrical forms, can be firmly dated to the 1530s. Inconveniently, though, the long wings of the front range on either side of them were not built then. Dendrochronology commissioned in the 1980s put the beams in the late sixteenth and in one case the eighteenth century (probably a repair), findings my father refused, with some passion, to accept. He liked to be able to tell Americans who came to stay that the bedroom they were sleeping in had been built in 1492.

So what did happen? The simplest suggestion is that when in 1533 John Baker bought the de Berhams' house on the site of the present orchard, he kept it. It was an important manor house, with a history of distinguished occupants and its own chapel. It had a moated garden beside it. What he undoubtedly added was a small, dignified and wingless modern gatehouse, decorated with its fashionable chimneys. The gateway would have led into a large walled 'base court', at the far end of which, a good three hundred feet away, stood the medieval house. Such a huge empty courtyard may seem odd to us, and certainly would not fit with later, Italian-derived ideas of proportionality of space, but could be found in many Tudor houses.

This simple picture fits both the man and the moment. It is essentially conservative. It does little but slot the Bakers into a pre-existing, de Berham-shaped mould. In John Baker's will, he asked his executors that his 'funeralls be done and made in honest maner with out pompe or pryde according nevertheless as vnto my deggree apperteyneth'. That was the style of his house too: dignified but not extravagant. The timbers used inside his gatehouse are not, intriguingly, of the best. Many were reclaimed from other places, with slots and peg holes marking their earlier use, and with nothing like the consistently high quality of oak that can be found in other, later parts of the building. The house he had bought was saturated in real, medieval, inherited status and was good enough to entertain both the French ambassador and, on one occasion, Queen Mary. John Baker was not a man to blow everything he had so carefully accumulated on a grand and a pretentious gesture; far too careful for that.

John Baker's enormous will, proved at Canterbury and preserved in the National Archives, is a measure of his methods and his ideals. It is, in fact, a picture of the Sissinghurst through which he moved, one which, not by chance, looks like a depiction of a great medieval household. 'I John Bakere of Cessyngherst in Kent Knyght one of the Kinge and Quenes Majestyes previe Counsell' presided over an entire community at Sissinghurst. It is the statement of a great territorial patriarch and magnate. Alms were to be given to the poor, masses and dirges sung for his soul in sixteen churches across his estate, and the old Roman road from Sissinghurst to Staplehurst was to be mended. His sons and daughters (one of them Cecily, married to Thomas Sackville of Knole), his in-laws and sisters and their husbands, the parents of his godchildren and the godparents of his own children, his knightly neighbours and their wives: all were remembered with rings, golden cups and money.

From them, he carefully steps down to his own servants, the people living with him in the great medieval house in the orchard. Mystris Marye Mustyamps, Benett Hale and Mother Water, all of whom had worked for him and his mother for many years, had generous legacies. Twenty-four of his menservants were named, including Anthonye of the Kitchen, James the Brewer and one John Nycolson, and all got money or gold rings.

Finally, in a string of codicils 'wrytten with myne owne hande by me John Bakere', he turned to his family. His 'good and loving sister Johanne Reames widow', who had married a Benenden man, was to have an annuity 'and two chambers in my manor of Cessingherst'. His other sister, Lady Wilforde, 'for her paynes taken with me in the tyme of my sicknes', had the leases of several properties. Everyone who had helped him and looked after him was attended to.

There was no question here of dividing the great inheritance into equal parts, as the custom of Kent had been. Baker had 'disgavelled' his lands so that the bulk of the estate could remain whole and in the hands of a single heir. To his second son John, Sir John gave 'Goddes blessinge and myne and £200 and such stuff I have in the Citie of London' and 'to you my doughters Marye, Cecyle and Elizabeth I gyve Goddes blessyng and myne requyringe you aboue all things to serve God and to be faithfull, assured, true, humble, lovinge and obedyent wifes vnto yor husbands'. They were off his hands. To his eldest son Richard, who was in his late twenties when this will was drawn up, he left the great prize that he had spent a life accumulating: the vast estate and Sissinghurst at its core.

Sir John's will is a paternalist vision, perhaps an old man's sentimentality, of what his world should be, with Sissinghurst as a place where many would be employed and his own relations looked after, a family widely connected with the higher gentry and with an ideal of stability and completeness standing outside the turmoil of Reformation England. Almost nobody knows of this paternalist Sir John Baker because his name will be forever bloodied by one of the great triumphs of Elizabethan Protestant propaganda, John Foxe's *Acts and Monuments*, usually known as *Foxe's Book of Martyrs*. This 2300-page compendium of crimes committed against the Protestant martyrs of the English Reformation, particularly in the reign of Mary, was more widely read than any book except the Bible. In Elizabeth's reign it stood by order of the archbishop in every cathedral in England as the companion to the translated scriptures. Cranbrook had opted hard and early for a fairly strict form of Protestantism and it is certain that in the independent-minded, entrepreneurial culture of the farmer-clothiers, there would have been many copies of Foxe's book, at least in the richer houses scattered through the surrounding parishes. And Foxe, in one incident after another, drawing on personal testimony and eye-witness reports, damns this great man as a cruel and intemperate persecutor of Protestants. It is the dark side of his desire for the order and consolations of the old world.

Sometimes the scene of the cruelty was Sissinghurst, sometimes in Cranbrook, sometimes in London. The earliest, in the reign of Henry VIII, concerned the persecution of a young Lincolnshire woman, Anne Askew, a friend of Henry's last queen, Catherine Parr, who had been disseminating Protestant literature. The Catholics in Henry's household wanted her to reveal her connections with the queen and put her on the rack in the Tower of London. Baker and the Lord Chancellor, Thomas Wriothesley, were there, asking the lieutenant of the Tower to rack her harder. He refused

> to streine her on the racke agayn. Which because he denied to doo, tendering the weakeness of the woman, he was threatened therfore grevously of the sayd Wrisley, saying that he woulde signifie hys disobedience unto the king: and so consequently upon the same, hee and Syr Iohn Baker throwing of[f] theyr gownes, would nedes play the tormenters them selves: first asking her if shee was with childe. To whom she aunswering againe, sayd: ye shall not neede to spare for that, but do your wylles upon me: And so quietly and paciently praying unto the Lorde, she abode their tyranny till her bones and ioyntes almost were plukt asunder, in such sort, as she was carried away in a chair.

When she was eventually burned, aged twenty-five, Anne Askew couldn't walk and was carried to the stake in that chair. In a later edition, Foxe cut Baker's name out of this story, perhaps because the Baker family had managed to coerce him, perhaps through the intervention of the old patriarch's son-in-law, Thomas Sackville, first earl of Dorset, a member of Elizabeth's Council, the rheumy-eyed earl who used to stare at me from the dining-room wall when I was a boy.

The reliability of Foxe's witness is never very certain – he is an advocate not a reporter – but Baker's rage and cruelty, often described verbatim, appear again and again in his book. When one Protestant, a Scotsman called Bland, came up before Baker as a magistrate in Cranbrook, the accused produced a Latin New Testament in court. Baker threw it across the courtroom (in the

George Inn), shouting, 'I wil geue sixe fagots to burne thee withal . . . Hence knaue, hence.' One of the Protestants Sir John condemned to death that day turned to him and said, 'My Lord, if we be killed at your hands for Christes sake, we shall liue with him for euer.'

The story that comes closest to home, dramatising the condition of Sissinghurst in the middle years of the sixteenth century, and its separation from the surrounding country, concerns Edmund Allin, a miller, who lived at the beautiful Maplehurst Mill in Frittenden, a mile or two north of here. He was a man full of concern for his poor neighbours and 'in a deare yere, when as many poore people were like to starue, he fed them, and solde his corne better cheape by halfe then others did: and did not that only, but also fedde them with the foode of life, reading to them the scriptures, and interpreting them'. The radicalism of the Reformation, its distrust and loathing of instituted authority, came in Allin's hands sifting into these fields and lanes.

Allin and his wife were reported to the priests, arrested and brought to Baker at Sissinghurst, where he kept them prisoner, in his 'house the one from the other'. Where was that? Almost certainly in some back rooms of the de Berhams' building in the orchard, now disappeared. Baker then began to play with his prisoner and 'entreated the sayd Edmund Allin to come to Masse in his Chappell the next day'. This must have been the chapel that had been there since the fourteenth century. After much persuasion, Allin agreed to go to chapel with Baker the next day, who then allowed him to

> goe lye with his wife that night, and desired him to perswade her to come also, and he would deliuer them both out of prison. When [Allin] was come to his wife, he told her what he had promised, and she with teares sayd, hee shoulde go alone for her. Then he likewise lamentyng the same, sayd, he would go with her to death.

I feel a kind of vicarious shame at this story, at this suffering imposed on young Kentish idealists, here in this house five hundred years ago. The next day, Baker came to Allin, asking him to keep his promise and come to chapel with him. Allin said: 'I will not: do what you will with me.' Then Sir John called out Allin's wife, Katherine, and berated her:

> 'Thou old whore, thy husband would be a Christian but for thee.' Then he beate her very sore with his staffe in his hand, and sent then both to prison the next day, sending with them a cruell letter that they shoulde be burned out of hand.

The manuscript notes from which Foxe wrote up this story (given to him by the vicar of Cranbrook) have survived, and it is clear that Foxe did not alter the evidence he had received.

Allin and his wife escaped to Calais, but there his conscience troubled him and he returned to Frittenden to continue his secret ministry. He and his wife were arrested again, his house was ransacked by Baker's men and in June 1557 Baker was given another chance to 'taunt and revile him, without all mercy and pity', as Foxe says, at a hearing in Cranbrook, at the George Inn. 'We are al kings to rule our affections,' Allin told Baker. One day, walking in Frittenden churchyard, the miller had realised he could never believe that a communion wafer was anything but a symbol. 'He considered in the Churchyard with him selfe, that such a litle cake betwene the Priestes fingers could not be Christ, nor a materiall body, neither to haue soule, life, sinnewes, bones, flesh, legges, head, armes, nor brest.' Baker could have no truck with this. 'Away with him,' he said. On 18 June 1557, Allin, his wife and five others, all tied to a single stake, were burned on King's Meadow in Maidstone, one of them a blind girl called Elizabeth and another 'a vertuous maiden cauled Jone Bradbrege'. As the wood was being laid around them, Joan

> turning to the people sayed, 'What is it a clocke?' They sayed, 'Ten.' Then she sayed, 'Thanks be to God! Bye xi we shalbe with our God.' And then, turning to the blinde mayde, sayd, 'Now sister Besse, be of good cher. Thou dyd never see, but soone yow shalt see Lord Jesus Cryst.' To whom she answred, 'I trust so.'

Is it any surprise that these stories sank deep into the psyche of the Protestant people of the Weald? Or that this exercise of orthodox power and the suppression of liberties should give rise to terrible, half-mythical tales, still current in Sissinghurst and Cranbrook, of John Baker as Bloody Baker and Butcher Baker, a Bluebeard murderer, rapist and oppressor? I remember my father telling me one as a boy, taking me to the place, in the old brew-house, just on the other side of the arch from our kitchen. There is an early-sixteenth-century staircase there, with a rubbed and worn newel post at its foot. At the top, shadowed and spooky when I was young, a big door gave on to a room that had been my father's bedroom when he was a boy. This, he told me, had been Bloody Baker's own room, and it was on this staircase that the most terrible crime in his long and terrible life had been committed. He was in the habit, my father said, of ravishing young virgins from the village. 'Do you know what *ravishing* means, Adam?' I did. And *virgin*? I did. Bloody Baker would summon them, they would come to the foot of the stairs and he would take them up to that room and in there *do his worst* with them. 'Do you understand *do his worst*, Adam?' I did.

One day a young woman arrived early. She was approaching the stairs when she heard someone coming down them and hid in the cupboard beneath. *This one here.* It was Bloody Baker carrying the body of his latest victim. As he reached the foot of the stairs a ring on her hand caught the newel post and in a rage of frustration Baker drew his sword and sliced the hand from the wrist. *Look, Adam, here, where the sword cut into the wood.* I saw how the newel post had been slashed and hacked as if with a hatchet into a worn and eroded stump.

Although this story and the many like it are all untrue, nothing I had heard had ever seemed more real. It is the kind of story told by the powerless about the powerful. It relies on the strangeness and distance of authority and the way in which power can suddenly land, terrify and destroy its victims out of a clear blue sky. It is a measure of the distance between Tudor Sissinghurst and the world around it.

In 1558, the old man died. In his will, he addressed his son directly from beyond the grave:

> To myne oldest sonne Richard Bakere goddes blessinge and myne and all suche my plate of siluer and gilt &e. and all other stuffe and utensiles of houshold in my manor mesuage and house of Cessyngherst. And I charge the[e] my sonne Richarde that above all things thowe serve God and thy soueraigne lorde and ladye the Kinge and quene, applye thy lernynge, be curtesse and gentill to euery bodie, be aydinge and lovinge to thy naturall Brother John Bakere and to thy susters Mary Cecile and Elizabeth, love well they neighbours, counsell, cherishe and help theym in theire necessities as righte and good conscience will requyre, avoyde Brybery, extortion, corruption and dissimulacon, eschewe Idlenes, applie the[e] to vertuose exercise, be faythfull and true in worde and deede and holly putt thy truste in Almightie God with humble callinge to hym for grace with laudes and thanks for all thy benefits and he wilbe thy keper and defender from all daunger, perill and evill.

The implication is clear: the ageing father, replete with his vision of strict social wholeness, distrusted his son. He was right to do so. In the most spectacular of Sissinghurst's generation shifts, Richard Baker, still in his thirties with a huge income from the inherited estate of at least £650 a year, took Sissinghurst in hand and drove it in a new direction: not ancient propriety but aestheticised glamour, not conformist strictness but Elizabethan romanticism, not rooted Kentishness but highly cultured, Italianate arcadianism, with a sophisticated interaction of building and landscape, large, grand and expensive, far beyond anything anyone had ever done here. Between 1558 and 1573, Richard Baker made of Sissinghurst an Elizabethan palace at the centre of its own dream world. It was the flickering ghost of that place, with all its ancient Sackville connections, which drew Vita here, to make a garden among the ruins.

There are many forms of evidence for what Richard Baker did: the remains of the buildings themselves; plans of other contemporary buildings which bear strong resemblances to Sissinghurst; drawings made of it in the eighteenth century which show the great Elizabethan palace from various points of view; accounts of one or two eighteenth-century visitors; the verbatim record of a month-long investigation made in 1761 into crimes that had been committed here, whose pages inadvertently describe the Elizabethan house's geography; the claims made by the owners against the government for damage done by prisoners held here; the marks left on the surrounding landscape by Richard Baker's great and encompassing scheme for the whole place; accounts of court cases held at the end of the century, which describe the relationship of Sissinghurst to the surrounding population; a very early seventeenth-century census of people living in Cranbrook and the surrounding parishes, house by house, which takes in Sissinghurst; and finally the accounts of Queen Elizabeth's visit here for three days in August 1573.

Although it is a fragmentary archive scattered across the country, in Cranbrook, Maidstone, Lincoln's Inn, Kew, Staffordshire and Sissinghurst, and although there are no contemporary maps, drawings or letters, there is richness and suggestion here, which, taken together with other Elizabethan theories of what the beautiful place should be, can be assembled into a coherent picture of what Richard Baker made. He overlaid the medieval inheritance with a mixture of classical detail and a simple version of an Elizabethan fantasy palace. By the time he died, everything was here: a great, many-courtyarded house; a garden beside it; outlying banqueting houses overlooking the Park; a prospect tower from which the Park could be viewed in its full extent; new barns in which the hay was kept for the Park deer; a bank and pale surrounding that Park; woods and open grasslands called 'launds' within it; a park-keeper's lodge; and necklaces of ponds dammed along the stream within the Park. Evidence for every one of these things remains at Sissinghurst today.

It was all made in the service of a deep and extraordinarily expensive form of play. House, landscape, woods and meadows were reshaped as theatre. Each of the elements was carefully integrated with the others, all contributing to an atmosphere in which the demands of getting and spending did not for a while have to be observed. The parishes beyond the Park gates may have been deeply embroiled in the accumulation of capital. Within it, those priorities were suspended. Central to this transformation is the fact that the Bakers were often not at Sissinghurst but at their London houses, either in Southwark or in Lime Street in the City. When a crisis with the local populace erupted in the 1590s, the whole Baker family was in London, and when a survey of communicants in Cranbrook parish was repeatedly made in the first decade of the seventeenth century, the Bakers were only rarely here to be counted. Sissinghurst was their dream place. It became a kind of toy.

Like the other gentry of Elizabethan England, Baker was not indifferent to enterprise or industry, and along with this theatrical construct of the new Sissinghurst was something else: a working and earning landscape. The woods grew coppice wood and standard timber; a large dam was built across the Hammer Brook and a fifty-acre pond made upstream of that dam; its head of energy powered the hammers and bellows of an ironworks; there were other mills, other ponds and sluices which provided extra head for the corn mills farther downstream.

What can be said about the world of this glamour-and-delight palace which Richard, the Elizabethan Baker, inserted into his father's adapted medieval-Tudor manor house? To begin at the centre: still standing in the orchard was the de Berhams' close-timbered manor house. Beside it on the eastern side was a large fish

0 _____ 40 metres
0 _____ 40 yards

Privy or Necessary House

Moat

Medieval
Manor
House

Passage
over

Service
Building

South
Banqueting
House?

Great
Hall

Well

Best   Garden

*Lower
Court*

Chapel?

Lodgings

Winter Parlour

Little
Hall

Gallery over
Lodgings

Middle

Court

Parlour

North
Banqueting
House
(Priest's
House)

Lodgings

Tower

*Upper
Court*

Barns

Stables

Steward's
House

Elizabethan
Barn

Porters'
Lodges

1530s
gateway

N

pond. Three hundred feet to the west was John Baker's twenty-year-old gatehouse with its out-of-date twisted chimneys. Between the two stretched a large open court. It was a bitty inheritance which needed ordering, regularising and aestheticising.

Using an architect whose name has not survived, but whose plans as seen in eighteenth-century drawings bear a strong resemblance to the drawings collected by John Thorpe and now in the Soane Museum in London, Baker inserted between the medieval house and the 1530s gateway a large Renaissance core to Sissinghurst. It consisted essentially of a prospect-tower-cum-inner-gateway with a *cour d'honneur* beyond it. The result was a three-courtyard house: the first a reduced base-court, paved throughout, into which horsemen could enter through the earlier arch. Dendrochronological dating of the timbers in the front range has shown that Richard Baker probably lengthened the wings on either side of the entrance arch at the same time, with stabling to the north and simple accommodation, perhaps for the steward, to the south. Both façades of both ranges were decorated with large black diamond patterns in the brick, visible in early-twentieth-century photographs but now faded.

These lengthened wings exaggerated an effect that has troubled rationalists (including my father and grandfather) ever since: the axis of the gateway is not perpendicular either to the Tower or the court beyond it, nor presumably to the medieval house, which has now disappeared. The unfortunate effect is that the upper courtyard is not rectangular but deeper at its northern than its southern end.

Why should this have been? No one has ever been sure: a possible reason is that part of medieval and early Tudor theory of the healthy building insisted that a gateway should not be directly aligned with the entrance to a house. Doors into the house should be either offset or misaligned so that a noxious wind could not find its way into the rooms.

At the far side of the first court stood the new Tower, still called 'the Great Gate' in the eighteenth century. Its form dramatises the story of its own insertion into a pre-existing plan. The side looking back to Baker's father's gateway is pierced with a flattened, Tudor arch. But the other arch on the other side of the Tower and the entire façade looking into the great court are strictly detailed in the correct grammar of a Tuscan order, with pilasters, entablatures, elegantly moulded cornices and the perfect semicircle of a Roman arch. As you passed under the Tower, you moved from medieval to Renaissance Sissinghurst. Steps led down then as now into the court. Horse and carriage had been left behind on the other side. You were entering a piazza in which the gentry strolled. There was no muck, noise or dung. It was the scene for a Kentish *passeggiata*. On either side, large mullioned and transomed windows gave on to apartments reached from separate stairs, much like an Oxford or Cambridge college. A paved path led across the court between lawns. Stone balls marked the breaks in the cornices. Those which had survived until the 1930s Harold put up on the garden walls. Over each doorway, small pediments held the Baker arms flanked by their surrounding dolphins. A fragment of one of those pediments still sits, unregarded, in the arch under the Tower. Another was taken by a visiting Baker descendant to Cranbrook church in the 1830s, where it was accidentally put up in the east wall of the nave, by the chancel opening, thought to be part of old Sir John Baker's tomb.

At the far end of the courtyard was an elaborated columned and entablatured doorway, like the frontispiece for an Elizabethan book. Harold and Vita used the shafts of its fluted and channelled columns, which they found lying in the ruins, to make a pergola called the Erechtheum outside their dining room on the edge of the White Garden, where a white wisteria grows over the frame and a rose spirals up one of the shafts. Part of the cornice is now used as a doorstop at the foot of the stairs up the Tower. Originally, the doorway had led into the screens passage between the hall and the buttery and on out into the third, medieval courtyard, now closed off with an Elizabethan range across its western side, and with a well in its centre.

Other, satellite buildings clustered around these three central courtyards. Two large-windowed pretty banqueting houses, one to the north (now called the Priest's House), one to the south (on the site of the Nuttery, still there in 1760 but now disappeared), gazed out over the parkland. Outside the entrance, Richard Baker also built a pair of beautiful brick barns to the north-west of the main cluster. One is still there but one was demolished in about 1800. Unlike the precision classicism of the Tower and its great courtyard, the barns were built with big strong Gothic archways, medieval buttresses and air-slits through which the hay could breathe. It is a manner and vocabulary which, for a 1560s building, may have been consciously nostalgic, a suggestion in the pointed arches that the barns had been here since time immemorial.

Slowly the ensemble of Elizabethan Sissinghurst begins to gather. Evidence from the eighteenth-century prisoner accounts, from a fragment recovered in 2006 in a drainage trench and hints from other sixteenth-century houses make it possible to describe something of the interiors here. Turn off the 'Pavement of the Middle Court of the mansion house', as it was called, step inside one of the doorways and you would find a staircase rising before you. On either side were doors giving into guest lodgings, or those for Baker's relatives. The stairs rising in front of you turned on a half-landing at the back of the range and climbed to the first-floor landing overlooking the court. Here on the north side was a long gallery, 17 feet wide and 120 feet long, wainscoted throughout, with a rich entablature and carved marble fireplaces. 'The ceiling', according to Horace Walpole, who saw it in 1752, was 'vaulted, and painted in a light, genteel grotesque'. Above it, in the attic, may have been the bowling alley referred to in the 1760s. Other rooms upstairs in these ranges were also panelled, probably with oak, probably with some classical allusion in the ornament. Alongside half an oyster shell, a small piece of classically moulded cornice, made of plaster, was found in a drain in the orchard in 2006, nothing very elaborate but cleanly and precisely done.

At the far end of the middle court the hall would have filled the right-hand part of the range and the butler's pantry and buttery the other half, across the screens passage. There was probably a smaller and cosier winter parlour upstairs here too. As the account of the prisoners' damage refers to the 'great and little halls' – both panelled – it may be that the great hall of the medieval house survived in the medieval court beyond it, and that a small, modern Renaissance hall was installed here in the Elizabethan range. There was nothing low status about that third court. Here the household continued to use the well. Beyond the medieval court, which still contained the chapel, stretched the garden, running up to the old fish pond as its eastern boundary. It may be that Richard Baker added two new arms, turning the old pond into what looked like an ancient moat.

This Elizabethan garden filled what is now the White Garden and those parts of the modern orchard not taken up by the great house itself. It was walled to above head height and fruit trees were trained against the walls. What this means, intriguingly, is that when Vita came to a bedraggled and broken place in 1930, and found, miraculously, an unknown *Rosa gallica* growing here on the edge of the ramshackle orchard, among the weeds and brambles, it was in exactly the place it would have been planted in the Elizabethan garden. The rose is particularly persistent. Vita claimed she could never eradicate it from wherever it wanted to grow, and it is not absurd to suggest that successive plants of that tough and hardy rose, which Vita named 'Sissinghurst Castle', had been growing there for 450 years.

Inside the Tower, Richard Baker had one of the rooms decorated with a set of carved heads of Tudor monarchs. They were still there in the 1870s and shown to visitors, but tantalisingly they had disappeared by 1930. Above them, though, was the real showpiece of the place, then as it is today: the prospect from above. Until the early nineteenth century, each of the two turrets was a room higher than it is now and in each face of those octagonal rooms a window gave the viewers collected there – no more than four or five for comfort – a panoramic view of the lands of which this tower was the node and hub.

This view from above was a central part of the Elizabethan experience. Big rooftop prospects, rooftop walks, rooftop pavilions, parties on rooftops, even romantic assignations on rooftops: all this was part of a sudden new sixteenth-century relationship to a place, not only dominating it from above but, by standing above it, seeing it for what it was and for what your place within it might be. The sixteenth century in England was the moment when people first began to draw and buy aerial views, when the first models of buildings were made by architects for their clients. And the view from the top of the Tower at the end of the building campaign of the 1560s would have been full of a very particular aesthetic pleasure, the experience, it seems to me, around which the whole ensemble was framed.

At your feet was the intricately made thing, many interlocking courts, with passageways and doors between them, a house not only as a machine for living in – there were thirty-eight hearths paying tax here – but as a kind of enlarged jewel, a device, a cleverly made object. It was placed in the middle of a landscape from which all apparent human influence had been removed. Beyond the perfect court at your feet; beyond the stable court to the west and the medieval court to the east; and beyond the little banqueting pavilions to north and south – lower cousins of this great prospect tower – came the free-flowing lands of the Park through which the hunt could pass. The farm on which the inhabitants of Sissinghurst had relied for so long, which they had worked and cultivated for perhaps a thousand years, was no longer needed. The 15,000 acres of the Baker estate provided enough money. So while the new house at Sissinghurst was made particularly refined, the land at Sissinghurst could be thrown back to an artificial naturalness, which was both self-consciously relaxed and self-conciously luxurious, a holiday zone for the well born, from which the poor and the industrious were explicitly and often officiously excluded. Intuitively or not, when Vita and Harold came here in the 1930s, they were responding to a place that had once been shaped into a model of Elizabethan Arcadianism.

The field pattern of modern Sissinghurst is not medieval, but a mixture of late eighteenth century and Victorian. The medieval fields had, in other words, been removed and replaced within the Park pale by a relaxed openness, a pretence at nature. It was a set of relations which embodied constraint and ease, order and freedom, the cultivated and wild. Stand on top of the Tower at Sissinghurst in 1570 and you could feel almost literally on top of the world. It may have given the pleasure that nineteenth- and twentieth-century Englishmen got from standing on top of mountains: the perfection of dominance.

An enormously expensive fence and bank – an oak pale – seven miles long had been built around the whole seven hundred acres. The Park was stocked with deer and, in a small part, just beyond the site of the Victorian farmhouse, with exceptionally valuable and highly prized rabbits. There were gates into the Park where the old roads entered it and stiles here and there over which a man could climb but a deer could not jump. On the northern edge, where the drove road from Charing to Cranbrook crossed the Park, an oak-framed park-keeper's lodge was built. It is still there: a one-up, one-down cottage now subdivided and buried under later extensions, but with the field next to it still called Lodge Field.

From the Tower, and to a lesser extent from the two little banqueting houses, Baker, his family, friends and guests could survey their world, one which, in the heavily commercialised and semi-industrialised surroundings of the Cranbrook cloth business, had been cut out of the new normality, and in its adopted and theatrical simplicity made to seem precious beyond price. This is a very early holiday house, or at least a beauty house, a place in which life could be seen and enjoyed like a ballet.

The landscape historian Nicola Bannister, in a survey for the National Trust, has made a richly interesting discovery about the relationship of house and Park. She took me with her one day that winter to show me what she had found. For about two-thirds of its length, Nicola had rediscovered the bank on which Richard Baker's Park pale had been built. Sometimes it snaked its way through modern woodland. Sometimes it was as much as five or six feet tall, sometimes no more than a ripple in the leaf litter. For much of its length the old drove from Three Chimneys to Cranbrook (now the busy A282) ran alongside it, and for another part the old lane from Frittenden to Cranbrook Common. But the intriguing point was this: for all the length that it survives (which is about 70 per cent of the complete circuit), it is laid along the skyline as seen from the top of the Tower. Both the pale and the tower-top rooms are about 230 feet above sea level. It is unlikely that this a coincidence. It seems as if the height of the Tower was calculated to make the house-and-park effect work most precisely. The deer in the Park were to be hunted. The height of the Tower guarantees that from its prospect rooms you would never lose sight of it. The vision of the Sissinghurst Park is precisely like one of the sixteenth-century tapestries Vita brought with her from Knole and which still hang in the corridors of Sissinghurst: open grounds, shady bowers, exquisite pavilions among the trees, and the hunt of the swine or the deer, at which the men with their javelins stand firm, while the horn is blown and all is happily and easily laid out to view.

The Park was important to the Bakers. In Richard Baker's 1594 will, his executors were empowered to have any of his woods and underwoods felled to pay off his debts, 'except only the okes and Beeches growing within my sayd parke of Sissinghurst'. Some things were worth more than money, and the family maintained the Park and had the pale repaired and renewed up until the end of the seventeenth century. Only then did it fall into decay. When Horace Walpole came here in 1741, he described 'a park in ruins and a house in ten times greater ruins'. In the late eighteenth century it was reclaimed for farmland and wood. Only here and there, magically, does a great tree survive. The huge four-hundred-year old pollard oak in which I spent a day in the early summer of 2006 is a relict from that Park. There is another down by the Hammer Brook, almost equally old and more venerable, its giant bole not to be hugged even by four people. The big beech pollards up on the crest, although much younger, probably germinating even as Walpole was looking at them, are from the last days of the Park, as are many of the younger oaks in the wood. They are now surrounded by dense chestnut coppice planted in the nineteenth century. Many lower branches of these oaks, which must once have grown out in the open air of a park, have withered and died where the chestnuts have shaded them out so that only the crown and the central trunk of the tree remain green and juicy. These lower oaky limbs hang out barkless and sapless, sticking out from their trees like narwhal tusks, the memory of an Elizabethan dream long since gone.

All this is to take the great house, with its precisionist workings and its surrounding spread of exquisite nature – so unlike the tightly knitted closes of the Wealden landscape – at its own valuation. It didn't look quite the same from beyond the Park pale. The court records at the end of Elizabeth's reign are full of trouble between the Bakers, their precious Park, their ironworks at Hammer Mill just outside it and the people of Cranbrook.

In the cases that came to court, one can see what Sissinghurst meant to anyone not admitted to its charmed circle. The landscape of exclusion and preciousness suddenly jumps into another form of life. One after another, young Cranbrook men appear before the magistrates accused of stealing Sissinghurst deer. In January 1597 Anthony Carpenter had been heard telling a friend that a deer had been killed in Sissinghurst Park. Old Agnes Greenyll, who had been roasting some meat in a house at Golford, heard Carpenter say it. And Carpenter had added something about a crossbow arrow. Had he done it? No, he said. He had seen the dead deer lying there, saw the man who killed it run away and then put the arrow up a tree (there were low pollards in the Park). He had gone to find someone to help him recover the deer, which he described as 'such a bootye as he should never meete with the like againe whelst he lived', but found no one, went back to the Park but the deer had disappeared.

He 'looked aboute in the bushes the space of an hower or better' – the thorny scrub that must have been growing in the Park. Why hadn't he told Jasper Glover, the keeper, who was presumably in the lodge on the other side of the Park? Because, Carpenter said, 'to what end should I hurt the fellowe that had killed the said deare and not benefytt myselfe thereby?' But what, the magistrate asked, was all the talk about an arrow? Nothing, Carpenter said, his lying now becoming desperate. All he had been doing was discussing some unsatisfactory *ploughing* that had been done recently. He had been at Branden, a farm outside the old Park boundary to the south, and he had said in a conversation there that the ploughman 'at the first setting on did not drawe the first furrow as straight as an arrow'. The quarter sessions records as usual have no account of what happened to the accused, but guilt can rarely have been so plain.

Jasper Glover, the keeper, appears again a year or two later, chasing young apprentices to Cranbrook, after they had been seen carrying away some Sissinghurst deer at midnight one Saturday. The two boys he had pursued were apprenticed to a Cranbrook clothier. Glover went after them all the way to the clothier's house in Cranbrook, where he found them sharing a bed in the attic, got them up, inspected them and asked one boy 'how his stockings became so bespotted with durt?' Because, one of the boys said, thinking fast, they had been driving some bullocks for his master the afternoon before.

In 1601, four men from Cranbrook, a butcher, a yeoman, a shoe-maker and a clothier – certainly not the poorest of the poor – arrived at Sissinghurst one November midnight and took two does worth six pounds: a dare by some young urban artisan-professionals, on a secret outing into the country, with some good venison as the trophy. There is something altogether more serious about an incident which occurred the following year when in broad daylight, at ten o'clock in the morning, a party of Cranbrook gentlemen, their servants and friends broke into the Park with their greyhounds, heavily armed with halberds, a combination of axe and spear on the end of a seven-foot pole. Baker's men caught up with them later, ordered them to 'yeld their bodyes', but the Cranbrook invaders attacked the Sissinghurst men, who then fled for their lives.

The case surrounding this attempted theft and battery rolled on for the best part of a decade, the court papers becoming ever more impassioned. Sissinghurst Park was 'impaled and principally employed for the breeding and cherishing of deer and conies'. The thieves, although one was a knight, Sir Alexander Culpeper, and another a gentleman, Walter Roberts, were said to be no better than 'common night walkers, deer stealers and hunters in parks and chases'. They had got together with alehouse keepers and other low sorts and armed themselves with 'bows, bills, guns, swords, daggers, long pick staves and other weapons'. Before their invasion they had been 'drinking great and excessive quantities of beer until about 11 o'clock of the night' at a house called Gaythorne (now opposite the garage near the roundabout at Willesley), and only then had gone 'in warlike manner weaponed into the park' with crossbows, seven greyhounds and long deer-catching nets called buckstalls. 'With outrageous violence they pluckt out 8 of the pales and entered into the park and there with the hounds hunted and chased the deer and killed 2 does and carried them away. And they spoiled and hunted many other deer and did other outrageous actions to upset the peace of the realm, to the terror of the inhabitants.' Baker's men had pursued them to Haselden, an old house, once belonging to Sissinghurst, just north of the village, to arrest them for this monstrous behaviour, and there the Cranbrook men, roaring drunk and armed to the hilt, attacked the Bakers' keeper, Jasper Glover, and two others brutally and immoderately, putting them in danger of their lives.

That, at least, was the accusation. The true story, according to the defendants anyway, was simpler. In the previous June, some deer had escaped from another park at Glassenbury on the other side of Cranbrook, belonging to Sir Thomas Roberts, Walter's father. Sir Thomas's son-in-law, Sir Alexander Culpeper, heard that there was a deer loose in 'a place called the Hammer', the woods near the Bakers' mill three miles or so to the east. Culpeper went over there with two servants, to look for the deer at night, failed to find it and early the next morning (but is this timing convincing?) was making his way back towards Glassenbury, along the road between the Hammer Mill and Cranbrook, the old drove road running alongside the Sissinghurst Park pale.

> Not finding the said deer, they returned homeward the usual and high road way [which] doth lead along by the pale of the enclosed ground ... Having two greyhounds running along by his horse and the said greyhounds winding [scenting] the deer in the said enclosed ground did without any instigation or knowledge ... break into the said enclosed ground and there killed one deer.

It was no more than a case of dogs off the leash and worrying the stock. Culpeper and his servants heard the deer 'bray' on the other side of the pale, two of them jumped across it near a gate and found one of their greyhounds with its teeth fixed in the neck of the deer. They caught the hounds and took the dead deer with them, climbing back into the road over a stile, where a third man was holding their horses. The only weapons they had with them were their riding swords and daggers. The rest of the story, the warlike invasion, the outrageous behaviour, the riotous affray – all of it seems to disappear into a bog of animosity and mutual loathing. Walter Roberts, one of the gentlemen defendants, blamed the Bakers' attack on their neighbours as nothing but 'malice and evil will without any just cause'.

But there were other issues in the air which hint at a troubled relationship between Sissinghurst and the world around it. There may be some continuity from the general loathing in which Sir John Baker, the Butcher Baker, had been regarded. In 1594 his daughter-in-law Mary, Richard's wife, had been fined for recusancy – for not attending services in Cranbrook church because she still held to Roman Catholicism. In the same year a plot had been hatched in Cranbrook to destroy the Bakers' most valuable asset: the ironworks that Richard Baker had set up at Hammer Mill in 1569. Baker had built a furnace in which iron was beaten out of heated ironstone ore. The source for the Hammer Mill ore was probably the wet, lumpy, glutinous wood just north of Sissinghurst still known as the Treacle Mines. You can see the yellow, rust-mottled ironstone in the bed of the Hammer Stream, just where the track to Bettenham crosses it. The Bakers had also built a forge in which the pig iron was made into tools and weapons. Mrs Hall, who lives in Hammer Mill Farm, still has a small cannonball which was found when the road outside the mill was repaired a few years ago. Her children used to play with it, rolling it across the kitchen floor, so often that it finally split in half. Soon after it was discovered, they took it to school in Sissinghurst to show the other children. The next day five of them brought in their own cannonballs, treasured in these houses since the sixteenth century. Iron sat alongside the woollen broadcloths as the dominant business of the Elizabethan Weald.

The ironworks needed stupendous amounts of charcoal made from coppice wood, largely oak and hornbeam, in the surrounding woodlands. It has been estimated that about four thousand acres of coppice would be required to fuel a furnace and a forge. The woods had to be near the ironworks because charcoal, if carted too far, shatters into dust. In Richard Baker's 1594 will, sixteen different woods are listed, of which half he had bought himself from his neighbours. One has to imagine every wood here under a tight and meticulous coppicing regime, every last fragment of the hewn wood collected up, a cleanness to it, the young shoots of the new wood rigorously fenced off from browsing animals, an intense feeling of nurture, harvest and use. You would have seen much farther across this country in the sixteenth century, as the pollards in the hedges would have been lopped and topped, the hedges themselves tightly laid into stockproof barriers and the woods never left unused or neglected. It would have been a shorn country, in which the dark and fiery ironworks, surrounded by their mounds of slag and with their giant hammers slamming into the half-molten ore, smoked and bellowed day and night. The wood was the source of heat but the streams drove both the hammers and the vast, industrial bellows with which the heat was kept high. And nothing was more important to the working of the furnace than continuous operation. Only when the fire remained continuously hot could satisfactory amounts of ore be reduced to iron, and for that reason every iron-works needed its dam or 'pond-bay' which held back sufficient quantities of water for operations to continue for days at a time. The pond-bay at Hammer Mill is still there, next to Mrs Hall's orchard, over seven hundred feet long and eight feet high, covered in primroses and celandines in April. It dammed up behind it a fifty-acre pond, covering those beautiful hay meadows in which I walked with my father when I was a boy. It also seems possible that the lakes in the valley at Sissinghurst, on our boat-race stream, were also 'pen ponds', reservoirs penned up until the ironworks (or perhaps other mills downstream) needed their water too. Every ironworks employed a man whose job it was to control the sluices on all the ponds in which the potential energy of the saved water was waiting ready to be released.

Cloth and iron were in competition for wood. The great vats in which the clothiers dyed their wool were in need of wood too. The annual processing of a million pounds of wool in the six parishes around Cranbrook consumed untold quantities of it. The problem was that the wood belonged, in large measure, to the Bakers, the ironworks had first call on it and on top of that wood merchants were exporting it to London. By December 1594, the clothiers of Cranbrook, and all the weavers, spinners, shearmen, teasel men, carters and mercers who relied on the cloth business, had put up with enough. They had already attacked a wood dealer in Biddenden. A conspiracy was hatched focused on 'Mr Bakers mill and woodes'. Secret meetings were held in Cranbrook houses urgently debating how 'to break upp Mr Bakers Hammer Pond'. The authorities began to hear whispers of the plot. Some poor Cranbrook weavers, egged on by the richer clothiers, remaining hidden in the background, were planning 'to put up the bank of the ponde'. Cranbrook had no wood to burn and so 'There is a rumor that they will put down the furnace.' The men of Biddenden and of Benenden were said to be part of the conspiracy. Old greybeards in Cranbrook were recalling the days, long ago, when ironworks were pulled down by teams of oxen. A weaver called Thomas Williams was summoned to a secret meeting in his brother's house in Cranbrook. The brother asked him 'What he would give towards a good deede'. 'What is that good deede you would have me doe?' Thomas asked. 'He answered he would put down or pull downe a Baye or Bayes of ponds.'

John Baker, Richard's son, had become the owner of Sissinghurst when this crisis hit. Hearing of 'certaine mutinus speeches tendeinge at the least to greate disorder ensuinge', he hurried down to Sissinghurst from his house in Southwark. The situation was complicated. 'The persons charged with these lewde speeches be verie poore men and greatlie charged with children.' It may have been tempting to put them all in jail 'for the greater discoredgment of the rest of their confederacie', but that wouldn't necessarily have the right effect. Reports were delivered to Baker. 'Sir Richard his father did set upp the said Iron Woorkes . . . for profit . . . but to the great dislike of many of the Inhabitants . . . because of the great scarcetye of woode thereby.'

Many of the conspirators were arrested while others were known to have fled. A shortage of corn for the poor added to the crisis. All the other gentry in the parish were away in London too and so the constable and some 'honest private persons' were co-opted to keep order

> bycause they be holden to be religious and honest, besides the
> which they are knowen to be riche, and thereby have great cause
> to feare, that if the rascal multitude should make any uproare,
> they would first invade them.

The chief clothiers were going to apply to the queen herself to have the ironworks pulled down and any new ones banned. But in the end there was no need for such extreme action. By mid-January 1595, the crisis seems to have ebbed; it is difficult to say why. There is a remote chance, as one anonymous report to the Lord Lieutenant puts it, that Baker himself had done something to quell the flames:

> Certain wealthy Clothyers would give to Mr Baker as much
> money for his Woodes, as any other would; and in that respect
> seeing it not only no loss to Mr Baker, but also ready Water to

> quenche all this fyre, I would yor Lordship that he might by you
> be persuaded to sell them to the Clothiers.

Is it likely that Baker would have agreed? If his ironworks were to make a profit – and they continued in production here until the 1660s, when the dam was broken and the fifty-acre pond drained – he would have to rely on local supplies. It was for the clothiers to find their fuel where they could.

Elizabethan Sissinghurst, which might have looked and perhaps to Vita did look like the moment of perfection, turns out to be a time of polarised identities: a fierce distinction between inside Sissinghurst and outside it; a pretence at ease and refinement within the enclosure; a hard-pressure world of unregulated business beyond it. The whole of the Weald, in the middle of which the parkland and jewel-like house sits, was a negotiated and contested space, full, not slack, taut and as tightly patrolled as anything now. In retrospect, there seems to be no privacy here. Those huge forgotten pollards, the mist-coated meadows by the Hammer Mill, the secrecy of the modern woods: all of them in their abandonment are relics of Elizabethan Sissinghurst; none faithfully records the world in which it began.

There is no portrait of Richard Baker and nothing written by him. We know only that he was a man of wealth and sophistication. He left to Mary, his Roman Catholic wife, 'such apparrell as she hath' in his will, 'And my better coatch with the horses and furniture thereto belonging.' He had a daughter Chrysogna, whose portrait as a girl survives at the Vyne in Hampshire, a miniature person in ruff and gilt lace, with a coral and pearl necklace and a red gallica rose in her hand, not unlike but not very like the *Rosa gallica* 'Sissinghurst Castle' discovered here by Vita. Richard Baker had his own silk clothes which he left to his eldest son John. He had been trained up by his father for a political career, but abandoned it as soon as his father died. Instead, he devoted himself to creating a vision of a perfect Sissinghurst. He loved Sissinghurst. He had taken his inheritance and profoundly reshaped it. Sissinghurst became his self-portrait. What he made of it was a denial of his terrifying, moralist father, a substitution of delight and playfulness for authority and violence. He had retreated from brutal Tudor politics into the play-politics of Renaissance aestheticism, a quasi-medieval, quasi-classical world of a pure pink fantasy castle surrounded by its lawns and woods and prancing deer.

A good house, according to Andrew Boorde, the leading English theorist on Tudor houses, had to be well away from others, with a beautiful prospect in front of it, on the edge of a low hill overlooking a vale, visible from afar and settled in its place 'comodyously'. Because, as Boorde explained, if

> the iye be not satysfyed, the mynde can not be contended, the harte can not be pleased, yf the herte and mynde be not pleased

nature doth abhorre. And yf nature do abhorre, mortyfycacion of the vytall and anymall and spyrytuall powers do consequently folowe.

Richard Baker's Sissinghurst could have slid into Philip Sidney's description of Basilius's house in Arcadia:

Truly a place for pleasantness, for it being set upon such an insensible rising of the ground as you are come to a pretty height before almost you perceive that you ascend, it gives the eye lordship over a good large circuit, which according to the nature of the country, being diversified between hills and dales, woods and plain, one place more clear, another more darksome, it seems a pleasant picture of nature, with lovely lightsomeness and artificial shadows.

This is the place to which, in an orgasm of anxiety and preparation, the queen and her court came in August 1573. By then the house was surely complete: the rents gathered, the coping stones on, the paving laid, the moat extended and filled, the garden manured and planted, the roses trained, the banqueting houses embellished, the glass polished, the panelling up, the light grotesque devised and painted, the tapestries hung, the chimneypieces installed, the fires lit, the Park laid out, the pale erected, the deer stocked, the meadows fenced, the woods coppiced, the entranceways smoothed, the pond-bay dug, the river dammed, the charcoal made, the furnace lit and the ironworks begun.

In August 1573, the queen had been on progress in Kent for a week or two. She had already stayed with the Culpepers at Bedgbury and knighted Sir Alexander, and with the Guilfords at Hemsted, and knighted Sir Thomas. Finally, on 14 August, she and her court arrived at Sissinghurst, coming up from Rye through the atrocious clay-stodged roads. The courtiers were not in the best of moods. Lord Burghley had written three days before to the earl of Shrewsbury in Derbyshire, saying he had much rather have been with him at Chatsworth than down here in the slums of the Weald.

It was the most dazzling sight ever seen at Sissinghurst. When the court went on progress, its baggage filled between three and five hundred carts. You have to imagine them coming through the heavy gate in the Park pale, lurching down the deeply entrenched road through the wood, pulling on to the level ground in front of the gatehouse, streaming in through that gate into the upper courtyard and there debouching their riches.

There is no record of who was on progress that year, but by chance an account has survived from the following summer of the rooms given to the court when it arrived at the archbishop's palace at Croydon. They had also been there in 1573. Most of the courtiers, as the document records, were given the chambers they had occupied the year before. Where the courtiers on progress differed, a note was made of who substituted for whom. The 1574 Croydon list, in other words, can be used to identify the people who came to stay at Sissinghurst in August 1573.

That summer day the whole cavalcade of Elizabethan courtliness arrived. There were the old men: the Lord Chamberlain, Thomas Radclyffe, earl of Sussex, a seasoned soldier in Ireland and the north, aged forty-eight, now in charge of the Household; the Lord Treasurer, Lord Burghley, the architect of Elizabethan security, now aged fifty-three, who as a young man must have known Sir John Baker well; the Lord Admiral, Edward Clinton, earl of Lincoln, now sixty-one, an experienced man of war, now turned courtier and diplomat. A generation down, and the glamour star of the whole performance, Robert Dudley, now aged forty, recently created earl of Leicester by the queen, was here. Loathed by Burghley, Lincoln and Sussex and beloved by the queen and her ladies, Leicester had already begun this summer, in secret, unknown to queen or court, a love affair with Lady Douglas Sheffield, who would secretly marry him and conceive a son later that autumn. She was not here but her sister was, the unmarried Lady Frances Howard, said to be just as far gone in love for the great courtier. Leicester could have acknowledged none of it, but as Master of Horse would have concentrated with Richard Baker on the hunting to be laid on for the party in Sissinghurst Park. The youngest of the courtiers here was the brilliant young poet, the earl of Oxford, Burghley's son-in-law, recently married, rich, of ancient lineage, the world at his feet.

Around the queen herself were her loyal and high-born ladies: the twenty-four-year-old Swedish beauty Helena, marchioness of Northampton, of whom the queen was intensely fond and whose task it was to warm up the queen's cold bed each night. Leicester's sister-in-law, Lady Warwick, was here, as was Lady Strafforde, Mistress of the Robes, Lady Carew and Lady Sidney. Armies of less high-born courtiers crowded around this jewelled core: Grooms of the Privy Chamber, Esquires for the Body, Gentlemen Ushers, 'Phesycos' and those in charge of the kitchen, the beds and the queen's own waiter all had to be fitted in.

The new Sissinghurst would have been built with this moment in mind. Baker would have had tens of rooms to play with: in the great new court, in the Tower and in the old medieval house. It was not unheard of for the hosts of the court on progress to farm out a few unimportant courtiers to neighbouring houses. The key concern, which the earl of Sussex would have overseen, was a set of rooms for the queen in which she could perform her political and public roles; and away from that, on the upper floor, more withdrawn rooms in which she could be cocooned in some privacy. If Sissinghurst followed the pattern in other houses, the court would have used the Hall as the Great Chamber to which all had access; the parlour as the Presence Chamber, to which many of the higher courtiers had access; and maybe a winter parlour as the Privy Chamber, to which access was strictly controlled.

On the floor above, probably overlooking both the garden by the moat and the great court on the other side, the queen's rooms would have been surrounded by her core household: Sussex within calling distance, Lady Carew and other gentlewomen of the bed-chamber and Lady Strafforde next door, 'the lady Marquess' of Northampton near by. The male counsellors would have been accommodated on the far side of the court in the opposite range: with Burghley, Leicester, Oxford and others over there in tense proximity.

What can it have been like? The queen, who had been given Lambarde's great book on Kent in manuscript by the archbishop to prep her for the county, would have been able to converse about her surroundings easily enough. But the Lord Chamberlain would have required, and Richard Baker would have happily ensured, that the days were tightly arranged. The form and patterning of Sissinghurst would have allowed that to happen.

From the first ceremonial greeting at the threshold, surely under the Tower arch, they would have moved on into the great courtyard. Each member of the court would have been shown his or her apartments. Hall, parlour, garden, the room in the Tower decorated with busts of the queen's father, mother, sister, brother and herself, the rooftop views and those from the flanking banqueting houses, the Park with its deer-hunting and rabbit-catching: all this feels like an amalgam of party architecture and landscape design, a complete universe in which life itself was a theatre of delight.

Sometimes people put on the most elaborate displays for the queen: gods, goddesses and fairy sprites, Arthurian swains and their wimpled ladies, verse-spouting shepherds and wild men of the woods, all popping up out of bushes as she passed. It didn't have to be as elaborate as that. Robert Sidney described to his friend Sir John Harington a relatively low-key, perhaps Sissinghurst-style visit to Penshurst:

> My son made a fair Speech, to which she did give a most gracious reply. The women did dance before her, whilst cornets did salute from the gallery; and she did vouchsafe to eat two morsels of rich comfit cake, and drank a small cordial from a gold cup. She had a marvelous suit of velvet borne by four of her first women attendants in rich apparel; two ushers did go before. Six drums and six trumpets waited in the Court, and sounded at her approach and departure.

Was that the tone here? Or had Richard Baker, like Sir Francis Carew at Bedington in Surrey in August 1599, dressed his cherry trees in canvas tents delaying their season, so that the fruit would be at perfect ripeness on the day the queen came? Or did he drive his

Park deer into a small paddock so that the queen might shoot one or two without much effort, as happened at Cowdray? Or did he make green houses in the Park, the walls of hazels cut and stuck in the ground, roofed in ivy, the interior hung with tapestries and the floor thick with strewing herbs and parsley, as the earls of Pembroke did in Clarendon Park near Salisbury? Did he have a young man serenading the queen under her window as soon as she awoke? Or did the Faery Queen with her accompanying maidens come dancing across the garden towards her, singing a song of flowery delight? Did the queen herself dance, in the high-stepping style for which this smallpox-scarred, wig-wearing forty-year-old was known across Europe? Or did she play the virginals in her own chamber, as she often did 'when she was solitary, to shun melancholy'?

All of this happened elsewhere on her progresses. Sadly, none of it is recorded for Sissinghurst. All we know for sure is that Richard Baker gave her

> One standynge cup, the bodie chaste [?] and cover partli christall, garnished with silver and guilt; in the top of the cover is a lion holding the Queen's armes cxvii oz

A rich cup weighing 117 ounces far outdid the offering made by the Culpepers (46 ounces), the townsmen of Cranbrook (47 ounces) and even the Guilfords (55 ounces). After three days, queen and courtiers left, perhaps with trumpets and drums in the court, and three days later, when they had travelled on to Dover, Baker followed them and was duly knighted, the reward which sealed his vastly expensive, entirely Elizabethan and father-denying efforts to make Sissinghurst a Renaissance palace in an invented park.

NINE

Disintegration

In the autumn of 2006, we set about salvaging the ideas for the farm. For all the catastrophe of the rejection in the summer, no one was going to let it collapse in a heap of figures. It was a sobering pause and there were many issues to address. A Sissinghurst dairy herd disappeared at this point, as a hop garden had earlier: both needed too much investment, both were subject to wildly fluctuating markets and both were dominated by large-scale producers elsewhere. We could not afford them. A beef herd was also looking marginal. The risks on fruit and vegetable growing were always huge. Raising chickens for the table and the egg market was both technical and tricky, particularly in terms of disease control. Pigs weren't easy. You could hire in some arable expertise – and the Pipers were keen to be involved – but every one of these enterprises became still more difficult under an organic system. Sheep were relatively easy but disease control was important and sheep were always getting diseases. I sometimes felt it might be better to carpet the whole place in polythene.

It was not as if we were able to reinvent Sissinghurst. We were having to engineer a new system inside the body of the old. The old had to continue to work and the existing visitor flow could not be disturbed. Everything we did had to fit. So we discussed, for example, at some length, the new cow shed. A high-quality building, which would be Sissinghursty, made of the correct materials to the correct design, would, it was thought, cost £200,000. Rob Macklin, the NT's head of agriculture, called it 'the gold-plated shed' phenomenon. 'Don't imagine', Jonathan Light said to me, 'that we enjoy having to live with these constraints. But they aren't constraints that can just be wished away.'

He revived an old suggestion: perhaps the Trust should buy the small and slightly run-down neighbouring holding called Whitegate Farm near the village. It had buildings, if not quite enough and not very swish, its land adjoined Sissinghurst, it would relieve pressure on the central cluster at the Castle itself, it could be made to look nicer, the local authority planning system would be working in our favour and the National Trust's own internal aesthetic bodies could not help but approve. Besides, Whitegate had been identified as a Sissinghurst priority for years. It belonged to Cyril Boulding, a local man who cared a great deal for the village and its surroundings, and who had always intended it should go to the Trust because he didn't want the land developed for housing. If the Trust bought it, the cost would be outside the farm project budget. Tentative negotiations were opened.

We pushed and stretched the plans and spreadsheets so that they could fit. Nothing should be done that could not be undone. Nothing should be done that could not be done elsewhere. And nothing should be done that would reduce Sissinghurst's income, although we would be given five years to get the new farm to break even. The glory days of a 15,000-acre estate paying for a luxury bauble were over. This would have to be a self-funding bauble.

Even though we had no clear idea of a way forward, it was decided to invoke the break clauses in the four old tenancies on the farm. If we missed this window, there would not be another chance for five years. As it turned out, one of the four tenants, June Munday, a grazier, was ready to retire; and two others, Ian Strang, the grazier from Lamberhurst, and the Piper brothers from Hawkhurst, who were arable specialists, were interested in taking part in the new scheme, either as tenants or contractors. They were all encouraging, if we could get it to work.

Only Ned Farris, who rented Upper and Lower Tassells for a game crop, was not entirely happy. His son told me they were moving the main focus of their business elsewhere anyway, to a shoot on the outskirts of Ashford, but his father was angry. I had a bad meeting with him one day on the edge of the wood, like something out of a Victorian novel. I had been ferreting that morning with Linda Clifford, and we had managed to catch three rabbits. Mr Farris was coming up the path out of the wood with a young magpie he had caught in a Larsen trap. 'We were joking about you in Ashford market,' he said as he walked up and put the bird in an old fertiliser bag in the back of his truck, tying the neck of the bag twice with a piece of baler twine. 'The big farmers down on the marsh. They think it's a joke. You're ten years late with this organic thing. That's about to run out. Hadn't you heard that?' He said he didn't care what anyone did with this farm. 'The National Trust won't allow the farmer to get on with it anyway, will they? They'll be all over him. I'm just going to leave them to get on with it. I won't tread on their toes and if they don't tread on mine, that will be all right. If they do there'll be trouble.' What sort of trouble? I asked, but he wasn't going to say, his eyes bloodshot and angry, his words apparently only saying half of what he felt. None of this was good. I knew there was support in the outside world and high up in the Trust but the neighbours, the local farming community, the Trust's professional advisers, the experts serving on their voluntary committees and several of their employees at Sissinghurst itself were all saying the same thing: the ideas I had were wrong.

I went back again to the longer story of Sissinghurst, to what I had always thought of as the long slide of a decline between the days of Elizabethan glory and the moment my grandparents arrived in 1930. Sissinghurst was not Knole. It had fallen from its great height, and that decline and collapse were the part of the story I now turned to. Again I found a surprise: as the great house had imploded, the land around it had thrived.

First, from about 1600 to the 1640s, Sissinghurst had continued as the Bakers' grand and occasionally visited hunting lodge, an increasingly out-of-date palace in a park. It was a period of profound inactivity. The Bakers were based largely at their house in Lime Street in the City of London and from the late 1630s onwards in a new, expensively rented and richly furnished house in Henrietta Street, Covent Garden, part of the earl of Bedford's development, designed by Inigo Jones, within spitting distance of the palace at Whitehall. Generation by generation, the Bakers trained as lawyers in the Middle Temple and Gray's Inn and hung around the edges of the Stuart court. They were among the first to buy a baronetcy in 1611 – the fee went to pay for the army in Ireland – while Sissinghurst remained occupied largely by their servants and filled with their possessions. Sir Henry Baker died at court in December 1623 from 'a contagious, spotted, or purple fever, that reigns much'. He left to his 'loving wife Catherine all the plate and furniture in her chamber at my house of Sissinghurst, her apparrell & my jewells, Rings, Bracelets etc and half the other plate and silver dishes & half the linen in my house'. His son Sir John had the other half but Catherine kept his 'plate and household stuff and furniture in London'. Loyalty to their servants appears in will after will, as it had done in the sixteenth century. Sir Henry left to 'the wife of one Lovell who nursed my son Thomas £55 . . . wch I have laid ready in gold for that purpose in my Cabinett att Sissinghurst'.

There is a hint that the Bakers may have continued as secret Catholics, drawing on the inheritance of the great Sir John, or at least as high Anglicans. In 1639, the chapel at Sissinghurst was, according to Thomas Philipott, the seventeenth-century historian, 're-edified'. Sissinghurst was 'in the wilds of Kent' and 'by reason of deep and fowle ways (especially in winter)' the latest Sir John Baker and his family were 'not able without much trouble and danger duly to frequent the church' in Cranbrook. Hence they needed their chapel here. The archbishop's licence describes it as 'newly built and decently embellished, apart from the ordinary part of the house', and so one can't say whether this seventeenth-century chapel was a refurbished version of the medieval chapel or an entirely new building. The licence says it was 'below' (infra) the mansion at Sissinghurst, which suggests it might have been in the orchard below the medieval house. One eighteenth-century drawing does indeed show a semi-detached building there, with a door giving on to the Elizabethan garden.

A further hint comes in the sermon that was preached by Robert Abbott, the vicar of Cranbrook, at the dedication ceremony in September 1639. The chapel was, Robert Abbott said,

> built and furnished with cost: profit therefore is engaged to give way to the devout worship of God heere. It is built by a garden of pleasure, a parlour of plenty: pleasure therefore is engaged to give way to the devout worship of God. *Iosephs tombe* was in a garden, to put thoughts of mortality into his delights, and this chappell is in a garden, to be a monitor (in the midst of refreshments) to the way of immortalitie.

Between garden and parlour, a 'chapel in a garden': this was the Sissinghurst version of worshipping God in the beauty of holiness.

Abbott addressed 'a large crowd', with some markedly Catholic names (Campion, Mounckton, Henley, Darrell) among them. And the chapel was furnished in a far from Puritan style. It had a communion table, pulpit, reading desks and thirteen pews 'all of wainscot', candlesticks and a branched candelabra, a 'fayre silver

To the noble Comittee for Examinacons
The humble peticon of Mary Baker
wife of Sr John Baker Barronett

Sheweth

That in Aprill last the Comittee in Kent did sequester the estate of your peticoners husband in Kent where his Mansion howse (about 40 miles from London) and all his Lands lyeth, to the value of above 2000 p and which Comittee he attended in person. and havinge a howse richly furnished in Covent garden; which he held at a greate rent: which goods were likewise sequestred: but vppon a tickitt issued from the comittee for the xxth being for 600 li the goods soe sequestred, were taken out of the hands of the sequestrators by a warrant from the Comittee (as yr peticoner is informed) for the xxth parte; and though of a very greate value, yet sold for 87 li yr peticoners husband, being much indisposed in his health, his whole estate sequestred, and so altogether disabled to pay a xxth parte. yet neverthelesse, a warrante was issued out against yr peticoners husband to make payment of the demaundes: whereas in truth yr peticoners husband is much indebted, and hath at this time noe meanes left to maintaine himselfe, and his wife and children. And being taken vppon the saide warrant, did gaue securities to appeare on munday the ... of this month of S... in the interim vppon motion made to this ho... Comittee by yr peticoner; libertie was given him in regard of his sicklynes to appeare on munday followinge.

May it therefore please this ho:ble Comittee; forasmuch as yr peticoners husband is a very weake and sickly man, and vnfitt for travell: that you wilbe favorable pleased to release him from his apparance and restraint, havinge noe meanes left him to make further satisfaccon for his said xxth parte; and yr peticoner shall pray &c.

bason, a silver pott for wine and a silver chalice with a cover for the communion and a silver plate with a bason for the font, all double guilt'. In 1639, this was the highest of church Laudianism, and you can be sure the whole of Puritan Cranbrook would have been scandalised. It was probably at this stage that the little Elizabethan banqueting house at the northern edge of the garden was extended so that the chaplain could be housed in it, and renamed perhaps by the locals the Priest's House, a term that in Protestant Cranbrook would have been dripping in contempt.

It was inevitable that this High Church, possibly crypto-Catholic family would side with the king against Parliament in the Civil War. Sir John was already off with the king's army in 1642, and in August that year his lands, worth £2000 a year, and his 'rich furniture in Covent garden' were seized by the parliamentary committees raising money for the war. His family struggled to save what they could, sending in petitions to Parliament, and in March 1644 Sir John petitioned the House of Commons itself.

The humble petition of Sir Jo Baker Barronett

acknowledgeth that hee hath beene at Oxford, in the Kinge's quarters where hee much disliked their proceedings. He never was in Armes against Parliament, nor ever advanced anie thing either horses plate or money to the King's forces but ever expressed his good affections to ye Parliament by his ready payment of all duties and assessments of Parliament so long as hee had any disposition of his estate and is ready to ingage life and fortune to the parliaments service. Hee is indebted 10,000 li and hath lost 3,000 pounds by the seizing of his estate to the use of the parliament.

In tender consideration whereof ye petitioner humblie praies he may be accepted into yr favours,

etc, John Baker

But the war had reached an implacable stage, and in May that year the parliamentarian Lord Warwick wrote to Captain Edward Boys, addressing him as 'my very loving friend'.

Ye are appointed by ye Parliament to bee sequestrator of all ye delinquents Woods within the County of Kent And for the felling thereof for the Service of the State.

The timber thus taken was to be used 'for the repairing of Castles & Forts & otherwise'. In the complex paperwork of the many overlapping committees by which Parliament administered the goods confiscated from the Royalists, I have been unable to find the inventory made, at some time in the summer of 1644, when Sissinghurst was raided for everything of value. But there are lists for neighbouring gentry houses whose goods fell under the hammer that summer, often sold to the local poor. At the Wottons' house in Boughton Malherbe, rugs for two shillings, 'a little round table', a coverlet, a chair, 'old pieces of stayres and lumber', 'the fruit of the Long Walk and the Privy Garden', 'nagges and geldings', 'two little turkey carpets motheaten for five shillings', 'a little pair of tongs': all were knocked down to Goodwife Andrewes, Goodman Albert, Mr Cogan (the sequestrator's assistant), Goodwife Gilbert or their neighbours.

It must have happened here too, and the evidence is in the woods. In the whole of Sissinghurst, there are now only two trees that were certainly growing here before the summer of 1644: the pollard oak in the big wood, in whose branches I once spent the best part of a day; another down by the Hammer Brook, its fat trunk scarred by lightning, its branches hanging out over the stream. Otherwise, they have all gone, and it doesn't take much to imagine the scene, the great old oaks and beeches which the Bakers had treasured, and even named in their wills, felled unseasonably in midsummer, the huge leafy crowns slowly descending to the park-land grass, the outer limbs cushioning the fall, splintering as they came down, the bodies of the pollards laid out like shot cattle, the timber wagons taking them away to the saw-yards. In other Kentish parks, payments were made by the sequestrator to the men doing the work for Parliament's cause. And there is one further clue. A description of Sissinghurst Park in 1695 says that 'The Growth of the Wood in it is most Birch, which is much in use for Birch-Wine'. Birch is the great pioneer species of Wealden woods, colonising any space vacated for it. For Sissinghurst to be covered in them in 1695 could only have meant that the oaks and beeches had been taken away fifty years before.

By July 1644, the Committee for Compounding proposed to fine Baker £5000, 'it appearing that he has been in service against parliament and has 2,500 l. a year'. Negotiations continued; the fine was reduced to £3000 but he didn't pay up and still hadn't by

July 1645. His indebtedness rolled on throughout the years of the Commonwealth. As late as 1652, 'on the morrow of Holy Trinity', he at last signed a mortgage on almost everything he owned in Kent: houses, barns, stables, 7 watermills, 40 gardens, 40 orchards, 2005 acres of arable land, 700 of meadow, 500 of pasture, 700 of wood and '40 acres of land covered with water' – the huge pond upstream of the furnace at Hammer Mill. Although Baker's London properties were not mentioned, 'the manor of Sissinghurst' was included by name. In return, Baker received £2760 sterling and with it paid the debt he owed the state.

Old Sir John died the following year and his son, yet another Sir John, inherited a heavily encumbered estate. He rearranged the mortgage in 1657, and with the money restored the pale around the whole Park, but Sissinghurst was now fatally burdened with its borrowings and the Bakers would never recover. This last Sir John died in about 1661, having committed the ultimate crime against his family's fortunes. He left a widow, four daughters and no son. The girls began by living with their mother in the huge house. Any number of others, unnamed, were living in the house with them. There were 38 hearths alight here on Lady Day in 1664, compared with 85 at Knole but only 21 at Penshurst. Inside the Park, at the top of the lane in the fields still known as the Well Fields, there was an 'old admired well', set with stones and basins, a 'curative chalybeate spring', much in use for those with infections of the urinary tract. Multitudes came. There were walks laid out. 'The park', it was said, had 'very great plenty of Stawberys in and about it ... Also near-adjoining ... is very good *Chery-gardens* and great plenty of Fruit: The best Sider is but Six pence the Bottle.' The district as a whole was 'much supply'd with Fish, there being much Gentry in the Parish, and many great Ponds of Fresh Fish'.

It didn't last. Lady Baker 'hated all the people and had the gates of the park locked to obstruct the same'. The stones and basins were removed as Sissinghurst sank towards its nadir. When the Baker daughters 'marryed into other counties', the old lady moved to her London house and Sissinghurst became half destitute and lawless. In 1673, the inhabitants of the mansion house attacked 'the possessors of a wood adjacent', the reason not recorded. An arrest warrant was issued, the parish constable came to the front gate 'with 16 or 20 to assist him'. The Sissinghurst gang refused to come out or give up the man named on the warrant. There was a stand-off but the constable and his men could hear them inside arming with staves. 'The constable and his assistants fearing mischief went away.' About fourteen of Sissinghurst's inhabitants then rushed out of the gate, chased the constable, 'the constable commanded the peace, yet they fell on and killed one of the assistants of the constable, and wounded others, and then retired into the house to the rest of their company'. The precise individual who had committed the murder couldn't be identified, but nine of them were arrested, all found equally guilty and all of them hanged, thus establishing the powerful precedent of the Sissinghurst House Case, by which membership of a murderous gang is considered the same as committing murder oneself.

Any question of Sissinghurst being the centre of a perfect world was long gone. It is not quite certain what happened here in the early eighteenth century. A very old pauper, interviewed at Sissinghurst in the 1830s by a visiting American descendant of the Bakers, 'said he remembered the last of the family coming to Church every Sunday with their guests and visitors in four coaches and four horses, long tails, etc., etc.'. There is no record of them. Sissinghurst and the larger Baker estate had been inherited by the four sisters, in equal shares. Each share followed a tortuous path down the different branches of the family, and although each of those four Baker girls, Anne (d. 1685), Elizabeth (d. 1705), Mary (d. 1714) and Catherine (d. 1733), returned from their husbands' estates to be buried in Cranbrook church, Sissinghurst was neglected. The buildings rotted. The Park pale collapsed. The unpaid mortgage continued to climb until by the 1750s the sum owing had reached £9000, nearly three-quarters the value of the entire Baker estate in Kent. Sissinghurst had become a lump against which money could be borrowed. The place, in a way that might be shocking to us in the age of preservation, was allowed to fall apart. But the eighteenth-century rich lived in a profligate world. Many families in England were overhoused. Each of the Sissinghurst heirs had their own satisfactory houses elsewhere. What good was a crumbling Elizabethan mansion, only as old for them as a Victorian, concrete shooting box might be for us?

The eighteenth century gave nothing to Sissinghurst. It only took away. I have often wondered what might have happened here if the Bakers' male line had not died out. Would there have been an exquisite Palladian pavilion placed on this gentle rise, surrounded by the elegances of its improved eighteenth-century park? Would Capability Brown have been brought in to dam the Hammer Brook and make a sky-reflecting lake in the valley? Would one or two Gothic eye-catchers have been built up by the pines in the wood? Maybe. And maybe Sissinghurst would have been coloured not with its air of romantic abandonment but with suede-lined riches, a title, perhaps an earldom for the Bakers, money from an advantageous marriage or two in the City. Perhaps Vita, pursued in 1912 by the earl of Sissinghurst, would have turned down him and his palatial residence as something too smart, too obvious, without poetry?

In 1752, Horace Walpole was touring the sites of Kent, and on 9 August wrote to his friend Richard Bentley:

> Yesterday, after twenty mishaps, we got to Sissinghurst to dinner. There is a park in ruins and a house in ten times greater ruins, built by Sir John Baker, Chancellor of the Exchequer to Queen Mary. You go through an arch of the stables to the house, the court of which is perfect and very beautiful ... This has a good apartment, and a fine gallery, a hundred and twenty feet by eighteen, which takes up one side: the wainscot is pretty and entire: the ceiling vaulted, and painted in a light genteel grotesque. The whole is built for show; for the back of the house is nothing just lath and plaster.

'Nothing just lath and plaster' is a mid-eighteenth-century view of the medieval house behind Sir Richard Baker's Elizabethan *cour d'honneur*.

Four years later, Sissinghurst entered the pit of its existence, when even the sad remains that Walpole had seen were effectively destroyed and the break with the sixteenth century was made final. The agents of the dispersed Baker estate found a means of making some money out of the old mansion. About 1400 acres of the surrounding land were let for £445 to a farmer called George Tempest, but the big house was reserved from the lease and let instead to the government. Britain had embarked on a Seven Years' War with France, and on 21 July 1756 the house at Sissinghurst was leased by the Admiralty's Sick and Hurt Board as a camp for French naval prisoners.

Up to three thousand Frenchmen were held here at any one time, most of them common seamen. There were rooms reserved for officers in the Tower (where their graffiti have been preserved in the plaster: their names and both brigs and square-rigged ships in full sail), but most officers, having given their word of honour, were allowed to live in Cranbrook, Tenterden, Sevenoaks or Maidstone. If any of them found themselves stuck here they were not slow to make their elegant and elaborate complaint to the Admiralty.

An Outside View of SISINGHERST CASTLE in the COUNTY of KENT dedicated to the Officers of the Militia.
Engrav'd from a Drawing taken on the Spot By an Officer 1760

au Chateau de Sissingherst
29 Juillet 1757

Monsieur

I take the liberty of writing to you to ask you to listen to me on the subject on which I have the honour to address you. I commanded a Calais privateer called the *Duc de Moncis,* in which I was taken about a fortnight ago.

I thought on my arrival I would be cautioned on my word of honour just as all others of my rank would be. But far from that. I found myself strictly locked up in a prison where I was mixed up with all qualities of men. Where I am suffering everything one might suffer in such a situation. I am the only captain here even though several others who are of a far lower rank than mine have been given permission to leave. So Monsieur, persuaded as I am that you are filled with Justice, I am writing directly to you, to ask you to help me obtain my freedom. On my word, I assure you, that I will never give you the opportunity to repent of having done me this favour. I await this favour of you, begging you to consider that here I am exposed to all sorts of things, riddled with vermin (please excuse the term) and thus unhappy.

This considered, Monsieur, may it please you from your generosity to grant your consent shortly to

Your very humble and very respectful servant

Charles Maquet

Captain of the privateer Le Duc de Moncis at Calais

I beg you, if it is your will, to grant me the same favour for my son aged 14 who is a prisoner with me.

The vermin by whom the Maquets were surrounded were guarded by revolving detachments, each of about 220 men, from various county militias: Surrey, to which the artist Francis Grose was attached as a lieutenant; Hampshire, in which the young Edward Gibbon was an officer here; and Leicestershire, which was the most vicious and almost entirely out of control. Officers of the guard lived either in Cranbrook or in buildings that have now disappeared at the top of the Lake Field. Supervising them on behalf of the Admiralty was a Mr Cooke, 'Agent for Prisoners of War at Sissinghurst', known to the French as 'Monsieur Cok' and suffering a little from the gout. He could speak no French but communicated with the prisoners through an interpreter called François le Rat. Cooke's relationship with the army officers was usually unsatisfactory and he was generally distrusted by both guards and prisoners alike for his 'Gouvernement', which according to one prisoner's complaint was 'nothing less than tyrannical and capricious'.

This broken-down and brutalised 'château', as they called it – a term then borrowed by the English; this was the moment at which Sissinghurst House became Sissinghurst Castle – was a strange and alien place for the French. Their letters refer to the 'Chateau de Sissengherst', 'Sisinchers', 'Chisterner', 'Sinsinhars' and 'Ste. Sigherts pres Cambrouck'. It was a zoo of abuse and maltreatment, the prison that Frenchmen in other prisons were threatened with if they misbehaved. The stories coming out of Sissinghurst became so bad that in November and December 1761 Dr Maxwell, the Commissioner for the Sick and Hurt Board, came down for a month and held an inquiry in a room in the great Elizabethan courtyard. From the evidence given to that inquiry, transcribed verbatim into a long manuscript now in the National Archives, a powerful picture emerges of the grief and suffering that thousands of men underwent here.

fait au Chatteau De St Sigberts pres Cambrielt Le 2 Juillet 1760

Mon Tres Honnorable Commissaire

Je vous Ecris Ce Deux Ligne pour Vous demander
Justice De Ce Quil peuts Nous Ette dû de Ce
Que Nous Avons Gagné Et Boits Du Roy de grosse
Marchant Venant De La Virginne Commande par Capitaine
Roberts Ribh Dont Le Capitaine Nous a Demande pour
Aler a Son Boits Et Quil Nous promit Trante chelin
Par Moy Dont il Avets Promis De Nous payer a Contes
Ce Quil faits Lancazion Que Nous Navons pas Ette payé
Cest Que Le Capittaine Est Tout Lequipage a Desendu
A Terre Et il Nous a Laisse aboit a Travaille Comme
Sil Nous avets Commande Je Voub Die quil y Est Venu
Un Bots pour Nous Venir Cherche De La par Du Roy
Et De La Lon Nous a Menne Elu Kins Armee Et De
La Lon Nous a Menne Dans Le Cattaux De Schennurk
Dont par Cette Aucazion La Nous Navons pa eû Le Tan De
Conté Noû Besoin Nous Avons Travaille Aboits pendant

The place was disgusting with 'great heaps of dirt in all the courts'. The moat was 'very foul and stinking', filled with all kinds of ordure and no proper means of cleaning it. The prisoners were packed into every available space on all three floors of all the buildings. They slept in hammocks strung from posts specially inserted into the rooms, converting Sissinghurst into the navy's equivalent of between-decks accommodation. The numbers of the wards and the number of men to be housed in each of them were painted up over the doors. There was no money to replace broken windows and so the prisoners blocked them up with bricks and clay to keep warm. They had coal fires but no scuttles or bunkers and so the coal lay in heaps on the floor and its dust blackened everything. Large numbers of unwashed men lived in virtually lightless and airless rooms, which Maxwell reported as 'dirty and very bad smelling' and 'very close, by the windows being shut up for want of casements and shutters'. The rooms of Elizabethan elegance became 'Bowling Alley Ward', 'Long Gallery Ward' and 'Great Parlour Ward'. Worst of all was a room known simply as 'Black Dog', and above it 'Black Dog Garret', both of which were 'very close, wanted air, bad smells in them'.

Every morning the prisoners were turned out of their wards, and on fair days when the ground was dry all the hammocks were taken out to be aired. The prisoners were given two long sheds below the Tower to shelter in during the day. There was a man working in a shed in the middle court making stockings. Others had small shops here, selling bread, candles or tobacco. Prisoners could be given licences to go out into the surrounding country, where they worked as cooks, lamplighters, postmen, waiters for officers of the guard or housekeepers for Mr Cooke. Money could be sent from France and was regularly distributed by Mr Cooke. It was said that 'arithmetic classes' were held for junior officers in the Tower, unless that is a joke. Some used the chapel to say their daily prayers.

They certainly gambled, drank porter and carved their names into the buildings. In the attic of the north wing above the stables, there is still the name of Pierre Mesnard, his letters cut deep into the 1560s oak, and each one carefully painted a smoky French blue.

They were mustered daily in the upper court, but otherwise the bulk of prisoners were forced to hang about in the middle courtyard, as they called it, in the medieval court below and in the remains of the Elizabethan garden beside the moat, some of which was still enclosed by a high wall. Where the wall had disappeared, the garden was surrounded by a 'paled fence with tenter hooks upon it of full 6 feet high'. This was 'the best garden', with the chapel to one side and 'a Necessary House', a privy, within it, giving on to the moat. One eighteenth-century drawing of Sissinghurst, recently discovered in Canada, shows a basic outline of walks and beds in the garden. There was another kitchen garden, perhaps on the site of the present Rose Garden, and another 'little court going into the garden', probably on the site of the present Delos. Throughout these courts and enclosures and beyond the moat stood sentries carrying loaded muskets and fixed bayonets, with sentry boxes and braziers on posts, from which light was thrown at night-time.

They were, at least nominally, well fed with a standard naval ration: three-quarters of a pound of beef to each prisoner, distributed in the form of 4½ pounds of meat to each mess, which six men would share. It was cooked in a building just outside the front gate, a delegation of five prisoners inspecting the meat every day before it was cooked. In addition they had 1½ pounds of bread each (which the French complained was 'glewy'), a quart of beer and on a weekly 'maigre day' they had cabbage in a bowl of soup, some bread and six ounces of cheese. But so bitter was the atmosphere at Sissinghurst that none of this was really as good as it sounds. In Dr Maxwell's notes there is a draft of what the daily ration of meat should consist of. Weight was not to be made up 'from the Coarse or boney part' and the meat was to be, he wrote, 'without Skirts or Kidneys, ~~Hearts Heads~~ or any other part'. Hearts and heads were considered on reflection a perfectly good part of the ration.

A deeply unhappy and rather chubby twenty-three-year-old Edward Gibbon, who was here for a few days in December 1760, hated every minute of it. Sissinghurst was 'a strong large old Seat, situated in the middle of a Park', with about 1750 prisoners housed there. The daily march to and from a 'miserable' Cranbrook was disgusting, the 'dirt most excessive' and the other officers despicable. He was already 'sick of so hateful a service, tired of companions who had neither the knowledge of scholars nor the manners of gentlemen' and was longing to begin again 'to taste the pleasure of thinking'. Life at Sissinghurst was 'at best, not a life for a man of letters'. It was 'both unfit for and unworthy of me'.

There is one curious side-note in young Gibbon's diary. His detachment was at Sevenoaks on 5 June 1761. 'We took a Walk to Knowles the D. of Dorset's seat, a noble pile, very much upon the plan of Sissinghurst.' The Knole–Sissinghurst connection was alive in the 1560s, when Richard Baker's sister was married to Thomas Sackville; again in the mind of a particularly alert young man in the 1760s; and again two centuries later in the 1930s, when a disinherited Vita recognised Sissinghurst as the nearest to a ruined Knole she would ever come.

Sissinghurst was a world of gossip and hate, bubbling with violence, threat and mutual loathing. Prisoners would spit in the face of militiamen, who in return would knock them down with their musket stocks. Brutal kicking and beating occurred almost daily. The lingua franca of the prison was foul abuse. Soldiers would habitually break the pipes in prisoners' mouths or smack them on the head. There were paid informers among the prisoners. At night, in revenge for insults heard or imagined, the militia would destroy the shelving and tables at which the prisoners would conduct their little businesses. Paul Escombre, the prisoner selling bread in the middle court, had his basket overturned and the bread tipped into the mud. The Leicestershire militia, as described by one witness to the inquiry in 1761, seems to have been almost anarchic:

> One day at the muster, the centinels who were posted as usual to keep good order at the muster maltreated many of the Prisoners

as they passed by, by striking of them on their backs with their naked hangers [swords], pushing off their hatts with them, pulling of them by their queues, and sometimes striking in among the whole body of those who had not passed with their Hangers. One of the soldiers with his firelock and bayonet fixed, being on the pavement in the middle court, came running along from the chappel. The prisoners seeing him coming did what they could to make way for him but he being too quick for them struck in among them with his firelock & bayonet and drove them off the pavement into the dirt.

Inevitably, this undertow of loathing and brutality now and then tipped over into murder. One guard, William Bassuck, was killed by a prisoner who dropped a filled pail on his head from the top of the Tower. A soldier who killed two prisoners in the garden said, when asked about it, at least according to one of the prisoners, 'if he had killed more it would not have given him uneasiness ... He sayd he would not have any more pity on us than if we were dogs. He took a stick in his hands. "I'll take care of these Dogs. They shall not move. If they do, I'll break their arms."' The soldier was said to have 'publickly boasted that he had long intended it & that he had a desire to kill 10 prisoners before he went off this duty'. The picture recently discovered in Canada shows this incident: the militiaman firing from the far side of the moat; the two men lying dead in the garden; the crowd of outraged prisoners; the ring of sentry boxes and braziers, a Lilliput-version of a human hell.

On 27 October 1759, Mr Cooke's assistant, Mr Ward, and an officer of the West Kent Militia, Mr Mortimer, were walking in the Long Gallery, on the north side of the Middle Court. It was about eleven o'clock at night, an hour after the regulations stated that all lights should be put out. They were looking across the court to 'the uppermost ward of the south wing'. Mortimer was convinced that the prisoners still had a light burning. Ward

spoke to Mr M and endeavored to convince him that there were no lights. That it was the Reflection of the Lamps. Upon which we walked up & down the room three times in the Long Gallery where I said I cannot be persuaded that there have been any lights in the room this night.

Philippe Hardie, one of the sixty or seventy prisoners in the upper ward in the south wing, sleeping next to a man called Joffe from Dunkirk, was asked at the inquiry what happened. 'The soldier called to them to put the candle out and there was no candle alight; as all the people were asleep nobody answered him.' Mortimer claimed that the prisoners 'bid him fire and be damned', but Philippe Hardie's testimony has the ring of truth:

> Everybody in the room was very quiet and I was laid alongside of [Joffe]. The reflection of a lamp shone upon a window in our ward & the centinel thought there was a light in the Room & he fired & the other prisoners say now he called out 2 or 3 times but I heard nothing of that & was asleep. The ball went through his thigh as he lay asleep in his hammock across the window.

The lead ball that hit Joffe in the thigh was found in his hammock. It had gone through one thigh and flattened against the other. But terrible damage had been done in its passage:

> A large hands breadth of the thigh bone [was] shattered to pieces the ball having taken an oblique direction. The wound was so near the head of the bone that amputation was impracticable. The man lived in excessive pain till the 31st then died.

Ferdinando Gralez, also of Dunkirk, was killed in 1758 'as he was putting his cloaths to dry' on the barrier on the east side of the garden, killed by a sentry on the far side of the moat. He had been shot in the back and the ball had come out 'about 3 fingers breadth on the right side of the navel'. Cooke had banned clothes being hung on the barriers but the prisoners were uncertain: 'some centrys suffered it & some did not'. Four of his friends carried Gralez to the hospital in the Elizabethan barn – a toxic sink of filth and unwashed linen, overseen by the incompetent surgeon, Mr Thompson – and 'there he languished till 11 o'clock that evening and then expired'. The dead were buried in the ground known as the Plain, the grassy patch in front of the entrance where visitors to Sissinghurst now picnic.

Most pitiable of all, though, are the letters preserved in the Admiralty files in Kew. One after another they describe their hopeless, slave-like circumstances: 'The sad situation I have been reduced to, having lost a leg in battle, unable to make a living with a large family'; a man who was the last of his crew left at Sissinghurst, all of them having been exchanged with English prisoners and now at home in France; men in need of money; a desperate young man, severely wounded in the face, wanting to be treated by a French surgeon, where 'he would be much better off than in an English hospital'. Hundreds of them, most of them written in an exquisite clerk's hand, are piled up in the Admiralty boxes, addressed to 'Ma Chaire Epouse', 'ma très Chere mere', 'Ma chere fame'. Others are from the prisoners' wives, still in France.

> from le havre 25 August 1757
>
> To monsieur Louis le Brun
> D'un navire Le Lizabeht
> commandé par le capitaine Pierre Double
> de present Prisonnier au chatau de Sissingnurst
>
> My dear husband
>
> This is to tell you of the state of my health which is strong, thank God, and that of our children. I hope that the present finds you in a good condition. I want to tell you that I long for your return at the birth

But she did not have much confidence that he would be there when his latest child was born. She had the good news for him that he would have a place for sure on a boat when he returned to Calais, but when would that be? They must have 'confidence in the Lord', but she begged her man to 'take any joy with moderation' for fear that things would not turn out as they might have wished. Louis must pray that the Lord will come to their aid.

Je vous prie de me faire response et de me faire scavoir si ce que vous marquerons fait plaisir je fini en vous souhaitans une parfaite santé je suis en attendans le plaisir de vous voir mon cher mary votre fidelle epouse femme Le Brun

I beg you to reply to me and to let me know if what you have learned gives you pleasure. I finish in wishing you perfect health. I await the pleasure of seeing you my dear husband. Your faithful wife, Mrs Le Brun

The most poignant aspect of these letters is that the prisoners never received them. They remain in the Admiralty files where they had originally been scanned for any intelligence they might have yielded on French shipping. And Mme Le Brun would have waited for a reply in vain.

The French prisoners took Sissinghurst apart, tearing up the woodwork, 'especially in a ward called The Black Dog by destroying the hammock posts and pulling up and making away with the Boards of the floor', destroying all the fittings in the chapel, parlours and Long Gallery, taking out the inside of the stables, making two barns and four oasts unusable 'by cutting out the principall beams', stripping off the panelling wherever it had survived, destroying 'the Palesade fence to the Kitchen Garden with other fences & gates Destroyed' and wrecking 'the best Garden, by the Wall fruite & other trees all destroyed and not even the stump of a Shrub nor Tree left'.

The owner of Sissinghurst was now Edward Mann of Linton, a Baker descendant who in 1762 had bought its 1402 acres from the other claimants for £12,982, plus £300 for the mansion house. When the war came to an end in 1763, Mann wrote to the Admiralty assessors, telling them that he was 'filled with a perfect Desire of bringing our affairs together to an Eclairissement'. He asked initially for £361 'in compensation for the great Destruction in every Particular which such a number of Prisoners have occasioned in every part of the Buildings & Mansion House & Gardens', but soon accepted fifty pounds plus the Admiralty's 'sheds and erections', which had remained here when the prisoners left.

1769

An Estimate of the damege don by
the Prisoners and forces at Sissinghurst
so farr as came to our Knowledge by
a Survey taken on the tenth & eleventh
of October last

1   To 2092 foot of Glass destroyed
and gon with great damge to the
winder frames by many Jams
& Iron Barrs being gon & winders
and may party of the winders stoped
up with Bricks Morter or Mud   100:0:0

2   To the Chapel by destroying the Pulpett
Pewes Pertition Carve work Table
floor Ceeling and all the timber of the
Ceeling Floor   40:0:0

3   To that long Gallery by Destroying
neer two hundred yards of Wainscott
with a Rich Carved
marvell Chymny piece Broke down
and wood work greatly damaged   50:0:0

4   To the Stables by 82 foot of Reck
and Manger four Stalls gon
by Doors & Door Cases gon   20:0:0

5   To the two Barns by floors great
Doors Breckts with many Breeches
in the Brick Walls   50:0:0

6   To the Oast House by four Oasts
being pulled down & gon & by cutting
out the Principall Beams   40:0:0

7   To the Great & little Halles
by destroying wainscott floor
Partition & Ornaments   20:0:0

8   To wainscott damaged & three Rumes
up stairs Front Door gon & one floor   11:10:0
To the Walls & Ceelings of the the
House broke Down   20:0:0

9   To Palesade fence to Kitchen
Garden with Other fences & Gates
Destroyed & gon   10:0:0

   361:10:0

2   To Great damage don in the best Garden
by the Wall frute & other Trees all
destroyed and not even the runniss
of a shurb nor Tree left

Sissinghurst had been utterly degraded, and this is the first moment when its history just leaks into the margins of living memory. In the 1930s, Vita met a 'very old' gentleman who had lived in the Castle in his boyhood. He had been a ten-year-old in the 1860s, when he met a ninety-year-old labourer, who had been about thirty in 1800, when his father-in-law (then about sixty) told him that he 'had been employed not only to pull down the walls, but also to pick the foundations in 1763'.

Most of the old house disappeared, probably as hard core for tracks and hard standing. Electronic resistivity surveys of the site have revealed next to nothing, and when drainage ditches have been cut through the lines of the old ranges, all that is revealed in their walls is dark scars of eighteenth-century earth filling the Elizabethan and medieval foundation trenches. All the fields around Sissinghurst are full of shards of tile and crumbled brick from the dismantled buildings. The value remained only in the land. The Park now disappeared. The pale was never recreated and a regular, eighteenth-century field pattern was laid over the open grounds. A survey was made of the trees here in June 1763 in Sissinghurst Park, Hammer Wood by Hammer Mill, Fludgate Wood next to it, Graylins Wood near Whitsunden and Legge Wood and Eleven Acre Wood, both near Wadd. In them, the indefatigable surveyors counted:

7981 oak trees

5012 beech trees

125 ash trees

320 chestnutt trees

3 walnutt trees

10 Sycomore trees

14493 tillers [young trees] and pollards of the above sorts

The Sissinghurst woods had begun to make their recovery from the depredations of the Civil War and were now valued at £5302, nearly eighteen times as much as the damaged house. Among these trees, so carefully counted, are most of the big oaks and beeches now growing at Sissinghurst.

In 1796 a lease was taken by the parish of Cranbrook on Sissinghurst Castle Farm, the idea being that the farm would provide work for those able-bodied men who would otherwise be incapable of earning their living, especially during the winter months. Among the thousands of documents in the files of the Kent County Archives in Maidstone, there are two giant vellum pages, stitched together along the bottom edge with vellum strips and carrying the seals and signatures of eleven different individuals. Each page is over two feet wide and eighteen inches high, and both are covered from top to bottom in the tiny, exact but very clear handwriting of the clerk who drew them up.

The document looks as if it might be medieval, or perhaps the translation of something medieval, written on a burnished sheepskin, with the vast Gothic headline '*This Indenture Tripartite*' painted across the top. It is in fact less than two hundred years old,

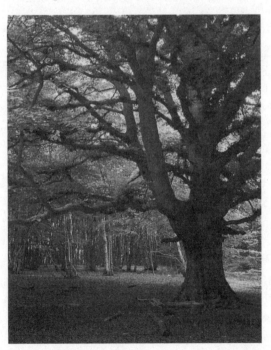

an agreement made in May 1811 between Sir Horatio Mann, Edward Mann's nephew, from whom he had inherited Sissinghurst, and a set of eight individuals, described as 'Yeomen of Cranbrook', who were renewing their lease on the farm here. It is both an ancient thing, dripping in its medieval inheritance, looking like a treaty drawn up after Agincourt, and a modern one, an arrangement for the welfare officers in Cranbrook, which is what these men were, to rent the farm on which the poor of the parish could live, work and support themselves: a job creation scheme of a modern and enlightened kind.

When I first read this lease, crawling my way across the curly, ant-like script, something else came bowling towards me. This, in its archaic language, its beautiful attention to the details of the land and the habits by which it was managed, was both a voice from the old world and a summons to do things like it again. It was not only a depiction of the world we had lost but a model of the frame of mind that Sissinghurst needed, a level of care and understanding of the place that the late twentieth century had entirely abandoned.

The indenture, with its wavy upper edge, was a lease for twenty-one years, renewing another which the Cranbrook yeomen had made a few years earlier. They were now to pay £318 a year as rent, in four equal quarters, in January, April, July and October. The land they were renting at Sissinghurst, called simply Sissinghurst Farm, was 'by estimation 342 acres and a half', in thirty-seven different parcels of arable, meadow and pastureland. The grass in the meadow was allowed to grow for hay; the pasture was to be grazed all year. There were eight acres of hops and extensive woodland.

In hunting for his game and in arriving to secure his timber, Sir Horatio and his agents agreed that they would do 'no wilful hurt spoil or damage to the Hay Grass or Corn'. There was some mutuality here; not for many centuries had landlords in England been allowed to damage with impunity the property that others had leased from them. But the burdens on the tenants were real and extensive. All hedges had to be preserved 'from the bite and spoil of cattle'. If any fruit trees died or were blown down, 'other good and young fruit trees of the same or better sort' had to be set in their place. Hedges had to be laid (every nine years) and good ditches made alongside them. If they cut any of the underwood, they had to give thirty days' notice to Sir Horatio's steward, 'so that the steward can mark and number the trees and tillers there growing'. They had to keep the buildings in good repair and pay for the window glass, leadwork, straw for any thatching and the carriage of materials. Mann's steward agreed to provide out of the rent enough rough timber, brick, tiles, lime and iron for the work to be done.

This has a modern ring to it, a negotiated sharing out of tasks and costs. But in relationship to the land there was something much deeper, to do with a vision of cyclicality and self-sufficiency that seemed both extraordinarily and deeply primitive, laying down rules for this place which embodied almost total self-sustenance, and a form of clarion call for us.

First of all, the tenants were not to pollute the land with any form of crop whose seeds tend to spread themselves at will and remain everlasting weeds, now to be seen on every motorway verge in England: 'The tenants shall not nor will at any time during the said term sow any hemp, flax or mustard seeds or any other prejudicial seeds on any part of the said demised premises.' If they did, they had to pay the Mann estate every time the punitive sum of ten pounds per acre in liquidated damages.

Nor, more importantly, and as a crucial part of this vision of completeness, were they allowed to carry away from the farm any of the farm's own produce. Any hay, straw, fodder, unthreshed corn, compost, manure or dung 'which now is or shall at any time during the said term grow arise or be made upon or from or by means of the said demised premises' had to stay there. Sissinghurst's fertility had to be kept at Sissinghurst because its long-term viability as a farm relied on those nutrients remaining to be recycled into the ground. The tenants 'shall and will there imbarn stack and fodder out all such hay Straw and Fodder'. They were to see that the compost, manure or dung 'shall and will in a good husbandlike manner [be] laid spread and bestowed in and upon those parts of the land which seem most to need it'. This is something the lease repeats insistently. 'They shall and will constantly during the said term use plough sow manure mend farm and occupy the said demised lands and premises in a good tenantlike manner and according to the custom of the country in which the same are situate. And so as to ameliorate and to improve and not impoverish the same.' I thought, when I read those words, that they should be set up on a carved board at the entrance to the barn. I realised that they encapsulated, two centuries ago, exactly what I hoped for from my modern farm-and-restaurant scheme, which was having such difficulties finding its way to reality. This sense of self-enrichment was exactly what I had been stumbling after.

Here at last was a template for what we could do, for another way of looking at this place, which ran deep into its roots. It was essentially a cyclical vision. It did not imagine that next year would be very different from this, nor was it an exercise in progress. It felt for the health of the land in a way that understood it as a body, with all the implications of that organic analogy. It was not a fantasy of wholeness, but a working system, tied to earnings, rents, money and returns. It understood about the need for money on both sides, and the careful regulation of costs and responsibilities, but it did not single out money over all other aspects. It understood that money was one outcome, not the only one. And it understood that the land could only give what was put in. It was a picture of constancy and interrelatedness, not in any Wordsworthian ecstasy of revelation or understanding, but in a lease, a formal document made between the baronet and the yeomen of Cranbrook, drawn up by the lawyers. There, preserved in the county archives, was an invitation to the future. It was a world based on cud. A love of cud – that slow, delicious, juicy recycling of the nutritious thing – was what Sissinghurst needed. This was its unfinished history, its folding of the past into the future in the way that a cook stirs sugar into a cake.

This Cranbrook poor-relief scheme was exceptional. The general rule at the time was to give outdoor relief as a supplement to low wages, the Speenhamland system, which had the effect not of subsidising wages but of depressing them, causing the widespread misery of which William Cobbett was the fiercest scourge and critic. Cranbrook's hiring of Sissinghurst Castle Farm meant that housing, shelter and food were provided for up to a hundred men at a time. The farm made a good profit, which meant that Cranbrook local taxation, the rates, did not rise too high and the desperate poverty of farmworkers in other parts of southern England was avoided.

Because of the income derived from the Castle Farm, Cranbrook rates throughout the early nineteenth century were consistently running at a third and even a half lower than in surrounding parishes. Farmers in need of casual labour could hire men from this farm, paying the parish a fee according to the current level of wages. Men could come and go from Sissinghurst whenever they pleased. Between 1813 and 1818, with grain at a wartime price peak, this farm earned £1000 profit, which was given to the parish for the poor. Even in the widespread post-war depression in the 1820s, Sissinghurst Castle Farm lost only a hundred pounds a year, a small price for its benefits as a whole. When the violent Swing Riots broke out in the 1830s and agricultural labourers, demanding a weekly wage of 2s 3d in winter, 2s 6d in summer, burned ricks, destroyed threshing machines and threatened and shot at employers, Cranbrook, almost alone of all the surrounding parishes, had no trouble. This farm, overseen by the group of Cranbrook men who had signed the lease, had done its part in maintaining some kind of social cohesion. The rest of England was in the full flood of laissez-faire market capitalism. Sissinghurst, not through any interest of the landlords, the Manns, who had by now become the earls of Cornwallis, but through the leaders of the local community, remained an island in which the poor had been treated as more than economic cogs to be used and rejected at will.

After the economy recovered in the 1830s, Sissinghurst started to pour money into Cranbrook's coffers. The Frittenden brick kilns were opened on the northern edge of the estate and there was a sawmill set up next to them, both making a profit. Between 1842 and 1847, £2500 was credited to the parish from the farm, which was fondly called 'The Old Cow', which could be milked and milked and would always deliver. Assistance was given to Cranbrook families wishing to emigrate. Money was provided for the repair of churches. Only with the downturn of the late 1840s, and an overdraft growing to £1500, did the parish trustees decide to pull out. Having first traded their way out of that debt, in 1853 they found themselves in pocket, surrendered the lease to the Cornwallises, handed £3622 to the parish, with which the Vestry Hall in Cranbrook was built, and considered sixty years of poor relief well done.

The buildings were in a fairly ruinous condition. The South Cottage was a thatched hovel. Both the Tower's turrets had lost their upper prospect rooms and in the 1830s were roofless. In 1839, the Mann Cornwallis estate repaired the roofs with oak-shingled conical caps, surmounted by some beautiful weathervanes marked 'MC 1839'.

Nevertheless, the Cornwallises were keen to get the farm back in hand. In 1853, when the farm here was still rented out to the Overseers of the Poor in Cranbrook, a report had been made on the condition of the Cornwallis estates. Of Sissinghurst, the Cornwallis trustees had written:

> This is the most important farm on the estate in the Weald. We incline to the opinion that it is much more desirable to have a respectable tenant residing on the farm and farming on his own account than to have so many non-resident Trustee tenants, who could not feel the same interest in it that he would feel. The only objection to this change which presents itself, is the heavy outlay which must necessarily be incurred in erecting a good farmhouse and suitable buildings, many of the present ones being very old and inefficient for an occupation of this extent. The farm is not in so good a state as it was ten years ago, and about half of it requires draining.

When the poorhouse was closed, Sissinghurst entered a period of high Victorian farming. A dynamic and highly cultivated young man, George Neve, whose father was a land agent, managing several large aristocratic estates, was chosen as the new tenant. George had worked with his father and this was his opportunity. A big brick farmhouse, called 'The Castle Residence', was built in 1854/55, a large family house approached by an asphalted carriage drive and sweep, with seven bedrooms on the first floor, a bathroom and a flushing loo, four more bedrooms above, four stalls for hunters and two loose boxes, a harness room and two coach houses. The house was surrounded by lawns, shrubberies and gardens. There was a greenhouse and a vinery, 'with the remains of Sissinghurst Castle close by, which are a prominent and pleasing feature to the property and full of historic interest'.

The new asphalted carriage drive, which is the present lane, was built in a long curve down from the main road to arrive at the front of the new house, where cedars, laurels and rhododendrons were planted. Twenty-five acres of ancient woodland were cleared from in front of the house, leaving only the older trees standing in a stretch of what became elegant new parkland, 'which is of excellent grazing quality and beautifully timbered with oak, chestnut, silver birch, ash and walnut'. Chestnut coppice was planted throughout most of the old woodland and over some of the older fields called Roughter near the Biddenden road, turning them into woods 'which produce some of the highest priced Chestnut and Ash in the district, as well as being Splendid Game Coverts'. The field pattern that had been imposed on the abandoned Park in the eighteenth century was regularised, some new, mainly hawthorn hedges planted and others taken out. A small stream between Large and Lodge fields was canalised. George Neve was a great advocate of dry land as a way of preventing sickness in animals, and drains were installed in most of the Sissinghurst fields. New oast houses with four kilns were built. There was stabling for ten carthorses, more for the bailiff's and shepherd's horses and a new brick dairy. There were cow sheds, fatting lodges with pits, two chaff steaming rooms, wagon and implement sheds. The large Elizabethan brick barn had the windows that had been opened for the prisoners' hospital filled in. Huge wheat and barley stacks were made on the stack plat to the north of the barn. Every winter the threshing teams would arrive with their giant steam-driven machines and the corn in sacks was hauled up by hoists in the barn and then stored in the upper floors of the granary beside it. Beyond the new dairy, there was a range of hop-pickers' huts with a cooking house beside them.

The Neves' coachman lived in the South Cottage and eight other farm families lived in the old buildings, a bailiff in the Priest's House, others in the front range and in the Tower, where both the archways were bricked in to make a room. A gamekeeper lived in Horse Race House, which had kennels and outbuildings. Fruit trees were trained on the south wall of the great Elizabethan courtyard and a greenhouse built near the Tower.

Neve had the 278 acres of Bettenham (where the farmhouse was divided into three cottages) as well as the 478 of Castle Farm. The brick kilns were 'in full working order with plenty of excellent brick earth close at hand', and next to them was the highly productive timber yard with four cottages for sawyers. The farm produced 'heavy crops of hops, grass and cereals'. It was even said that the finest hops in Kent were grown here. A large flock of sheep and many head of cattle were fattened on it, and there were 'extensive piggeries'. There were six acres of allotments on the southern side of the wood, let out to people from the village.

Payments made by the Cornwallises' agent to men at work on the Sissinghurst estate describe a world of unbridled energy and productivity. All fencing and gates were made from the wood grown here. Ladders, stepladders and brick moulds were all made in the timber yard next to the Frittenden brickworks. The brick 'lodges' in which the clay for the bricks was dried before being fired were made from oak cut in the neighbouring woods, roofed in the tiles dug from the neighbouring brick earth and held on the riven oak laths with pegs cleft from the same oak. Hundreds of payments are made for 'hewing and sawing', including for up to five hours at a time to one 'Elizabeth Eldridge'. Hired-in labour worked in the woods, 'setting and planting', weeding around the new chestnut plants, picking up nuts at a shilling an hour, ditching, digging, carrying manure, 'letting off water' from the rides in the woods, brushing the roads, cleaning the carts after they had come out of the thick clay, making bridges over the streams. In all this multifarious work, there was one constant: the men and women who did it were paid a pittance.

It was, amazingly, a farm still worked largely by oxen, creatures that would remain in harness here until the First World War. To feed them, 110 acres of the farm were given over to grass, including the Park. Arable covered 108 acres, hops were grown on 59 acres and then carted in their giant sacking pockets to Cranbrook railway station and from there to London. There were 13 acres of orchard and 265 of wood. When the Neves had some time off, they fished for trout in the Hammer Stream and hunted deer with the Mid-Kent Stag Hounds, which met here every winter. There is not even the faintest suggestion that Sissinghurst, as it arrived in the twentieth century, was an abandoned or declining place. It was a living monument to farming excellence, to Victorian enterprise and to all the sustained and sustaining virtues of 'imbarning, stacking and foddering out'. The ruins of the Elizabethan house stood there not as the focus for nostalgia but as a kind of memory, full of half-mythical stories. The Neves' children used to dig in their garden for the secret passage Bloody Baker was meant to have built from here to Cranbrook. Frederick William Neve, one of George's sons, listened agog as he heard 'a tradition handed down among the peasantry that when Queen Mary came to the castle, she alighted from her horse and the footprints which she made are still there. Even when ploughed over they would return. However, as flagstones cover the ground, there is no way of testing the truth.' The first postcards of Sissinghurst were made. One or two tourists used to come and for a few pence would be shown the top of the Tower, its room full of carved Tudor heads and, intriguingly, its museum. A note written by Vita survives among my father's papers:

> A curious old couple came to Sissinghurst in the spring of 1942, to visit the garden. The woman told me she had been a midwife in Cranbrook many years earlier & had often been up the towers. She asked me what had become of the things from the 'museum' that used to be at the top of the tower, and mentioned that there was a ceinture de chasteté there. I must have looked surprised, for she explained 'What the gentleman locks the lady into when he goes away.' She said her daughter was one of Epstein's favourite models.

When the Sissinghurst Castle Estate was sold by the Cornwallises at auction on 25 June 1903 in Maidstone, in twenty-one lots, it was advertised as 'an unusually fine sporting property in this lovely part of Kent', on which 'the estate has been well farmed & looked after for a long period'. The 1083 acres of Sissinghurst, including a great deal of arable land, meadow, pasture and wood that no longer belongs to it, went for £16,500 to the Cheeseman brothers, one of whom, Barton, came to live here in the farmhouse. In 1925, he left and the castle and farm were sold to a sixty-eight-year-old coal and feed merchant, William Wilmshurst, a rich man, who was already dying of cancer. Against the wishes of his son and heir, he wanted to spend his last years doing something worthwhile and had decided, after driving round Kent and Sussex, to pour his money into the ruins of Sissinghurst Castle. His nephew, John Wilmshurst, lived in the South Cottage and ran the farm, while his niece, Dorothy, was living only a mile away, married to the farmer who had bought Bettenham four years earlier, Captain Ossie Beale.

Wilmshurst died in 1927 before he could do anything for the Castle ruins, and his son, also called William, who had thought his father's plans absurd and romantic, decided to sell the whole place. Ossie Beale started to rent the Sissinghurst fields on the Bettenham side, but England was just tipping into an agricultural depression and Sissinghurst sat on the market unsold for more than two years, increasingly glum. The farm started to slide away from its Victorian condition. Then one day in April 1930, Ossie's brother Donald, who was a land agent, brought two women over from Sevenoaks to look at the place, a pair of aristocratic women poets: Vita Sackville-West and Dottie Wellesley, her lover, to whom four years earlier she had dedicated her long pastoral poem *The Land*. My thirteen-year-old father came with them, appalled at the mess. Vita fell 'flat in love with it'. By 6 May, she had bought Sisssinghurst, its lands, woods and buildings, less for the overbrimming excellence of its farm than for what the agents' particulars described as 'picturesque ruins in grounds'.

TEN

Acceptance

QUITE UNEXPECTEDLY, James Stearns, the last man to have been the farmer at Sissinghurst, died at the end of February 2007. He was on the way back from South Africa with his wife Pat. Their children had given them three weeks of holiday as a fortieth wedding anniversary present. He was sixty-five.

I went to see Pat on the morning she returned from the airport. A packed cluster of cars in the driveway of the farmhouse and frost in the puddles. Her family was all there in the sitting room and the hall. The whole of George Neve's Victorian house was busy with them, and a feeling of sweetness and gentleness filled it. We had coffee and biscuits, in a strange and heightened party, sitting on the sofas, everyone bright in the bruised air, people coming and going, the friends and neighbours, all of us suddenly allowed an intimacy we had never had. Pat was pale and brave, sitting expectant in the centre. James's mother, Mary Stearns, was there, her cheeks flushed, and his sister Linda and his daughter Catherine: these four strong, capable women who had surrounded James and sustained him in his lifetime. I hugged Pat and kissed her and we talked about his death. They had been side by side in the aeroplane on the runway when he died. They had been sorting out their seat belts, she looked away, heard him cough a little, looked back and he had gone. They had been so happy on the holiday. There had been no build-up to this death. It was just a sudden removal, a hole cut in their lives. It felt as if the family had been stabbed, or attacked in the street, and had gathered here now to dress the wounds. Mary Stearns held my hand as she spoke to me. Hurt and affection were so close to the surface that morning, they were like a scent hanging in the rooms.

I thought as I went back home of the long talk I'd had with James two years before about the farm and its history. He had told me how everything in his life had been bound to this place. His grandfather, Ossie Beale, stood at the foundations. As a young man, Oswald had his own farm in Sussex at Hadlow Down, and at the beginning of the First World War he had enlisted as a trooper in the Sussex Yeomanry. But his own father, Louis, a great, waist-coated, bearded patriarch, who was running the Beales' construction and property business in Tunbridge Wells, had taken him out to dinner, told him to go to Sandhurst and get himself a commission. So it was that Ossie fought the war as a commissioned officer in the Bedfordshire and Hertfordshire Regiment, The Beds and Herts, at the Somme, at Passchendaele, in Italy and then on General Ironside's staff during the Murmansk expedition, returning as Captain Beale in 1919, a veteran, with the MC and the Croix de Guerre and a shrapnel wound on his forehead. His admiring father gave him £17,000 to buy the farm at Bettenham in 1921 and the family had moved in: a lovely but draughty and earth-floored medieval house, surrounded by a moat – disgusting because the drains ran into it; two hundred acres of good valley land; hop gardens; some stables and huge, marquee-sized barns; a herd of beautiful, milky Guernseys. Every one of the Beales loved it there.

James told me this over his dining-room table in the Sissinghurst Castle farmhouse, in his deep, reverberating voice, while his hang-dog, rather lugubrious eyes looked into mine now and then to con-firm that I was getting the picture. This was the other Sissinghurst. To begin with, the farming went well. Captain Beale rented the eastern half of Sissinghurst Castle Farm, up to the Sissinghurst moat, planting an expensive new hop garden in Lodge Field, man-aging it with expertise and tailor-like precision. Everything was orderly and the whole place breathed well-being. Vita immediately took to him, charmed by his gentlemanly, buccaneering manner and charming him in return. Both, from their different sides, liked the antiquity, the half-formal almost-courtship of their neighbour–landlord relations. She loved his knowledge and he loved her romance and perhaps her aristocratic allure, that inexplicable seductiveness she could summon at will. He was a self-consciously wonderful man, a showman and a commanding figure. As his party trick for his grandchildren he would blow cigar smoke out through a hole – a childhood defect – just below the bridge of his nose, like a smiling dragon in a tweed jacket. His daughter Mary called him her 'BM' – the Blooming Marvel – and between him and Vita the relationship was one of long-sustained, mutual flattery and delight.

This happy time was not to last. In the late 1920s farming started to slip into a catastrophic depression. Every year the milk had been sold locally, delivered by van, the potatoes were sold, sheep and cattle came and went to Ashford and occasionally Biddenden markets, the apples were packed and shipped to London, the hops picked and dried and sent to London in their giant pockets, first by wagon on the road to Cranbrook station, and from there to the brewers in London. Every year the produce going out was a guarantee of the year to come.

Mary Stearns can still remember the late autumn moment in her teens, at some time in the late twenties, when one day at Bettenham they all heard and then saw a train of wagons coming back rumbling down the lane towards the farm. On them was the whole of the Bettenham hop harvest returning from London unsold. The market had failed them. There was a glut of hops. Supply far outstripped demand. All the work and investment in the hop gardens that year, all the setting up and stringing of the poles, the manuring, weeding, spraying, picking, carting, drying, packing and dispatch: all had gone to waste. The hops were worth nothing. The wagons were unloaded, the pockets taken out on to the land, slit open and the precious contents spread as a mulch on the fields.

The Beales only just got through the depression and emerged from it financially damaged. In 1936, after Vita's mother had died and left her a fortune, she bought Bettenham from them, the debts were paid off with the purchase price and Captain Beale took on the whole of Bettenham and Sissinghurst Castle Farm, now as Vita's tenant. With some reluctance among his womenfolk, he moved the family up to the Victorian farmhouse at Sissinghurst (at Vita's suggestion) and left Bettenham behind. Their capital had largely disappeared but in Ossie's hands the whole joint farm nevertheless became glowingly beautiful, perhaps never more beautiful in its history: the Guernseys down at Bettenham, the dairy shorthorns up at Sissinghurst; hops; apples, pears and cherries; blackcurrants and potatoes; a large flock of sheep; peas and beans, wheat, barley and oats for milling and cattle feed; kale, turnips, rape and mangolds; fifty acres of meadow; men and women at work, working horses and the first tractors arriving, a kind of bright, rich, ancient modernity. Vita had added Brissenden Farm (in 1940) and Little Bettenham (a year later) to the estate. And Captain Beale was riding high, presiding over the county, becoming chairman of Ashford cattle market, a Justice of the Peace (with Vita) and a governor of Wye

Agricultural College, from where one or two students always came to live and work here.

During the war Mary had married Stanley Stearns, a Canadian pilot with Coastal Command, who after the war and a spell training pilots in Canada came to work here in partnership with her father. The Stearnses lived at Bettenham and the Beales lived in Sissinghurst Castle Farm. Vita and Harold were in the Castle itself, Jack Copper and the cook, Mrs Hayter, lived in parts of the front range and a cowman and the head gardener were in new cottages built beyond the oast houses. There were other cottages in the village, where other gardeners lived, and still more attached to Bettenham.

Ossie Beale, called The Captain by the farm staff and students, presided over this beautiful and multifarious kingdom until his death in 1957. In 1952 the Sissinghurst shorthorns were sold and the Bettenham Guernseys moved up here, but apart from that there was no shrinking of the enterprise. New orchards were planted, new machinery bought and, after Stanley Stearns took over, much the same was true. He too was a go-ahead farmer, bought a new efficient hop-stripping machine, which made most of the hop-pickers unnecessary, and became chairman of the Kent NFU.

So when, I asked James, had it all begun to unravel? First, he said, when Nigel, my father, was forced to sell Bettenham in 1963 to pay his mother's death duties. The Stearnses had to surrender the tenancy there (for which my father paid them £6000) and the size of their farmed area shrank by almost half. That was a body blow. The Stearnses should have bought it themselves, James said, but the capital wasn't there. The Bettenham house and land were sold separately and for the first time since the Dark Ages that unity was broken. Then, in 1967, James's father died suddenly and young – 'he was a smoker, sixty Senior Service a day'. James in partnership with his uncle John Beale took the farm over. John was a distinguished virologist, Scientific Director of the Wellcome Research Laboratories in London, and at the weekends he did the book work for the farm. James was the hands-on farmer. The business was laden 'with quite a bit of debt and no assets'. I asked James why he had taken it on? 'Because I loved it,' he said. 'I always loved farming. And I loved it here.' There were seven men working on the farm, looking after a flock of sheep, the Guernseys, ten acres of hops, two orchards and the big arable fields on the eastern end of the farm. A capital injection from Pat's father, who was a big vegetable grower at Offham near West Malling, paid off the overdraft, but it was not long before the first disaster struck. In 1967, the hops in Frogmead became infected with verticillian wilt, an ineradicable fungal disease, and the hops, always the most treacherous of crops, expensive to grow and threatening low prices in a high-yielding year, lost the Stearnses more than they could afford. James pulled them out in the following spring.

The Guernsey herd also seemed wrong. James and his father had started a move towards more productive Friesians in the early sixties but the Milk Marketing Board had insisted that each farm stuck with a single breed. So James kept the Guernseys, even though he never felt particularly drawn to the life of a dairy farmer, until they too stopped making financial sense and finally left the farm in 1980. His father-in-law was an expert in vegetable growing and under his encouragement James started with Brussels sprouts and lettuces in 1968, labour-intensive crops that involved management of the gangs of pickers, but nothing on the farm was singing.

'Lack of capital was beginning to strangle us,' James said. There was no financial cushion, nor assets to borrow against, nor any sense that they could easily weather a crisis. The debts were looming larger. From 1968 onwards, the family was running the tea room for the visitors in the now redundant oast house. Mary was making her famous apple cake, and the wonderful unpasteurised cream straight from the Guernsey herd lay at the heart of the teas. In 1971 Pat started up a farm shop, supplied from Covent Garden market, and they began doing lunches. All of these were buoyancy aids: without them, the small farm, with no ability to make large capital improvements, and with a debt burden on its shoulders, could not possibly have kept afloat.

Then the hammer fell: in 1982, the National Trust, itself looking for income to maintain an increasingly expensive property, told the Stearnses they wanted to run the tea room themselves. Two years later the transfer was made. Now James and Pat were faced with the hard fact: the farm had become unviable. 1984 had been an extraordinary bumper year for grain but still it was no good. They were 'getting deeper into real debt' and James was living night after night with racking anxiety, the feeling that everything he loved was dissolving around him. He hung on until Christmas 1989. '"We're bust," I said to Pat. "I don't know what to do."' Only the bed-and-breakfast business that Pat was now running in the farmhouse was going well. They struggled on with the farm for another decade. All the work on it was now done under contract by outsiders. No one was employed here. Finally, in 1999, it came to an end. James surrendered the farm and the Trust gave the family a fourteen-year tenancy on the farmhouse. No other farmer came in. Sissinghurst was divided up and let to four separate farm businesses, whose main focus was elsewhere. It was the saddest possible end to the three generations and eighty-eight years that the Beales and Stearnses had been at Sissinghurst.

James's life had coincided with the worst years that the farm had seen for centuries. No one had suffered the decline of Sissinghurst as much as he had. He had experienced the deepest change in the ways of farming, not as a business phenomenon, a technological or market shift, but as something of a personal and private crucifixion. Once, before James died, Pat Stearns heard me giving a talk at a charity lunch in Tenterden, when I had spoken about what I wanted to see happen on the farm here. She came up to me afterwards and said gently and kindly, 'That was interesting, Adam, but I don't think you know just how difficult it was.' I could only say to her then, as I do now, that I hope I was at least trying to understand.

The question remained whether this story could be reversed. Could the farm ever return to the rich, mixed condition it had enjoyed until the 1960s? I was increasingly certain that my ideas could only become a reality if the farm was not viewed in isolation. Sissinghurst needed to be seen as a whole financially, as well as in terms of its landscape. House, garden, restaurant, shop, bed-and-breakfast and farm all needed to be seen as different aspects of a single organism. They needed to be mutually supportive. Some of the large profits made on the garden, in the shop and the restaurant needed to be fed back to the farm, into the surrounding land. The farm would provide both the food and the ambience on which the restaurant would thrive, but a small, complex farm taken in isolation would never compete in the open market. To look at it in that way, though, was missing the point. The essence of the idea was to stop seeing things in isolation. A small mixed farm was no longer viable. A small mixed farm integrated with a restaurant, shop and tourist attraction certainly was.

On 16 March 2007, James's funeral was held in Cranbrook church. The pews can fit five hundred but the crowds for James were so large that lines of people stood at the back to hear his friends pay their tributes. One described him as a 'yeoman', a word, with its roots in the Sissinghurst earth, which brought tears to my eyes, for its irony, for its taunting understanding that James had been a yeoman at a time when yeomen were not wanted or their qualities understood. I stared at the small stone pediment fixed up on the wall in front of me, brought here in the 1830s from the remains of Elizabethan Sissinghurst. Others talked of his kindness, his warmth and jokiness, his generosity, the way in which he was loved by everyone who knew him, his love of Kent and Sissinghurst. We sang 'Jerusalem' and 'I Vow to Thee My Country'. His mother, wife, sister and daughter were there to mourn him like four queens. I thought of him as an oak in the wood, which had fallen and left a gap, a big present absence where the crown had been, something rooted now down and gone.

In April, the Soil Association delivered their final report. We had met and talked through it often throughout the winter and spring and we had come up with something that looked quite like Sissinghurst in its glory days under Captain Beale. There was to be a suckler herd of Sussex beef cattle, and a flock of Romney ewes. Most of the farm would be grass and there'd be 50 acres of crops. Cow Field was to have its vegetable patch of 2½ acres. Twenty-five acres of mixed fruit orchard would have grazing under the trees. There would be chickens in mobile houses. All of this needed a capital investment of just over £300,000. After five years, there would be a small working profit.

We imagined that, this second time around, our proposals would look as if we were on the money. We weren't. In May, the plan was rejected for a second time. Unaffordable. Yet another report, by yet more consultants, delivered in July 2007, concluded that the whole idea was impracticable unless it were part of a bigger enterprise. We had spent yet another year trying to get this right and it was still as dead as it had been the previous summer. There were only two grounds for any optimism. Jonathan Light and Louisa Freeman-Owen had successfully steered the acquisition of Whitegate Farm through the National Trust approval processes. This acquisition meant there would now be a place for the Sissinghurst cattle to spend the winter and for much of the hay and straw to be stored. The need for new farm buildings had shrunk by a half.

The other development was more ambivalent. Pat Stearns had in the end decided, after talking to her children and her friends, that she could no longer live in the great battleship of the Castle farmhouse. It is a Victorian brute of a thing, expensive to heat and laborious to clean. She and James had run a successful B&B business there for more than twenty-five years. People came back year after year, every time booking their next season's visit before they left. At the height of the summer you could never get in. It was a sad day but Pat could no longer think of running the six-bedroom business on her own. What this meant for Sissinghurst, though, was that a house for the farmer and more significantly a bed-and-breakfast business for the farmer's wife or partner had suddenly become available. The farm business no longer had to stand on its own. Tied to a bed-and-breakfast, it was surely a viable proposition. It is the greatest irony that this opportunity should have occurred because James Stearns died. I hope it is not too sentimental to think that if the farm at Sissinghurst does work in the future it is because his death allowed it to.

These elements seemed at last to be pointing in the right direction. A candle flame flickered, if only just. Jonathan Light asked me to come to the meeting of the NT Regional Committee at Sissinghurst on 9 August to talk about my 'vision' – a word that by now had acquired something of an ironic tinge.

I stood at one end of their table and talked to them. The farm scheme was fighting for its life. We could, I said, reduce the ambition, set up a partnership with local growers and end up at

Sissinghurst with a superficial gesture towards the original idea. It would be highly compromised. The heart would have been taken out of it, because the essence of the idea was 'an intimately close connection between food, people and landscape'.

Do you know those moments in meetings when you are more fired up than everyone else around you? When you notice a sudden balloon of your own passion come wobbling out over the table and hang there as a form of radiant embarrassment? While people shuffle in their chairs and look at their papers? This was one of those moments.

But I was going on. The other option was to increase takings in the restaurant. Sell more of what we grow and/or charge more for what we make. Don't be idealistic about it: be entrepreneurial about it. The sums were pretty straightforward. The restaurant turned over £600,000 a year. About half of that was on prepared food. A 10 per cent rise in that half of the revenue would deliver an extra £30,000 a year. The projected shortfall was in the region of £75,000 a year. Half the solution to the problem lay in the market. And there was another figure: the Chatsworth combined farm shop and restaurant turns over £5 million a year and makes a £1-million-a-year contribution to the Chatsworth estate. I had been to talk to them about it and the key word was *processing*: not leeks but leek pie, not apples but apple cake. If you add the value, you get the profit.

I have no idea if these Regional Committee meetings usually have speeches of this kind made to them. Maybe not, but after so long and after so much hope denied, I was in a state of high frustration.

Don't abandon the ideal, I said to them, because the ideal is the only thing worth having, but go slowly and build a ramp towards it. But don't kick it back again. There were only a certain number of times you could fell a scheme like this and expect it to come bouncing back as before. If they inserted another year into this process, the air would come leaking slowly out of the balloon, a long slow wheeze, and nothing would change. Or at least other places would change and Sissinghurst would only have to catch up later.

I would like to have seen me, to see just how Billy Graham-ish this was. As so often in this process, I looked for the nods around the table, for the scepticism to ease. I didn't dare look at Jonathan Light, who was sitting next to me. I can't think this is what he expected me to say.

> Why was only the whole idea worth doing? If we go for a dilute version of this scheme, reliant on other local growers, Sissinghurst-lite, there would be nothing to shout about. 'We buy our raspberries from within a ten-mile radius.' 'Our lamb comes from the south-east of England.' 'Our salmon is not from Nagasaki.' That is not a message for which anyone nowadays is prepared to pay more. The word 'local' is well on its way to over-used exhaustion.
>
> But if we can say, 'Here, for a small premium, is lunch for 50,000 people a year from 250 acres of farmland at Sissinghurst,' that is a story to tell.

The battle lines were clear. You either thought that there was nothing to be done against the large-scale, globalising forces of international commodity agriculture; or you stood out against it, found other ways of establishing a relationship with the land, which were not 'romantic', but attentive to a modern appetite for real food from enriched places. By establishing something here that was full of hope and optimism, it could generate its own market. The farm at Sissinghurst could, like the garden itself, become something to which people would want to come, and from which they would want to buy. If you think you can't do anything except the homogenised, the cost-cutting and the mediocre, it's true: you can't. You can only if you think you can.

Jonathan Light's response to the new situation was to gather every-one together and make us find a solution. The original timetable was now shot. We could not start hiring people to run a project that had not been given the go-ahead. If the orchards and new hedges were ever to exist, they would have to wait a year. Everything would slip, but a slipped something was better than a nothing, so we all went along with it. The old tenants were each given an extra year on the ground. But there had been a curious shift in atmosphere. We still had a hundred and one things to agree on. There were some horrible gaps in the budget and yet somehow, now, without anyone quite saying so, it was understood that this idea would not be allowed to fail again. A Scottish fisherman I knew used to claim that he could tell whether the tide was rising or falling by the different sounds that waves made during the ebb or the flood. There was something of that here in the autumn of 2007: I felt, without being able to put my finger on it, that, for all the negative signals, our boats were somehow just lifting up off the sand.

I know now that Jonathan Light was doing a great deal of preparatory work high up in the Trust. He won't tell me what he did – 'I asked people to look at the wider canvas,' he has said to me – but somehow he changed the weather. People started to ring up asking how they could help. Clearly the word had gone out that this should now be given a fair wind. There were anxieties at Sissinghurst, still largely unaddressed, about how the restaurant would respond to the challenge of its own farm; and what effect all this would have on the workings of the place as a whole. Those difficulties would soon emerge, as the scheme started to swing into operation. But now at last a way to the future seemed to be opening. Revised ideas slipped over their hurdles in late November, arriving at the NT's Central Projects & Acquisitions Group meeting in Swindon on 4 December 2007. Sally, Jonathan and Sue Saville all went and that afternoon Sally rang me from her mobile. 'It's a yes,' she said. We had the go-ahead. We had five years to get it right. I went out into the Cow Field and stared into the dark of the evening, up along the line of the old drove to Canterbury, across Sissinghurst's wet and lovely fields, and wondered what would become of them. Would this scene in 2020 or 2030 be a model of delicious productiveness, of the land as its hundreds of owners would have recognised it? I thought and hoped so. I could people this place now with layer on layer of different ghosts. I could bring to mind that long flickering film of its bogs and woods, meadows and orchards, streams and lakes, its herds, flocks and draught animals and the ten thousand years of bird song which had been sung in these hedges and skies. The phrase 'an unfinished history' ran on in my mind. That was surely the point: nothing was over. The land at Sissinghurst was no longer staring at a sterile and redundant fate. It would be more than just an adjunct and backdrop to a famous garden. Sissinghurst would be a place that fed off its own richness again. None of it would be easy. But now, here, in the cold and dark, looking to the north, with my coat wrapped around my chin, I thought I saw coming towards me the future of which I had long dreamed.

ELEVEN

Admiration

AT THE END OF THE SEASON at Sissinghurst, the gardeners always find spots on the lawns where visitors have stood and gazed at a particularly seductive rose or luscious wisteria, and under their feet the grass has withered and the lawn gone slightly bald. They call these 'Admiration Patches', and they need to be aerated and revived each autumn. There is no doubt that in the history of Sissinghurst the period from my grandparents' arrival in 1930 until Vita's death in 1962 is one of those exaggeratedly looked-at and slightly worn patches, the most famous moment in ten thousand years of Sissinghurst's existence.

The story of their arrival and life at Sissinghurst has been told over and over again, in private and public. This fame was nearly all due to my father's persistence in the 1960s, '70s and '80s. An element of it was commerce. He knew in his parents' story there were valuable publishing properties. He knew, too, that the National Trust was anxious that when Vita and Harold died, the interest in Sissinghurst would wane and its financial basis would collapse. He became, in the last forty years of his life, Sissinghurst's custodian, librarian, archivist, publicist and entrepreneur. All through the peak of the Bloomsbury boom, he carried on an enormous and global correspondence with scholars and fans. One could tell, each year, where the latest foreign editions had appeared, as first American and French, then German, Dutch and Danish, Latvian and Russian, Hungarian, Greek, Turkish and, finally, Japanese and Korean enthusiasts for Sissinghurst and its literary-lesbian-hortico-aristocratic amalgam arrived at the gate to drink at the shrine. My sisters and I used to stand there trying to spot the territories my father's publishing campaign had recently conquered.

But if this was canny, it was not cynical. It was also a form of honouring his parents' memory. Nothing in his life mattered more to him than them, and Sissinghurst became in effect a portrait of their marriage. They framed his life and he remained their perpetual son, bound to them both, but in polar-opposite ways. His relationship with his father was one of overwhelming love and admiration. Harold played with him, told him stories, drew him pictures, empathised with him as he made his way into the world, understood his nascent homosexuality, urging him to keep it in perspective, and always pressing on him the central virtues of a civilised life: tolerance, kindness, energy, civility, integrity. They discussed everything all the time. 'He always claimed', my father wrote of him, 'that it was impossible for a father to transmit experience, but in fact he did so, for his advice was always practical, and by understanding the exact nuances of our dilemmas, he dissipated them.' My father felt he lived not in his father's shadow but in his light.

Towards the end of his life, my father sold nearly all of his parents' letters to American universities, but before he died, he told me that if I were to sell anything, as he imagined I might, the one thing he would like to remain at Sissinghurst for ever was the file of letters that his father had written to him and his brother Ben during the war. It is a thick typewritten folder which contains what is, in effect, a manual of fatherhood: of love, anxiety for his children, a flattering ease in the telling of news and the testing of opinions, a fascination for the world, a brilliant play across anything that amused, stirred or worried him, in his life or theirs, written from the House of Commons where he was an MP or from the Ministry of Information, where for a time he was a junior minister in Churchill's government, to the battlefields of North Africa and Italy, page after page drenched in a form of love that was so strong it could be easy, funny, courteous, dignified, articulate and challenging without ever losing its undernote of deep and passionate affection. My father kept this file in his bedroom until he died.

With his mother, it was different. She had neglected him and his brother when they were children, leaving them for months on end when away with lovers or friends; and when, in the second half of her life, she returned from her adventuring, to embed herself at Sissinghurst, she was absent there too, in the Tower, and when in the Tower in the world of poetry, from which her children felt – and were – entirely excluded. Whenever my father wrote about her, that sense of exclusion, almost of expulsion, was the dominant note. She 'withdrew into preferred solitude'. Poetry was 'her secret life, the life of the tower, into which we never attempted to penetrate'. He was constantly anxious that he might wound her. There was a 'gap between her and us. It had been there since we were babies.' If she talked to them or wrote to them, her tone was 'constrained'. She 'thought herself a failure as a mother, but it was as much our fault as hers. We never made the necessary effort to know her well.'

This double emotional inheritance, of warmth and cold, transmitted through my father, has soaked into Sissinghurst. Its image has become fixed in a binary vision of the twentieth century here. Harold was classical, Vita romantic. Harold was kind and engaged, Vita distant and unintelligible. Harold was clever, Vita passionate. Harold was civility, Vita poetry. Harold my father knew; Vita he didn't. Harold he loved, Vita he didn't. These polarities became our governing myth.

I knew the story of my grandparents' lives from the moment I was conscious. My father used to stand on the dais at one end of the Big Room and tell it to visitors while I stood at his side. The climax would always be that, after his death, 'Adam, and Adam's Adam, and Adam's Adam's Adam' would live here, far on into the unforeseeable future, words that would make me glow with significance and squirm with embarrassment while the people stared from three steps below us on the polished oak floor.

The family mythology swirled around us, planets orbiting above our heads in ever wider and more distant circles. There was a Nicolson element, to do with generation after generation of public servants and military men, backed by layer on layer of Edinburgh lawyers, and going on beyond them, mistily, to chieftains of the clan in Skye and Assynt in the far north-west of Scotland. But the

Nicolson story was not at the heart of Sissinghurst. It was never important enough. Two coats of arms stood on either side of the entrance arch: three Baker swans on the right and the chequers and bars of the Sackville Wests on the left. It was Vita who had the money, who bought and owned Sissinghurst, who conducted negotiations with Captain Beale, the farm tenant, whose flag flew over the Tower, whose room in the Tower silently oversaw Sissinghurst and whose spirit infused the place. Under the Tower a memorial stone put up after she died remembers her as the person 'who made this garden'. Harold is not mentioned.

She dominated the present and behind her stretched an inheritance of pure glamour. Her mother had persuaded Sir John Murray Scott, the vast, five-foot-waisted, lonely owner of the Wallace Collection, to leave her half of it in his will. The legacy was contested by his relations ('dumpy, dull and middle class', according to my father), but as soon as Victoria Sackville established her claim, in a spectacular court case, she sold the collection en bloc to a Paris dealer, adding £270,000 to the £150,000 in cash Scott had left her too. These figures can be multiplied by at least fifty for their modern equivalents. Vita would inherit most of it; it became the fund on which Sissinghurst floated for Vita's life. Her mother's mother, Pepita, had been a Spanish gypsy dancer, whose hair was so long that it dragged on the floor behind her, with whom her grandfather, Lord Sackville, had fallen in love after seeing her dance onstage. Behind them lay receding avenues of Sackvilles going back towards Restoration, Cavalier and Elizabethan heroes, all set in the huge grey Kentish palace of Knole, the house in which Vita had been brought up and which, if she had been a boy, she would have inherited. Against this bouillabaisse of a story, the Nicolson aspect, the element of middle-class normality and sanity, was thin fare.

Vita had been lonely as a child. She had looked with a sceptical eye at the Edwardian indulgences of her mother's friends, fell in love with poetry as a girl, and more than that with Knole and with the romance of its stories. She was wooed by the great heirs of Edwardian England, could have had dukedoms and county-covering estates for the asking, but never stooped to that. She refused the giant houses offered her by Lord Lascelles (Harewood) and Lord Granby (Haddon Hall and Belvoir), largely perhaps because Knole was greater than either, not in the gilded richness of its rooms, but in something less articulate: the pale grey simplicity of its ragstone walls; its succession of courtyards and the buried secrets they promised; the way you could push into Knole, uncovering layer after layer, one court folding out from another, linked by intricate route-ways, through flagged back halls and into other high, narrow spaces, where the windows of the surrounding galleries looked down blankly from above, suddenly coming by chance at the foot of a stair on a cupboard full of gilded porcelain or the delicious eighteenth-century statue of a duke's mistress, nude and prone on her velvet blanket, her body resting on cushions as luscious as herself.

Knole is more maze than house, a private coral reef of accumulated riches, where under its four acres of roof, and within layers of encrustation, its long galleries are filled with the pictures still hanging in the order in which they were inventoried in the seventeenth century, furnished by successive Sackville Lords Chamberlain, who brought down to Knole everything rejected by each change of fashion at court. It is the most beautiful beach in England, thick with the successive tidelines of English taste. It would be difficult to imagine a more powerful stimulus to the imagination than this: Knole, loneliness, the flamenco brilliance of the Spanish-gypsy-dancing gene, dusty brocades, the looming portraits, the charm and volatility of her seductive, plutophile, intemperate mother, the mulch of Englishness, the badge of illegitimacy only a generation back, a sense of herself as the heir to this slow, deep river of fading beauty, something which poured over and through her as if she were more weir than heir.

As a young woman, Vita added to all this a love of Italy and the jewelled life of the Renaissance, the scents and tastes of the Mediterranean world. Benozzo Gozzoli, Venetian colours, cistus and rosemary, almond and apricot blossom all combined to intoxicate her as a teenage girl. She began to feel in herself what she thought of as the fire of her own Spanish blood, mixed with Kentish earth, and began to sense even in her earliest poems her own self to be strung between these poles. Nothing in her was ever parochial or limited, but that exoticism, and a wilful streak of selfishness and dominance, played over a deep and almost stagnant bed of Kentish rootedness. Richness and melancholy joined hands across her own inner divide.

Instead of one of the grandees of aristocratic England, she married a young Third Secretary in the Foreign Office, who came, in his own description, from a family of 'impecunious high civil servants'. He was a matching combination of contradictory talents: high minded, with a belief in the central role public service should play in a man's life; homosexual, with an almost unassuageable appetite for clever and beautiful young men; a brilliantly witty and delighted describer of the world around him; multilingual, passionately internationalist, in love with the civilisations of Greece and France; and above all filled with curiosity for anything that life might bring. Only one man in a thousand is a bore, he told my father, and my father quoted repeatedly to me, and he is interesting because he is one man in a thousand.

Again and again my father would tell me when I was young about his father's comparison of his life and career to an alpine meadow, spotted and lit with flowers, and how preferable that was to a single crop of maize or lucerne. But this multiplicity, and the love of the shimmering surface, was always to be allied to work, love and loyalty. Harold longed for rootedness himself. 'I wanted to feel autochthonous, the son of some hereditary soil,' he wrote. These desires and interests, and this appetite for a life that combined wide horizons with a sense of enriched belonging, were what made their marriage. They felt, immediately, mutual. When he and Vita were married, at Knole in 1913, and lived first in Constantinople, where Harold was attached to the embassy, and then at Long Barn, a cottage outside Sevenoaks, which they called their 'little mud pie' and could have fitted inside one of Knole's courtyards, they thought of each other as playmates, self-consciously innocent, young and happy.

All of these threads would, in time, find their way into Sissinghurst, but after the end of the Great War, two devastating events changed this happy, pretty picture of their early lives. The effects of both could have been foreseen; neither was; both left them changed; and both became, in opposite ways, shaping influences at Sissinghurst.

The first was Vita's long love affair and elopement in 1918/19 with Violet Trefusis, the daughter of Alice Keppel, Edward VII's mistress. It began in 'a mad and irresponsible summer', as Vita described its early phases, 'of moonlit nights, and infinite escapades, and passionate letters, and music, and poetry. Things were not tragic for us then, because although we cared passionately we didn't care deeply.' Violet, according to Victoria Glendinning, was 'a damaged and damaging young woman'; to Harold 'some fierce orchid – glimmering and stinking in the recesses of life, throwing cadaverous sweetness on the morning's breeze'. She undoubtedly wanted to destroy Vita's marriage. Vita was more equivocal and, in letter after grief-stricken letter, wrote piteously of the love she had for a husband she claimed to be deserting.

In 1920, as the affair's fire was dimming, Vita wrote a long manuscript account of it, which she kept in a Gladstone bag, stamped with the gold letters V.N. It remained hidden first in her sitting room at Long Barn and then in her turret room in the Tower at Sissinghurst for the rest of her life. It was never shown to anyone before her death and was only finally published by my father in 1973, after Vita, Violet and Harold had all died, as the central element of a book he called *Portrait of a Marriage*, a title in which he packed the pain and grief of this affair in the cushioning tissue paper of his parents' lifelong, often declared love for each other.

I remember with great clarity the moment the book came out. He had written to me at school to warn me of the coming scandal. I now know, from his own papers, how anxious he was. The prospect of its publication left him 'terrified by the reproach I might draw on myself'. He felt guilty,

> knowing that even if it was true that Vita wanted it published, Hadji would have deplored it. He was the figure that haunted me throughout. I argued that it was a confession which only a son could handle with delicacy and love, but this was an excuse. I wasn't doing it out of love, but to set a new style in biography, of total honesty, to make a stir, earn me money, show that I was capable of taking a risk,— not only with my reputation but with Vita's.

He had justified it, he wrote in his own self-reproaching memoir, written twenty years later, as 'a eulogy of marriage, [which] had lessons for other people who found themselves lesbians and homosexuals, but could still have a very happy marriage. It might "help" people, I wrote, but this was special pleading. I was finding excuses for my guilt. That guilt has still not dissolved.'

Violet Trefusis's sister, to whom Nigel sent the typescript, called it a 'distasteful book'. 'It seems incredible to me', she wrote to him, 'that while professing to revere your mother's memory, you are prepared to publicise for profit details of her infatuations of over half a century ago.' Lord Sackville, who 'had affection and great admiration for your mother', told Nigel that 'these feelings have been tarnished by your book'. Admiration poured in from much of the world but none of it ever quite washed away his own sense of betrayal. When the serialisation of the book started to run in the *Sunday Times*, he could not bring himself to look at it. 'Ben knew', Nigel wrote in his memoir, 'that my love for Vita was very shallow, his shallower.'

I was back at Sissinghurst the day the papers came with the reviews in them. He had been told that Bernard Levin had reviewed the book in the *Sunday Times*. The paper lay on the kitchen table unopened between us. My father finally steeled himself to look at it and turned to the review section. He leant over the pages with both elbows on the table and his head in his hands, reading between the protective grid of his fingers. Levin had fixed on what he saw as the narcissism and self-indulgence behind this story of late, luscious, moneyed romanticism, the urge of the wild 'gypsy' spirit to break free of the tedium of a civil servant husband, of children and normality. The skewering sentences, on which Levin fixed, were these:

> I saw Violet twice more. Once in my own house in London; she looked ill and changed; and once in the early morning at her mother's house, where I went to say goodbye on my way to the station. There was a dreary slut scrubbing the doorstep, for it was very early, and I stepped in over the soapy pail, and saw Violet in the morning room. Then I went to Paris alone.

Levin said my father should have burned the manuscript. Rebecca West said the same. Cyril Connolly had been friendly about the book in private but in his *Observer* review was cold. After reading them all, my father went upstairs without a word. My sisters and I read with some delight the copy of *Private Eye* that ran a spoof introduction to the book. Under a large picture of an Edwardian country-house party, 'Nigel Sackville-Nicolson' wrote that he had published this account of his mother's homosexuality only 'after long and careful consultation with my family, my dearest friends and my bank manager ...' It left his reputation enlarged but, in some quarters, damaged, and it made him £80,000.

Violet, Vita had written, very rarely came to stay with her at Long Barn, their house near Sevenoaks. Whenever she did,

> the antagonism between her and the house was ludicrous and painful. The country would seem deliberately to drape itself in tenderness and content, and she, feeling the place to be an enemy, would turn yet more fierce, yet more restless, while I

stood bewildered and uncertain between the personification of my two lives.

My house, my garden, my fields, and Harold, those were the silent ones, that pleaded only by their own merits of purity, simplicity, and faith; and on the other hand stood Violet, fighting wildly for me, seeming sometimes harsh and scornful, and riding roughshod over those gentle defenceless things.

Engagement with the draped tenderness of the Weald, the mud-pie life, competed in Vita with something larger, unsweet and more domineering. The traumatic affair, 'a vortex of unhappiness', had revealed to her in the starkest possible form the contesting elements of her own personality. That polarised view of herself, both domineering and tender, both private and theatrical, both rotted and filled with a love of the exotic, would in time come to shape Sissinghurst.

The second transforming event of their lives was the death of Vita's father in January 1928. It was the moment when Knole passed into the hands of her Uncle Charlie, when the fact of dispossession was finally confirmed. The house and its lands had in the nineteenth century belonged to two of her great-aunts. There had never been a question of women not being able to inherit Knole. But Vita, who possessed it in a way more deeply than anyone ever had, was now finally denied it.

On 16 May that year, as she wrote to Harold, now in Berlin,

> I allowed myself a torture-treat tonight. I went up to Knole after dark and wandered about the garden. It was a very queer and poignant experience, so queer and so poignant I should almost have fainted had I met anybody . . . I had the sensation of having the place so completely to myself that I might have been the only person alive in the world, and not the world of today, mark you, but the world of at least 300 years ago . . . Darling Hadji, I may be looney but there is some kind of umbilical cord that ties me to Knole

At the end of May 1928 she heard that Charlie, the new Lord Sackville, and his American wife were moving into Knole and were thinking of selling some of the great paintings and furniture she most treasured, a dismantling of her store of memories. She went there, had lunch with them and came home in tears, unable to drive for them, with the rain streaming down the windscreen outside.

It was in the light of this dispossession that the cottage at Long Barn no longer seemed enough. My father always maintained (perhaps relishing something of a myth) that a few years before they had flirted with the idea of buying the moated stone keep of Bodiam Castle in Sussex. Each of the four of them – Vita, Harold, Ben and Nigel – would occupy one of the corner towers, meeting occasionally for a ham sandwich in the central hall, a model of Nicolson family life to which they all apparently subscribed. But Bodiam had been too expensive.

The search for a substitute Knole was already under way when in March the next year they heard that the fields next to Long Barn were to be turned into a battery chicken farm. In April 1930, with the poet Dottie Wellesley, Vita came to Sissinghurst for the first time. They found the ruin, dripping with wet. It bore every mark of its long history, a place of broken grandeur, looking, in a curious way, like a ruined Knole, with a tower and a succession of courts, filled with the ghosts of Sackville ancestors and rubbish where life might have been. It was crying out for redemption, an opportunity to make a garden that drew on the sense of its own abandoned past. Perhaps its fragmentary and broken state made it more satisfying than Knole. A ruin, in these circumstances, was better than anything gilded and complete. The disintegrated Sissinghurst could stand in for a ruined inheritance.

The sales particulars described the splendid Victorian farmhouse – the 'excellent family residence and grounds', 'well clothed with choice creepers, approached by a Carriage Drive and Sweep', ten bedrooms, 'well matured grounds with lawns and rhododendrons' – the five hundred acres of wood and land and, almost as an afterthought, 'the Towers of Sissinghurst Castle in the background'. It was, of course, that background to which Vita and Harold were drawn: gaunt, partly unroofed, damp and bleak. They wavered. Harold, on 13 April, after a second look, considered it 'big broken down, and sodden', but Vita had the money, and it was her choice. They bought it for £12,375. There was no electricity, no running water, no drains, no heating and scarcely a fireplace that worked. One or two of the windows had glass in. But this was the invitation: to pour their energies into redemption of the past.

It was here in 1931, in her room on the first floor, that Vita wrote the poem that she called simply 'Sissinghurst'. It was the best thing, Harold thought, she ever wrote, and she dedicated it to Virginia Woolf. Far more than Vita's garden-writing ever could, the poem addresses the core of Sissinghurst. It is a place apart:

> Buried in time and sleep,
> So drowsy, overgrown,
> That here the moss is green upon the stone,
> And lichen stains the keep.

Time has almost stopped. A kind of enriched stagnancy colours the place and her vision of it. Sissinghurst, like the depths of its darkened moat, becomes a pool in which Vita can feel both ecstatically alive and at the same time suspended from the real world:

> For here, where days and years have lost their number,
> I let a plummet down in lieu of date,
> And lose myself within a slumber,
> Submerged, elate.

Those last two words are the essence of Vita's Sissinghurst, a freedom found in a deep absorption with place, land and the sense of a treasured past, a past that was better than the present, drenched into these bricks and this soil.

There was a chance here to revitalise a once-great but deeply neglected place, to take a ruin and make it flower. Again and again, whenever Vita wrote about Sissinghurst, the atmosphere she summoned was of that embedded history, a certain rich slowness, even a druggedness, as if evening, when colours are soft and thickened, were its natural and fullest condition:

> The heavy golden sunshine enriched the old brick with a kind of
> patina, and made the tower cast a long shadow across the grass,
> like the finger of a gigantic sundial veering slowly with the sun.

Everything was hushed and drowsy and silent, but for the coo of the white pigeons sitting alone together on the roof . . . They climbed the seventy-six steps of her tower and stood on the leaden flat, leaning their elbows on the parapet, and looking out in silence over the fields, the woods, the hop gardens, and the lake down in the hollow from which a faint mist was rising.

The garden became, inevitably, a reflection of its makers. The received idea is that it was a marriage of sensibilities: a certain classical elegance and even austerity in the planning by Harold; a rich and romantic profusion in the planting, mostly by Vita, what she called the 'cram, cram, cram, every chink and cranny' method, the verve of 'exaggeration, big groups, big masses'. All that is true, even if not in quite so schematic a way. Often it was Vita who advocated a simplicity and straightforwardness in design; often it was Harold who wanted a more baroque and theatrical effect.

Letters from many of Harold's passing lovers, now preserved along with the rest of his papers at Balliol but never published by my father, describe him as masculine and assertive, a manly man, with his yacht, his pipe and his familiarity with the powerful and the great. His reputation among those who lived and worked at Sissinghurst was for brusque coldness and indifference. It was Vita who used to come and sit on the kitchen table in the farmhouse and talk to the children, who was always amused by the jokes and joshing of the men who worked on the farm or in the garden. She always used to come to the birthday parties of the young Stearnses in Bettenham. Harold was away in London much of the time, only to be spotted leaving for or arriving from the station in his dark blue pinstripes. The distant and reserved Vita in the Tower, always calling herself Vita Sackville-West and never Mrs Nicolson, seems largely to be a product of my father's emphasis on it. In fact she was known at Sissinghurst only as Mrs Nicolson or, after Harold was knighted for his biography of George V, as Lady Nicolson. Most of her books in the Tower are initialled 'VN'. 'V. M. Nicolson' was how she described herself to the War Agriculture Committee. And although Nigel rarely went to her room in the Tower, many others did, spent long hours there with her, talking deep into the night. Jim Lees-Milne, Harold's friend, lover and biographer, remembered a bewitching, dusky evening talking up there:

> There were no reservations of any kind. No topics were barred. Her curiosity about and understanding of human nature in all its aspects were limitless. Her sympathy with every human frailty and predicament was all embracing. This was the Vita I knew and most dearly loved. As dusk faded into night I watched the outline of her noble head against the chequered Tudor case-ments of the tower, would watch the tip of her cigarette from a long holder glow fiery red as she drew upon it, with constant but imperceptible inhalations so that her profile – always her profile of drooping eyelid, straight nose and soft rounded chin – would emerge from the darkness as in a momentary vision. I would smell, when I could no longer see, the cloud of Cypriot tobacco peculiarly her own; and listen to that deep slightly quavering,

gently swelling voice, broken by eddies of short sharp laughter. 'Oh do tell me what happened next.' Then I understood what this unique woman's love meant to Harold.

Even in the way the garden developed, the received picture is not quite true. Many of Harold's plans for Sissinghurst, including a wall of busts of himself and his friends, loggias and 'caves', are far from the picture of the cool, Mozartian rationalist struggling to impose order on Vita's bubbling chaos. In the early days he suggested vast flower beds to fill the upper courtyard – not the cool green pools of lawn that are there today – and a Versailles-style fountain occupying the Rondel in the Rose Garden. It was often Vita who had to slim down his grandiose fantasies. The story and its interactions are subtler than the received idea often allows.

The relationship of exact form to luxuriant planting is almost a cliché of twentieth-century garden design. Sissinghurst's planterliness, its love affair with the Mediterranean, with spring bulbs and roses, with yew, brick, stone and grass – all of this is simply the lingua franca of twentieth-century gardening. Much of it was there in Vita and Harold's first garden at Long Barn. And it has mistakes. The colour of the new brick walls, despite an enormous amount of care taken over them, is not good, too brown and too dead, never glowing. Even the curved wall at the west end of the Rose Garden is a little pretentious. The Yew Walk is too near the Tower, the two rows of yews are too near each other, its entrance to the orchard is poorly designed and it isn't aligned properly with the paths in the Rose Garden. The small north-facing Delos they never got right. Harold's additions to the Priest's House and the South Cottage are a little lumpen. This is not an exercise in perfection. The genius of Sissinghurst's design – Harold disciplined by Vita – is in its self-deprecation, its lack of egoism, its courtesy in playing second fiddle to the plants, the place, the surrounding country and its deeper meanings.

I am sure the reason that Sissinghurst continues to stand apart from its many near-contemporaries is the way it is slipped so discreetly into the ruins of its site, its interfolding of building and garden, garden and farm, farm and country. The garden, as a design, merely fills the frame that the place provided for it. It is subsidiary and subtle, no more than the dancing partner for an existing ancientness. It has sometimes seemed to me as if the fullness of the planting in the garden is merely drawing up the stories that are soaked into Sissinghurst's bones. Harold's design does not compete with that. As Jane Brown pointed out, there are no elegant drooping curves at wall-ends, no rich Italian stone frames to openings, no niches of plum-coloured brickwork to enliven the Elizabethan pink. A garden was not imposed on Sissinghurst; it seems as if Sissinghurst was allowed to have its garden.

The bones of what they did were outlined extraordinarily quickly: by 1932 what is now the White Garden, the Tower Lawn, the Spring Garden, the Cottage Garden, the Yew Walk and the Nuttery had all been laid out. The hedges and trees that would in time give the garden its form were already largely planted. By the end of that decade, the new walls closing off the Rose Garden and the north side of the upper courtyard had been built and the orchard designed.

Innocence had no place here; there was to be sophistication in the ruin. Rareties and subtleties came from the very beginning. Colour schemes were devised before the plants that were to fulfil them. Harold collected foxgloves from the wood in an old pram and by accident brought up bluebell bulbs with them. They would have preferred to make the paths of York stone as they now are, but there wasn't enough money, so paving-stone-sized slabs of rough concrete were cast on-site. What statues they bought were cheap. Some have aready disintegrated and been replaced with copies. Only what they inherited from Vita's mother after her death in 1936 – the bronze and lead urns, the statue of the Bacchante now in the Spring Garden, the bench at the head of the Moat Walk designed by Lutyens – was of undeniable quality. The beautiful stoneware pot in the centre of the White Garden, a seventeenth-century Chinese oil or ginger jar, had been bought by Harold in Cairo for ten pounds.

Sissinghurst was not, it was always said, a winter resort. The cold and the discomfort were intense. The hessian on the dining-room walls in the Priest's House would billow in a wind. Lunches usually ended with inedible roly-poly pudding. There was no spare room, although visitors often slept in Nigel's and Ben's rooms when they were away and even occasionally in Harold's bed. (I remember my father telling me that and shuddering: 'How he must have hated it!') The electric heating system in the library had unaccountably been installed in the ceiling, creating the conditions for a deliciously warm attic, but a persistently frozen and scarcely used room beneath. Even so, Harold and Vita did not live in poverty. They had two gardeners, a chauffeur, a cook, a lady's maid, two secretaries and other servants. Grapes, peaches, apples, pears, raspberries, gooseberries, cucumbers, tomatoes, mangetouts, cabbage, aubergines, squashes, pumpkins and quinces were all grown for their table. Scenes are fondly remembered of the butler and his wife, the kitchen maid, walking gingerly across the winter garden, trays in front of them, from the kitchen in the Priest's House through the snow-encrusted White Garden, leaving their tracks across the lower courtyard, through the Yew Walk and to the South Cottage, where Vita was lying ill in bed,

Sissinghurst
1930s–1990s

N ←

to Bettenham

Dionysos

Herb Garden

Moat

Gazebo

Moat

Orchard
Dovecote

Site of
Medieval
well

Moat Walk

Nuttery

Boathouse

South
Cottage:
VSW &
HN's
bedrooms;
HN's
writing room

Cottage

Garden

Spring
Garden/
Lime
Walk

Yew Walk

White
Garden

Tower Lawn

Rose

Erechtheum

Delos

Tower:
VSW's
writing
room

Rondel

Garden

Priest's
House:
Dining room;
kitchen;
Ben's room
above

Upper Courtyard

Pigs   Hideout
1960s
Logs

Elizabethan
barn

Big Room:
Library/
sitting room

Brewhouse:
Nigel's
bedroom

Start

Coppers Hayters

Finish

Vegetable
Garden

Granary above;
cowshed below

Copper's
garage

Pond

Dairy   Oast house

Greenhouses

Adam's bike
route 1960s

waiting for her lunch or supper. In wartime it was worse. Vita wrote to Leonard Woolf in January 1940:

Dear Leonard,

I ought to have answered your letter long ago, but both the boys came home for 24 hours leave and immediately took to their beds with 'flu. You may imagine that Sissinghurst is at no time an ideal place for invalids, but when it means carrying trays, hot water bottles and other requirements through snow-drifts some sixteen times a day it is really hell. Then George got it; then I got it; then Mac [her secretary] got it. Nigel lost his voice. I lost my voice. Pipes froze; lavatories ceased to function; snow came through the roof and dripped on to my bed. So perhaps you will forgive the delay.

Something of the atmosphere in the early Sissinghurst emerges in a letter from Vita to Harold describing a day in April 1936:

How people can say life is dull in the country beats me. Take the last 24 hours here. An extremely drunken man had left his pony to be tried in the mowing machine. So it was put in the mowing machine; I watched; all seemed satisfactory; I went away. So did the mowing machine. Kennelly [the gardener] sent it away without saying a word to me or to Copper [the chauffeur/handyman] who is responsible for it. Copper arrived in my room and abused Kennelly. I went and cursed Kennelly, who indeed was in the wrong. In the evening at about 9, I was told that Punnett [the builder] wanted to see me. I went out. He was in tears, having just found his old father drowned in the engine tank, and a note written to himself saying it was suicide.

Next morning, ie today, George [the manservant] came to fetch me: Copper would like to speak to me. I found Copper in the garden room covered in blood with a great gash in his head. Kennelly had come into the garage and knocked him down without any warning. He had fallen unconscious, and had come round to find Kennelly throwing buckets of water over him. He had then tried to strangle Kennelly, and they had only been separated by the arrival of Mrs Copper. So I sent Copper to the doctor in George's car, and meanwhile sent for the police. Accompanied by the policeman I went out in search of Kennelly, whom we found very frightened and white. He was ordered to go and pack his things and leave at once. So that was that and we are now without a gardener.

They first opened the garden to the public for two days in 1938, the entrance fee sixpence in an old tobacco tin, if you noticed it, on an old card table in the entrance arch. There must have been some pent-up demand: eight hundred people came that day. Vita would happily meet and chat to the visitors who accosted her. Harold could be ruder: 'A dreadful woman bursts in upon us,' he wrote in his diary of an unexpected photographer from *Picture Post*. 'I am very firm. But Viti with her warm-heartedness is weak. She calls it "being polite." Anyhow I refuse to be photographed, and go off and weed. I am weeding away, grunting under a forsythia, when I realise she is behind me with her camera. All she can have photographed was a large grey-flannel bottom.'

The family had little to do with the farm. Captain Beale was the farmer, and Vita would negotiate rents with him, or object to his planting ugly crops (which meant everything except corn), and there was an orchard in the present car park. East Enders came down in scores for the hop harvest, and Vita, who, according to my father, 'thought their squalor romantic', would go down in the evenings to join their campfires. My father 'went with her once and they gave us evil-smelling and tasting mugs of tea. Dutifully I drank her mug as well as mine, for she hated any tea, and seeing her mug empty she said "Oh I must have spilled my tea" and they gave her another which surreptitiously I drank too.'

This was never really a landed family. 'Granpapa Sackville left us his Purdy guns,' my father wrote, 'which Vita encouraged Ben to use, but we did only once, when Hadji took one of them, saw a rabbit sitting still on the wood-path, aimed, fired, missed, rabbit didn't move, missed again, then it loped off, and we laughed with a delight that is still remembered. After that the guns were given to Copper, and he sold them after Vita's death.'

The war interrupted progress, and for six years Sissinghurst roughened and thickened. Hay crops were taken off the lawns. Weeds invaded the beds and haystacks were made in the orchard. Vita extended her ownership of the surrounding land, buying Bettenham and Brissenden, trying to buy Hammer Mill, but at £12,000 it was too expensive. Captain Beale organised the Home Guard and a watch was kept on the Tower for German parachutists. But the cycle of the year continued; the lumbering wagons brought up the cordwood for her fires; the 'classic monotony' of the rural life persisted, heightened and even made perfect by the threat hanging over it. In the autumn of 1940, they watched the fighters in the Battle of Britain, cutting white patterns against the blue of the summer sky, tumbling silently overhead like butterflies. One night, unable to sleep, Vita

went down to the lake where the black water gave me a sense of deepest peace . . . the moon gave no reflection into the darkened waters. The only things which gleamed and glowed were the water lilies, whitely resting on the black pool. Taking the boat out, I cut the milky stalks of the lilies in the moonlight and as I did so drifting aeroplanes appeared over the lake, chased by the angular beams of searchlights, now lost, now found again; now roaring out now silent, traceable only by their green and red lights sliding between the stars. A fox barked at them, like something in a fable. I tried to compose the fable for myself, something which would combine the fox, the lilies, and the white bodies of the young men up there aloft, but nothing neat would come to me . . .

Jack Vass, the head gardener and mainstay of Sissinghurst from 1939 onwards, volunteered for the RAF in 1941, saying to Vita as he left: 'Look after the hedges. We can get the rest back later.' Dutifully, if a little amateurishly, Harold and Vita clipped the yews and pleached the limes until he returned. Vita knew she couldn't make Sissinghurst without him. One year he planted 12,000 Dutch bulbs, and in 1946 she prayed to her diary:

Oh dear kind God, please let Vass live strong and healthy until he is eighty at least, and never let him be tempted away to anyone else's garden. His keenness is so endless, and nothing is too much trouble. Besides he's so good looking, so decorative.

Vita's long series of articles in the *Observer* from 1947 until 1961 subtly and even surreptitiously, without actually naming Sissing-hurst, advertised the garden to the wider world. It was something she longed to put on show. Vita was enthusiastic when the BBC wanted to make a Sissinghurst documentary in the mid-fifties. Harold was not keen on 'exposing my intimate affections to the public gaze'. But when both of them were first conceiving of the White Garden – and it is scarcely ever remembered that the plant-ing was as much Harold's as Vita's idea – it was with a view to what it would look like to the public. 'I believe that when we scrap the delphiniums,' he wrote to her on 5 July 1949, 'we shall find the grey and white garden very beautiful . . . I want the garden as a whole to be superb in 1951 for the British Fair or Festival, with heaps of overseas visitors, and many will come down by car.'

Vass finally left in 1957, after he and Vita had argued over something to do with the Sissinghurst Flower Show. He was succeeded by other stopgap gardeners, but Sissinghurst entered a new phase with the arrival in October 1959 of Pam Schwerdt and Sibylle Kreutzberger. They remained joint head gardeners until 1990.

The Sissinghurst they found on their arrival was rough and untended. When Vita interviewed them for the job, she had a hole in her breeches which she held together with her thumb and finger. Vita was in the habit of digging up the odd plant while a visitor was with her and offering it to them, leaving a hole in the flower beds. The glasshouses were full of scraggy and rather shameful plants. In the White Garden, the bricks on the wet ground squelched when you walked on them and water squirted up your trouser leg. The fig trees in the Rose Garden were occupying three-quarters of the flower beds, with no room for flowers. Sibylle Kreutzberger remembers Vita and Harold setting off for a winter cruise in late 1959 and leaving the two new gardeners to tackle the pruning:

> We hacked away for weeks while she was away. There used to be a winter secretary who came in and sent Vita's post off to wherever they'd gone to. One day this secretary came round the corner and the whole Rose Garden was strewn with branches the thickness of your thigh. 'I do hope Lady Nicolson hasn't got second sight,' she said.

As Harold had predicted, Vita's entire inherited fortune poured into the creation and maintenance of Sissinghurst. Even when ill, she continued until 1961 writing her articles for the *Observer* because she needed the income. Only in her last years did she have to start selling her possessions at auction, some silver and a pair of the bronze Bagatelle urns, of which six now remain in the garden.

When Vita died in June 1962, she knew that she had created something of lasting value. 'We have done our best,' she wrote to Harold in November 1961, 'and made a garden where none was.' He survived her by six years, sad and lonely. Visitors would see him sitting on the Tower lawn with the tears running down his cheeks.

My father was 'awed by his desolation', but when Harold died in 1968, my father also collapsed in tears of a depth he had never known.

For a week or two after Vita died in the summer of 1962, my father tried to use her room on the first floor of the Tower as his own. But he was haunted. 'I could not endure it. I ceased to be myself: I became a ghost of her.' Ever since, it has remained as she left it, carefully curated by the National Trust, packed away in a thousand leaves of tissue paper every winter, carefully revealed every spring, so that visitors can peer in through the metal grille that now fills the doorway, allowing one to look but not to touch.

My father had been in there only half a dozen times in thirty years, and it is now a shrine, a preserved ensemble, drenched in a peculiar faded, organic, tobacco brown, 'the verdure brown', as Vita called it, of a tapestry or an autumn wood. One morning the other day I sat and worked for a few hours at her desk when the garden was closed. Vita's Sissinghurst remains more present in that room than anywhere outside it. A French blue-brown tapestry, of a pool in a garden, where a pair of swans drifts in the water and oranges

Tuesday
Oct. 27.
'59

Keep

My darling Hadji:
I was thinking this morning how awful it would be if you died. I do often think that; but it came over me all of a heap when I looked out of the bathroom window and saw you in your blue coat and black hat, peering into your scoop. It is the sort of sudden view of a person that twists one's heart, when they don't know you are observing them. They have an innocent look. almost as a child asleep. one feels one is spying on some secret life one should not know about. taking advantage as it were, although it is only the most loving advantage that one takes.

Anyway, the scoop would be the most poignant coffee-cup ever made.
I often think I have never told you how much I love you - and if you died I should reproach myself. saying Why did I never tell him? Why did I never tell him enough?   I am Mar.

hang from the trees in pots, lines the wall in front of me. Looking at it, I write down the words: 'a curved arcade of shadowed trees' and feel the Vita-ism creeping up on me, the ghost, another generation on. On the rough oak desk itself there are ink rings where a bottle tipped or was spilt. There is a photograph of Virginia Woolf, her lover, that long saluki face from which the person, it seems, has withdrawn half an inch below the surface, and is apparent only in the heavy, tented eyes. 'The human contact others can achieve is not for such as her,' as Ethel Smyth described Virginia to Vita. Opposite her, there is a photograph of Harold by Karsh, with a cigarette in one hand, a pencil in the other, his curly hair oiled back and on his face half a smile, more in the eyes than the mouth, as if about to speak, the person not sunk into the face, but barely contained within it.

This room is an assembled world. In the drawer of the desk

there are amber beads, a screwdriver, a Moroccan dagger in its sheath, a book of matches and some envelopes, a label saying 'Potentilla Nitida' and a dried seed pod like a small artichoke. There is nothing thin or refined. Everything is richly itself: the eighteenth-century leather-bound memoirs of Mademoiselle de Montpensier stand beside a selection from Landor. Sticks of sealing wax lie with some pens in a Mexican earthenware tray. There is a small alabaster pot and some tarnished gilt scales on which letters can be weighed. Everything is rich and faded, a fraying of stuff that was once valuable and is now merely treasured. Nothing here was ever renewed. It arrived and, as soon as it arrived, like a picked flower laid on a desk, it began to fade. Vita allowed her possessions to age, silks to wear, wood to darken, terracotta to chip and fail. 'Her possessions must grow old with her,' my father wrote. 'She must be surrounded by evidence of time.' It was a vision and an aesthetic of gradual withdrawal, the bass line of music in which the high notes were the growing and flowering of the garden around her. In here was the lower register, a kind of melancholy, a saddened music. Sissinghurst as a whole, as Jane Brown wrote, also became one of the 'crumbling shrines of the ancient garden gods of Florence and Rome'.

It is a more reflective, slower and deeper place than much of modern Sissinghurst can really allow. On the morning I worked there, trying to understand this place by absorption, osmotically, one of the gardeners, Peter Fifield, was mowing the lawn, and the burr of the mower's engine and the smell of the grass came up the spiral Tower stairs. I realised, as I never had before, that nowhere has quite the relationship to Sissinghurst that this room does: central and presiding, the onion rings of it spreading out from here, across the garden and the other buildings, the farmyard and the farmhouse, the closer fields, to the woods and the shadowed trenches of the streams. This Tower room is the gravitational middle of all of that but it is also hidden and enfolded, buried in the layers of the place like its heart, a presiding secrecy.

Inventories have been taken here, and the Trust has carefully numbered every object, book and paper. But you can read this room as more than a catalogue of objects. It is a form of self-portrait. There is a layer of imperial richness here: a chipped lapis tile on which a vase can sit. And another, on the other table, a brown and amber medieval floor tile, made of English clay. On the bookshelf next to her desk, there is *The Rhymers Lexicon*, in which in pencil on the title page she has written 'a rhymer, that's what I am', and in which many words are ticked as used and not to be used again. Some are added: *peristyle* between *puerile* and *reconcile*; *coracle* between *cruelle* and *demoiselle*.

In a Venetian notebook there is a letter from Freya Stark, describing the olives and lemon orchards of the Mediterranean scene then spread before her eyes, and a long list, stretching over thirty years, of the books she lent to her children, to her cousin Eddy and Uncle Charlie, to Dottie Wellesley and other lovers, even to her mother. There is a letter written by a woman who loved her, from 17 Montpelier St, SW7, undated:

> Thank you for a very lovely day. I shall long remember the rain sliding on the panes, the chanting fire and your voice coming from a long distance as if suddenly you were speaking to me across the years. An echo – or a warning – I shall probably never know – but thank you for everything
>
> Madeleine

There are duplicate order books from the great nurseries for hyacinths, Roman hyacinths, jonquils and narcissi, for tulips, and crocuses, for *Iris reticulata* and a hundred dark fritillaries. In a secret drawer in one of the wooden cabinets, there is an ivory paper knife in the shape of a tiny shoe. Vita's grandfather had it made when Pepita, his mistress, died, having the ivory cut to the shape and size of the sole of one of her dancing shoes. Beside it, a small coral brooch is pinned to a photograph of Pepita surrounded by her children. There are photographs here of Victoria's brother's children and grandchildren, Vita's lost Spanish cousins.

All the English poets are in her writing room, but in the small turret room off it are her gardening books, books of literary criticism and biographies of the poets, Frazer's *Golden Bough*, Bergson's *Le Rire*, and a shelf of Elizabethan history. Above them is a complete run of Havelock Ellis's *Studies in the Psychology of Sex*, initialled 'VN Long Barn' and with an inscription on the flyleaf from Verlaine in the hand of Violet Trefusis:

> *On est fier quelquefois*
> *Quand on se compare.*

Beside it, in *Sex and Character* by Otto Weininger ('VN Polperro July 1918'), Vita underlined: 'Men who are merely intellectual are insincere. All that they care about is that their work should glitter and sparkle like a well cut stone.'

Tucked high in one of the rather damp shelves in the turret I found the proofs of her poem 'The Garden', which she composed here, at this desk, through the war years, and which was the last poem she wrote. It was her final claim on poetry, in which she had once felt secure, but even then sensed slipping from her. I read it, with the April cold in my fingers and the mower outside, as the thudding ringing of the bell came down from above on the hour. I wanted to redeem what she had written, to find the Sissinghurst music here, but, strangely, and for no want of trying, I could not make her poetry take hold. It lacks the final, unanswerable authority of real poetry. There is an emptiness to the rhetoric and it does not get you by the heart, or the throat. Its lines seem always to be more interested in their form, their appearance, than in what they might mean. Vita's misfortune was that she was so much greater as a gardener than as a poet. In the end, everything she wrote was nothing compared to what she did in this place. 'Gardener,' she calls out at one point in 'The Garden', 'poet unaware/Use your seeds like words.' Perhaps in those few words there was a moment of knowledge and recognition.

A life and its griefs are soaked into the fabric of this room. At the foot of one of the bookcases, I found a calfskin attaché case. In it was a note in pencil from my father: 'These objects and papers were found on VSW's desk when she died.' They were mostly the stuff of everyday life, interrupted by illness – she had cancer – and death. Some little notebooks, with lists of what to pack, sachets of photographs of the donkey Abdul, Harold and various women I could not identify. An engagement diary, with dates stretching on into the summer of 1962 beyond her death. A seed packet of Sutton's wallflowers, 'Persian Carpet', 5s. A small note saying '*Foie de veau veneziana*' and 'Sultanas in apple pie'. A quote from Xenophon: 'There is nothing that does not gain in beauty when set out in order', and a poem by Thom Gunn cut out of the *New Statesman*. But alongside those daily, transitory things, two others remained from her long distant past, kept here, not in some hidden uninspected repository of a filing cabinet or a drawer but on her present desk, as much to hand as the photographs of Virginia or Harold. First, a letter from my father to his, written in December 1925 when my father was eight and his father had gone to the embassy in Tehran for two years.

Darling Daddy,

Last night I felt so sad about you being so long and far away
and I cryed a bit. Oh Daddy I do miss you, it is horrid to think
of you all those thousands of miles away, and two years is a long
time to wait for a person whome one loves very much which I do
you. I love you more than very.

Gogy [his French governess] has litten the fire in your little
sitting room, and I am writing on your desk.

I hope I will no longer be sad about you,

Your loving,

Niggs

That letter is the only sign of her children in this room. Alongside
it, still on her desk nearly forty years after it was written, was its
opposite, something a few years older, evidence of another kind of
love. Nigel's little letter is in pencil, carefully corrected by Goggy,
neatly tucked into a small, neatly addressed envelope. This other
thing is rapidly and even wildly written in heavy black ink in short
hurried lines on the back of the telegram forms of the Hotel
Windsor in Monte Carlo. It is a poem in French, written by Violet
Trefusis at the end of those 'four wild and radiant months' between
December 1918 and March 1919 when Vita, dressed as Julian, the
wounded soldier hero, had lived her life of ecstatic freedom
away from the bonds of bourgeois normality, from Harold and the
children. But this poem, the passion of its writing still apparent,
comes at the end of all that, the moment, or at least one of them,
when Vita rejected her most dangerous lover. It is Violet's admission of defeat, when Vita made her choice for Harold and her
family. It marks the moment, one could say, when Sissinghurst
became possible. 'Adieu Mon Ange,' Violet had written,

> Si triste échange
> Tant pis pour moi.

Sissinghurst itself is the monument to the choice Vita made.

TWELVE

Renewal

IT IS THE MIDDLE of June. Warm-weather clouds are sailing across the Weald towards Canterbury. I watch them, drinking coffee by the barn, my legs swinging beneath me on the edge of the tall brick step on its northern side. A wonderful day is laid out in front of me and I feel as happy as a dog: a pale blue sky, a rippled earth. It feels like an arrival. The warmth is finding its way between my shirt and skin. I watch the cloud-shadows slide over the wheat, following them as they hurry across the Eight Acres, the corner of Frogmead, on to the long flat of Large and then Lodge Field, across the lane and into Robert Lewis's seamless arable ground stretching to the north. The shadows slip across the grain of the country in the way that fish cast shadows on the bed of a stream: each patch eases over the bumps and hollows as if gravity did not exist.

The larks are up above Frogmead and the Lower Moat and they are brightening the morning like sequins, glimmering spots of song heard against the sky. Last night with some friends, I went out into the fields and we listened to a single nightingale in the scurfy wood, beginning its song again and again, each time a new variant on what had come before, as if nothing inherited or borrowed was worth considering. Every snatch of its song was unfinished, an experiment in gurgle-beauty. You wanted him to go on but he didn't, always stopping when the song was half-made. We listened, standing in the warm wind, waiting for the next raid on inventiveness. Every part of that bird's mind was restless, on and on, never settling on a known formula, an unending, self-renewing addiction to the new, to another way of doing it, and then another, all in the service of a listening mate and the survival of genes. That is the nightingale's irony: his brilliantly variable song is indistinguishable from his father's or his son's. Invention is nothing but the badge of his race. It is as if new and old in him were indistinguishable. That is the nightingale lesson: inventing the new is his form of repeating the past.

Is that the model here? Is that how we should do it too? I have been making some radio programmes about Homer and his landscapes. Reading the *Odyssey* now, at the end of this Sissinghurst story, brings something home to me. People think of it as the great poem of adventure and mystery, of a man travelling to strange worlds beyond the horizon, of the threat and challenge of the sea. That is true but it is only half of it. The second part, as long as the other, is devoted to something else: Odysseus's homecoming to Ithaca and his ferocious desire, in the middle of his life, after twenty years away, to reform the place he finds, to steer it back on to a path it abandoned many years before. Homer certainly knew about homecoming. Odysseus thinks that all he need do is re-create the order he remembers from his youth, to cleanse the place of everything wrong that has grown up in the meantime and re-establish a kind of purity and simplicity over which he can preside. I hear the echoes of what I have done. 'Nowhere is sweeter', Homer says, as Odysseus bends to kiss the green turf of Ithaca, 'than a man's own country.' That is what we might like to think, but the truth is harder. Nowhere is the desire for sweetness stronger than in a man's own country and nowhere is it more difficult to achieve.

Odysseus soon realises that home is not safe or steady. If he is to re-establish the order he remembers, he has to use all sorts of cunning and persuasion, and in the end even that is not enough. His longed-for sweetness clashes with the realities of imposing it on a place that has changed. The resolution the poem comes to is terrifying: Odysseus slaughters every one of the young men who have been living in his house and corrupting it. He leaves the palace littered with their bodies and his own skin slobbered with their guts – his thighs, Homer says at the end of the killing, are 'shining' with their blood – and then, with the help of his son, strings up the girls those men have been sleeping with, their legs kicking out, the poem says, like little birds which have been looking for a roost but have found themselves caught in a hidden snare. Odysseus thinks of it as a cleansing, a return to goodness but the poem knows that the desire for sweetness has ended only in horror and mayhem. He thinks that order can be imposed by will; the poem knows that the vision of perfection brings war into a house and leaves it broken and bloodied.

It is a sobering drama, an anti-Arcadia, with a deep lesson: singular visions do not work; only by consensus and accommodation can the good world be made; returning wanderers do not have all the answers; and anything which is to be done in your own Ithaca can only be done by understanding other people's needs and their unfamiliar desires. Accommodation, not simplicity, is all. It was a lesson I had taken many months to hear.

So the nightingale has it. Newness is not a new quality. Ingenuity and inventiveness are central parts of life, human and non-human. Stay loose, it says; don't rigidify; accept that you have inherited from the past many beautiful and varied ways of being. And once you know that, sing your song, which attends to the present, and is even a hymn to the present, to the long sense of possibility which has the past buried inside it. Elegy, which is a longing for an abandoned past, is not enough. Elegy, in fact, may do terrible Odyssean damage. It feeds off regret, and even though regret is beautiful and moving, it gives nothing to the future. Regret is a curmudgeon with a way of stringing up the innocent girls. This story, then, is a lyric, a song to what might be, not a longing for what has been. There is no reason when I look at what we have done here and what we are all doing here now, that we cannot say, in future, 'This is what we did then, wasn't it wonderful?'

It has been quite a year. After the decision to go ahead had been made in December 2007, things started to happen. Advertisements were put in relevant papers for a project manager; for a vegetable grower and a deputy; and for a farmer. Early in 2008 we had a string of open days on which candidates came to Sissinghurst for their interviews and to be walked round in the cold and the wind. We took them up the Tower, told the story and showed them the land and buildings. There were some oddities – people whose main experience had been in growing mangoes; a man who wanted to cover the whole farm in geodesic domes for his tomatoes; a woman who didn't want to walk out in the fields because it would get mud on her high heels; a father and son who talked about the ways in which they would drive the place for maximum profit: 'Are all these hedges really necessary?' – but it was exciting. Here at last, living in flesh and blood, were the people who were going to make the change.

The first to join was the new project manager. Tom Lupton is a huge, big-voiced man, Oxford-educated, with a hunger for order and eyebrows that jump at each emphasis in a sentence. 'We REALLY do need to get this into a BANKABLE document.' He is now in his fifties, lives nearby in Biddenden and has behind him a long career in the developing world, setting up vast agricultural and forestry projects, or as he puts it 'getting half-nebulous desires into practical, sequenced action'. None of us could believe that such a qualified man should have applied for this job. It was like having the engineer on the Aswan dam supervise the building of your pond. Why was he doing it? Certainly not for the National Trust salary. More because it was 'an ideal thing to get involved with. It was an idea with a very holistic view, doing things I have spent all my life doing, using land to improve people's lives at the same time as protecting the environment, and done by an organisation which takes a long-term view. It was a marriage of all those things.' When Tom arrived, and his voice started to boom around Sissinghurst's fields and buildings, it felt as if the admiral had joined the fleet. 'You need to be aware', he said, 'that there are many, many risks associated with this and one of my qualifications is that I will be able to extract you with minimum damage if it all goes wrong.'

Next was the vegetable grower. The ad in *Horticulture Week* came out in February. Amy Covey, a twenty-three-year-old, with a big-teeth smile and a blonde, tanned presence as buoyant and English as her name, was working in a private garden in the Midlands. 'I remember looking at it at tea break. We always looked at *Hort Week* and this ad ticked every single box I ever wanted to do. Growing, supplying, being in charge.' She laughs. 'I have known what I wanted to do with my life since I was fourteen.' After training in Sussex and then with the RHS in vegetables and fruit, she was looking for 'the next layer. I didn't expect to do what I am doing now for another three or four years. When I saw the job advertised my heart leapt, it was everything I ever wanted. It was coming home.' She was young to take it on, but we all felt when she came for an interview and we showed her the bleak unploughed, wind-exposed stretch of ground that was going to be her vegetable garden that her sense of enthusiasm and capability, her wonderful undauntedness, was just what Sissinghurst needed. Energetic, open-minded, wanting to learn, neither arrogant nor set in her ways: if any single factor is going to make Sissinghurst's vegetable garden work, it is Amy Covey.

Third in this flow of new blood were the new farmers. The advertisement in *Farmers Weekly* made it clear that the job was for two people, to run both the farm and the bed-and-breakfast in the farmhouse. There were forty different applications, six were shortlisted and out of the pile came Tim Prior and Sue Watson. He had been a London policeman, with all the policeman's under-standing of quiet authority, and then a lecturer in an agricultural college. She had experience of organic sheep and cattle in Devon and running an upscale B&B. Both were clearly business-canny people and understood that the proposition here was more than just a straightforward farm job. They would thrive by tying together what they grew with an enveloping, everything-connected environ-ment for people to enjoy *as a whole*. That was the point. Bed-and-breakfast, farm, restaurant, café, meat sales, wool sales, sheepskin sales, enjoying the garden and the woods: it was all one thing.

When they'd seen the advertisement, Sue had done some research on the internet, ordered an exceptionally obscure pamphlet on the history of the parish in the nineteenth century and had come up with the fact that Sissinghurst Castle Farm had generated a sur-plus of £3600 in the 1850s. 'We knew then that is what we wanted to do,' Sue says. 'I was the one that saw the ad and I thought "Ooh that's us." The whole profile of what you were wanting to achieve here. I thought, "I've done that, he's done that, I could do that, he could do that. That sounds really good." I felt that the farm project could be such a wonderful part of the history of the place. And it would be so wonderful to be part of a history that will still be going on in a hundred years' time.'

What appealed to them was exactly the coming together of history, business, the land, people, animals, farming, the place and its natural life which Sally, Sarah, Jonathan and I had been pushing for so long. They would have some capital to back them up, as well as a small herd of British Shorthorn pedigree beef cattle, which they could bring with them, a flock of Romney sheep and another of Shetland sheep whose caramel-coloured wool would go into jerseys, designed by Sue and made up by a team of knitters. Commerce was at the heart of their idea, as it needed to be, a version of retail farming which could feed off the Sissinghurst name, while putting its own qualities of top-level stockmanship and land management back into that name. They understood from the start that a virtuous circle was waiting for them here.

> *Tim:*
> It is a jump into uncertainty but then life is uncertain. I could be made redundant from the college in a year's time. If you don't take risks you are never going to get anywhere are you?
>
> *Sue:*
> There is an element of arrogance about us, thinking 'We could do that, we could make it fantastic.' We may be wrong and we'll fall flat on our faces but we thought we could give something to it as much as it could give something to us.
>
> *Tim:*
> We are middle-aged but we are very ambitious about things. Even if we hadn't seen the ad for Sissinghurst we would still have been out there looking for something. Rather than just sit on our laurels and think we've got fifteen years before we have to call it a day.

Adam:

I remember you saying when you came here on the interview day that the farm didn't have to be driven for all it is worth because the thing that was going to keep your family going was the B&B. And the farm is almost an entrance ticket to the B&B.

Tim:

The B&B is going to be the banker, the monthly cheque coming in. As far as the farm goes, it is going to take time to get it running, getting the right system. We woud have to learn the land here, what we can do and what we can't. We were told 'Ooh that field is dreadfully wet down there,' and we walked down there and said, 'Where's this wet field?' The one down by Whitegate.

Adam:

Oh yes, that is really wet down there.

Tim:

Not in Devon it's not! If it was really wet, you'd be up to here in mud. So where's this wet field?

Sue:

We have never seen anything quite like this advertised before.

Tim:

We would want this to be a complete circle so that everything that is born here goes off it on its legs, or in the stomach of a customer. The sheep will follow the cows round and the arable follows the sheep, so that you get a complete system. Twenty tons a year of the cows' manure from their winter housing is going on the veg garden and then whatever is produced here is sold locally or to south London or whatever and we could build up the brand name of Sissinghurst Castle Farm.

Sue:
We could be selling the pedigree stock live. I would like to sell it all live if I could but I know we can't. We could also change the herd name to become the Sissinghurst herd.

Tim:
That's what their names will be: Sissinghurst Brian, Sissinghurst Boris, Sissinghurst Gordon. You could name a cow if you like, Adam.

Adam:
Sissinghurst Vita?

The possible appointments of these new people to the Sissinghurst world felt like the dawning of a new day to me. Tom was there from early March, Amy soon afterwards. Ben Raskin and Phil Stocker from the Soil Association came up with a design for the vegetable plot: three and a half acres, nine different segments, the crops rotating through it year by year. Peter Dear had it manured, drained, ploughed, fenced, gated and hedged. An extra segment was added for the children of Frittenden school to grow their own veg. The site for the polytunnels was set up behind a screening layer of oak trees. Irrigation was put in. Plans were made for the drained-off water to be collected in a pond in Lower Tassells and then pumped back up to the top of the site where it could re-used to irrigate the crops. Peter and a party of volunteers made windbreak panels from the wood, using chestnut poles and sliver-thick chestnut slices which he wove between the uprights. Birch tops and hazels were cut for the peas and beans to climb. Peter drew up a plan for the whole farm in which all the hedges, gates and stiles were carefully and exactly detailed.

I loved it all. Suddenly, this new life was springing up out of the inert Sissinghurst ground. It was slightly rough at the edges. Despite some ferreting earlier in the year, the rabbits wrought mayhem with the early plantings and the beds had to be surrounded by low green electric fencing. Black plastic mulch marked out each strip of veg. The soil was not as good as we all had hoped and the gardeners had pushed grapefruit-sized lumps of clay to one side so that they could get each bed half-level. The sown lines were a little wobbly and there was an ad hoc feeling to the garden, but it was this

The Farm at Sissinghurst

Key

Grassland

Meadow

Arable / ley rotation

Vegetables

Woodland

Marsh

National Trust boundary

Sound fences

Field boundary

Lane / path

Gate – single, double, pedestrian **P**

Sissinghurst Park

Wood

Horse Race House

Mount Cottage

Irrigation Pond

Upper Tasse

3

Corner Field (Nut Orchard)

Upper Horse Race

Lower Horse Race Orchard

Car Park

P

Spencer's Shaw

Birches

Nine Acres

P

Park

Birches Wood

Bull Wood

Long Field

NW Well

NE Well

Young's Field

SW Well

SE Well

White Gate Farm

Entrance Lane (Driveable)

← Cranbrook

N

Old Hop
Pickers' Huts

Lodge

Flat
Field

Lower
Tassells

Brick
Kiln

New
Wood

Banky

Banky

P

P

Ten
Acre

Frog

Old
Hop
Garden

Great
Meadow

Meadow

Hanover Brook

Calf

Barn

Upper
Meadow

The
Twelve
Acre

Lower
Moat

Upper
Moat

Dog
Field

Lake
Field

Hazel
Copse

Long
Orchard

Boat Race Stream

Roundshill

Park

Wood

Biddenden

0   400 metres

0   400 yards

hand-made quality of the vegetable garden which touched me. Not for decades has someone attended to this ground in this way. The paths worn between the rows by the boots of the gardeners and their volunteers; the picnic tables for the Frittenden children; and the *Handbook of Organic Gardening* left on the tea-shed table: all were marks of a new relationship to this place. They were the signs of Sissinghurst joining the modern world, the same movement which had re-invigorated allotments across the country, which understood the deep pleasures and rewards of growing your own, which loved the local in the most real way it could. Did it matter that flea beetle was massacring the brassicas, the rocket was bolting, the gooseberries dying, wire-worm making hay with the carrots or the rabbits were eating everything the Frittenden kids had sown? Not really. Because all of that could be sorted out with time and this new presence of people out on the ground – bodies in the fields – was exactly what I had dreamed of four years before: land not as background, as wallpaper or flattened 'tranquillity zone', but the thing itself, engaged with by real people, the plants sown in it bursting into a third dimension, the soil the living source of everything that mattered.

A second grower, David Reynolds, was recruited to work alongside Amy. Sarah drew up a planting list of what the veg garden could and should grow, a cornucopia menu that stretched across the months and years. Intensely productive but not labour-intensive salads, herbs, leafy greens, chard, spinach, courgettes and beans. Alongside them all the tomatoes, pumpkins and squash, carrots and sugar snaps (peas themselves were thought to be too labour intensive for the kitchen – too much shelling for not enough product). Third were 'the unbuyables' – unusual herbs such as lovage, the edible flowers, red Brussels sprouts, stripy pink-and-white beetroot, as well as yellow and purple French beans. All of them, as Sarah said, 'for flavour, style and panache'. Kales, leeks and purple sprouting broccoli, 'the hungry gap crops', would grow through the winter and be harvested in March and April when the restaurant opens. Raspberries, blackberries, gooseberries and red and black currants were planted in long lines between the nine sections of the garden, both to provide windbreaks and to give the plot a visual structure. Fifty new volunteers were recruited to help work there and in the polytunnels.

Tom, Peter and Amy drew up plans for the orchard. A third of it was to be filled with 90 big old-fashioned apple trees (mainly juicing varieties so that the apples could be collected from the ground and no one would have to climb high in the trees to pick them). The rest, just over three acres, was to be smaller modern trees, 1500 of them, no more than eight feet tall, for easy picking and tons of fruit. Plums, apples, pears and a few cherries: a vision of blossom and fruiting heaven. I had the idea of putting thirty acres of hay meadow back into Frogmead along the banks of the Hammer Brook and meadow experts came to advise. Peter was designing wet patches for birds and dragonflies along the streams and a new rough wood to extend the habitat for nightingales. We bought some new disease-resistant elms to place around the landscape as the great towering tree-presences of the future. Architects and landscape designers looked at Whitegate Farm to see how that could be made more efficient and less ugly: a complete rebuild. Other architects redesigned the farmhouse as a modern B&B, in which Tim and Sue could live on the top floor. Meanwhile, the Priest's House was done up for the new farmers to live in until the farmhouse was ready.

Everywhere you looked, all through the spring and early summer at Sissinghurst, change was underway. More people, new people, new structures, new land uses, new relationships. All these changes were exciting but it also felt like a long, slow earthquake heaving up under this most stable and intricately defined place. Inevitably, the stress and grief began to tell. Difficulties, tensions and rows started to break out. There were tears and snubbings, huffs and confrontations. No one had quite understood how deeply these ideas for the place, and all its emphasis on re-invigoration and the re-animation of the landscape, would seem disturbing to the people who lived and worked here.

One afternoon I sat down and talked to Sam Butler, the National Trust's Visitor Services Manager at Sissinghurst, a funny and warm-hearted woman, who has been here since 1994. She had started as a part-time secretary, one of three office staff. 'We are still in the same office now. There are fourteen of us with seven computers which we all have to share. And there are five telephones which have got to be answered. It does take up quite a lot of the day.'

The stress levels went through the roof. People were getting angry, offended, offensive and dismissive. Thirty-five permanent staff, fifty to sixty seasonal staff, one hundred and twenty to one hundred and thirty volunteers, plus another fifty volunteers coming on for the vegetable garden, not enough office space, not enough computers, not enough desks or chairs, and the great cuckoo of the farm project and all its building implications landing itself in the midst of this. Everything I wanted for Sissinghurst – rerooting it, reconnecting the parts, generating some overall well-being – all of that was the opposite of what happened.

Change is hard in any business but when many of the people live on the site, when they have worked there for years and feel that their lives, their ideals, their work and their homes are entirely bound up in a vision of a place as it is – as they have made it – then change, however good or bad it may inherently be, is even more difficult to accept.

I talked to Tom Lupton about what was going wrong. He is almost the definition of a wise dog and one of the problems, he said, was that I had not properly understood how deeply attached other people were to Sissinghurst. I had assumed I was the only person to whom it meant a great deal.

> There is a lot of emotion tied up in this project. From you, of course. You have obviously staked a lot of emotion in it. But that's true of a lot of people who live and work here. Sissinghurst is not like going into Tesco's. People come here and very quickly form emotional bonds. They love it. It feeds many individual needs, which are very difficult to get fed in many places these days. Sissinghurst spoonfeeds it to people. As you walk from the car park, you are given these wonderful, sensuous experiences. In through the gateway, the tower, you wander into the garden. It's beautiful but it's obviously been beautiful for a long time. That is very reassuring and very comforting. It's a refuge but it does a bit more than that. I can't believe that many people don't leave here feeling better. It's a recharging point and for people who work here it has an increasing value to them the more they are steeped in it. You, Adam, need to be aware how many other people have loved being here.

It was well said and I heard it clearly. I asked Sam about this too. Why were people so attached to Sissinghurst? Was it just a tranquillity balm? I had always thought of it as a place that should have life and vitality, which should feel enriched by all the things going on here, by a sense of a living landscape not an embalmed one. Sam gave me a sceptical look.

I know you would like to bring the farm up close around the garden so that there was more of a contrast. I can see that, but I quite like the feminine, soft, National Trust sanitisation. I quite like that because that is where I am comfortable but what you are proposing is much more masculine and that's unknown territory. I am not sure how I am going to respond to that.

Really? Was a sanitised, blanded-out soft zone really what was needed?

I like it and most of our visitors like it. It makes it accessible and for those who don't know the countryside, they need their hands holding, giving them a comfort zone so that they can access it without it being too threatening.

How was she feeling about the whole transformation? A week or two before, at a meeting, she had suddenly coloured up at something I said.

It was like a slap in the face. I had been listening to you and Tom and I suddenly realised that this place was going to change for ever in the way I felt about it. When I drove up the lane, the place that I had known for such a long time, that drive up the lane would be bringing me to a different place and I wasn't sure. It didn't matter whether it was good or bad. I just didn't know how I was going to respond. I knew it was different and that for me was a loss, because I have been tied to this place for such a long time.

We have visitors who come here every Saturday morning to read their papers in the orchard, who have come here maybe with a partner or a husband or a wife or a child they have lost and they come here to reflect as well as to enjoy the flowers and the views and the vistas. And you know we must look after those people too.

All this was an education for me, almost the first time I had ever listened to the stories other people at Sissinghurst were telling me. Alexis Datta, the head gardener, continued to be worried, but she too has seen out many years and crises at Sissinghurst and thinks it will only be a source of short-term grief. 'I am hoping in a while it is all going to feel like part of the place. I think it probably will. At the moment it just feels as if everything is "Oh my God, what is going on?" A sympathetic farm will be an improvement,' she said.

> I'm hoping it is not going to be a mock historic farm. Having livestock will enhance it a lot. You don't see a tractor now. It is nice to see people working on the land as long as they are not dressed up in smocks. It is slightly sentimental if we are going to have nut trees and orchards which everyone else is ripping out. But now we have got Amy attempting to grow things on the land and we will soon have a farmer and they are doing it for real and it will be real. I think it is going to be ok.

Those sentences were undiluted music to me. 'I think it is going to be ok': I had been saying that for months. Now people were saying it to me.

The real pinchpoint, though, was the restaurant. It was vital that the restaurant changed to reflect what was happening in the wider landscape. It would make little sense to set up all these connections between land, place and people if the restaurant continued to produce food that was much as it was before. Sarah, who has a decade's experience of growing and cooking vegetables for her gardening school in Sussex, took on the task of introducing the restaurant to these new hyper-local sources of produce, urging on them a new responsiveness to what would be coming in off the field. For months, over these questions, there was an agonised non-meeting of minds.

Both sides felt deeply unappreciated by the other. Ginny Coombes, the restaurant manager, who has been generating quantities of cash for Sissinghurst year after year, while also responding to the Trust's own local and seasonal agenda, felt bruised by the whole process.

> There is no appreciation of how far we have come, or of what we have taken on. A lot of ideas have been thrown at us and it isn't easy. We are moving in the right direction and we are doing a

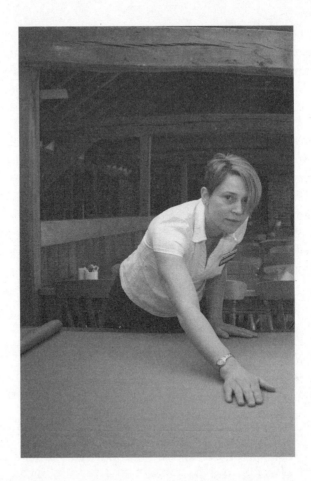

lot already with local and seasonal. That's my mantra! It is something the Trust has been working towards for years. And we are improving year on year. Someone needs to say, 'Listen to the staff, they run it, they know what they are doing. We want to help you improve what you have got already.' But we don't feel that anyone is saying that.

It was never going to be easy. For chefs and restaurant managers used to high-pressure, high-volume production of meals for hundreds of visitors, often in less than perfect circumstances, all our talk of 'the dignity of vegetables' was not even funny. Mutual frustrations erupted. Sarah pursued her gospel: vegetables are cheaper to grow than meat, better for the environment, better for you, utterly delicious when they are so fresh, and make you feel good when you know exactly where they have come from. And Ginny said 'Look, do you know what it is like in here on a busy day?'

When you came to me three years ago and said 'What about growing our own veg here?', I thought that would be a wonderful thing. But it's all got so over-complicated. I love what Sarah does at Perch Hill and I listened when Hugh Fearnley-Whittingstall came here and said we should have a Tart of the Day. That is all fine when you have fifty people to feed. When you have got a thousand people a day, they want choice. That is the plain and simple fact. And, now, people are looking at their purses more and more. If they have to choose between something usual, what they know, and something more expensive and localised, they are going to choose the cheaper option more and more.

Early in June 2008, to get some understanding of what Ginny and her staff were having to deal with, Sarah and I worked in the restaurant for two days, her in the kitchen, me on the tables, behind the counter and doing the washing up.

Seeing it all from the other side was pure reality-check. The customer demand was relentless and the need to shave costs unbending. The building – a restaurant inserted into an old granary-cum-cow shed – is badly laid out. For the staff it is often unbearably hot as wafts of hot air come from the industrial dishwasher, the heated counters or the ovens. The clearing away system does not help the waiters and there is a lot of double handling. The queue for a pot of coffee gets muddled with the queue for the hot dishes. Space behind the counter is cramped and, where different routes cross, inconvenient. Everybody works unrelentingly hard and remains cheerfully nice to each other through the heat and harassing customers. And everybody ends the day exhausted. I felt I had been in a trawler for eight hours. Only when one of the visitors said 'This must be such a nice place to work,' did I very nearly ask him if he had just landed from Mars.

Of course this restaurant finds it difficult to embrace any

change. An irregular supply of vegetables from the plot, in variable volumes, is going to need an elastic frame of mind. Working in this tight and difficult environment allows no room for elasticity. I asked Ginny about this. 'People here don't see our side of it, our passion for it, the work and energy we put in here,' she said.

> I know you saw it the other day, how drained people are at the end of a working day. But nobody gives us credit for it. And nobody knows exactly what is needed. It is all big ideas, everybody thinks they know better than us. We are taking on board the advice that everyone seems to be giving us, but give us time.

One of the problems is that the market is moving fast. A couple of weeks ago the first salad leaves from the Sissinghurst plot were served and sold in the restaurant. They looked lovely, fresh and perfect. I had seen Amy washing them with the hose at the plot only an hour or two before. I asked a visitor, queuing there, if she realised this lettuce had been grown in the field out there. 'Really,' she said, half-engaged, 'I would have thought most things in this restaurant would have been grown on the farm.'

Young people now are obsessed about feeding themselves and their children the right things. And here it is, the definition of the right thing: unbelievably local, unbelievably organic and unbelievably fresh. If it is going to continue to be successful, the restaurant has got to run with that. Soon, not growing your own will look strangely old-fashioned. The Trust knows that, Ginny knows that and has a policy to support it, but to make the change, when the change has to be made with a hungry public waiting for its lunch, is exceptionally difficult. It is clear to me now that we need a radical redesign, making the building and the kitchen all more open, easier to work, more efficient, more staff- and customer-friendly. That means more investment and yet another project but I am sure that unless it happens, the meaning of this transformation of the farm is not going to reach the public. Of course there are problems ahead. As Jonathan Light, the Trust's area manager, says, 'Remember: implementation is a slog.' Ginny has some doubts that the farm could ever provide everything the restaurant needs. But that doesn't mean to say we won't get there in the end.

*   *   *

A couple of days ago, tidying up the files in my workroom, I came across a letter I wrote to my father nearly twenty years ago, in July 1989. It is entitled rather grandly 'A Long-Term Vision for the Future of Sissinghurst', and in it I was surprised to find this:

> Central to Sissinghurst is the idea of a garden embedded in the country around it. The surroundings of the garden should not be divorced from it. There should be, in effect, a conversation between the two, a mutually sustaining relationship between the garden and the land. And one of the elements that binds them together should be a true responsiveness to the beauty and subtlety of nature.

The place should be farmed organically, I said, and Sissinghurst could become a byword not only for gardening, but for a fully integrated relationship between nature and culture, people and land, beauty and use. If we did this, I told my father, 'it would be a way of making Sissinghurst not simply a garden with a shop and café attached but a future-looking place with a new vitality.' I had entirely forgotten I had ever said this. Neither he nor anyone else took it up, but with it in the box file was a carbon copy of his reply. He couldn't tell if the idea was any good but one day, 'When The Time Comes', I would have a chance to try these ideas out in the real world. I should wait.

Later on, I went to see Linda Clifford, James Stearns's sister, Stanley and Mary Stearns's daughter and Ossie Beale's grand-daughter. She was born in Bettenham in the 1950s, now lives in Mount Cottage on the edge of Sissinghurst Park Wood and is as much tied to this piece of landscape as anyone alive. 'I feel as if it is my place but it is not my place,' she said. 'I feel I have this pro-prietorial interest in it, which is ridiculous, but I still want it to be a working place. Don't mess with the land. It has got to be done right. Don't make it a theme park. Make it properly productive again.' I asked her how she would like to see it in twenty years' time.

> I would like to see the farm as it was in the fifties - a true mixed farm, alive and productive. It can't be exactly like that, of course,

because it won't be the more intimate, privately farmed family enterprise it once was. And modern farming methods make different demands on the land. Quite simply, I would like it to be doing well. That's all. A farm doing well. And if that's the case, then Sissinghurst will be a contented place.

Just down from her house, at the top of the Cow Field where the vegetables are now growing, a blackbird was sitting on the new gatepost shouting fearlessly about his life. To the north, the wind was blowing catspaws through the yellowing wheat. In Banky Field, on the far side of the Hammer Brook, the oats were still a blue lime-green. Along the edges of the far woods, where the oaks reach out across the headlands, the sun was making shadowed hollows, like the eyesockets in a skull. It all looked concordant, a place brimming over with its own life. Each field was as full of wheat as a saucer full of milk. Within a few years those five fields below me would be divided into eleven different compartments. Hedges would be running on the ancient lines. Peter's new nightingale wood would be growing on the banks of the Hammer Brook. Shorthorns might be grazing in the old Hop Garden, sheep in the Twelve Acres. Flowery hay would have thickened in the bottom of Frog Meadow where it had grown before for so many thousands of years. Scattered through the hedgerows, the new elms would be starting to lift into their cumulus towers above the fields. Behind me, the nut orchard of Kentish Filberts and the fruit orchard would be shady groves over grazed grass. And just here in front of me, Amy and David's vegetable garden would be busy with the chefs and the waiters harvesting the beans and sugar snaps for the visitors' lunch. It is not far away now. I can sit here and see it, fully alive in a way I could never have guessed or hoped for.

I realise now that, until my father died four years ago, I had remained a Sissinghurst child. I looked to it for stability and comfort, for a kind of certainty, even while not quite understanding what Sissinghurst meant or what it needed. That has changed, and Sissinghurst to me now has become less a parent than a spouse, not hovering reassuringly above me but standing alongside, with its own demands and idiosyncrasies, its own beauties and generosity, its ability to change and reluctance to do so. My relationship to it has, in other words, at last, grown up. I see it now for what it is.

I am leaving this story when it is still unfinished. There are a thousand and one steps still to take. I look at the clouds streaming away in front of me to the north-east, and that is what the future looks like too: avenues of bubbled possibilities. The future here seems just as long as the past that extends behind it. Everything that Vita and Harold responded to when they came here nearly eighty years ago is still alive, but I also remember what John Berger wrote in *Pig Earth*: 'The past is never behind. It is always to the side.' That is true. The past is everywhere around me, co-existent with present and future, soaked into this soil but not sterilising it. There is no hierarchy. Past, present and future are all equally co-existent and

Sissinghurst is becoming a place that responds to all three. And through that re-connection Sissinghurst will once again reacquire, I hope, a sense of its own middle, a confidence that it can turn to its own resources and find untold riches there. It will become, in the best possible sense of the word, its own place. That is the word, I now realise, to which this book has been devoted: place as the roomiest of containers for human meaning; place as the medium in which natural and cultural, inherited and invented, individual and communal can all fuse and fertilise. I don't remember anything in my own life which has made me look at the world with such a surge of optimism and hope.

ACKNOWLEDGEMENTS

The length of this list of acknowledgements is itself a sign of how many layers of thought and direction go into running a place like Sissinghurst. It is a deeply complicated business.

First, I must thank the four people without whom the farm project at Sissinghurst would never have happened: Sally Bushell, the Trust's property manager; Jonathan Light, until recently the area manager; Sue Saville, regional director in the south-east; and Fiona Reynolds, director-general of the Trust. Sissinghurst owes them all untold thanks.

Beyond them, I would like to thank everyone in the National Trust who has given me and Sissinghurst their help and expertise over the last few years, in particular David Adshead; Jane Arnott; Mike Buffin; Tony Burton; Tim Butler; Sue Clement; Michelle Cleverley; Andy Copestake; Ivo Dawnay; Ed Diestelkamp; Jane Fletcher; Louisa Freeman-Owen; Harry Goring; Sue Herdman; Rob Jarman; Lynne Kemp; Sue Knevett; Rob Macklin; Maggie Morgan; Simon Murray; Peter Nixon; Matthew Oates; Dottie Owens; William and Merry Proby; Stuart Richards; Richard Saville; Emma Slocombe; Sarah Staniforth; Caroline Thackray; Richard Wheeler; and Sue Wilkinson.

The changes this book describes have not been easy and I am immensely grateful to everyone working at Sissinghurst for tolerating the disruptions I have caused, especially to Claire Abery; Stephen Barnett; Maddie Bell; Di Bennett; Sam Butler; Ginny Coombes; Amy Covey; Alexis Datta; Emma Davies; Peter Dear; Stacey Deaves; Sue East; Peter Fifield; Gavin Fuller; Anita Goodwin; Jo Jones; Matthew Law; Tom Lupton; Daniel Mead; Clemmie Mendes; Philip and Joy Norton; Lynda Pearce; Tim Prior; Heather Reece; David Reynolds; Victoria Roberts; Sarah Roots; Jacqui Ruthven; Jean Shill; Wendy and Tony Tremenheere; Sue Watson; Barbara White; Maggie White;

Caroline Wilding; Nathanael Wilkins; and Michelle Woodcock.

Mary Stearns; Brian and Linda Clifford; Pat, Catherine and the late James Stearns are all members of a family which has been at Sissinghurst since the 1920s. They have helped me enormously with their time, memories, insights and the loan of precious photographs and documents.

My own family has been encouragement itself, none more than my wife Sarah Raven, who from the beginning has poured untold amounts of energy and time into the farm project; my sisters Juliet and Rebecca Nicolson; my children Tom, William, Ben, Rosie and Molly Nicolson; my cousins Vanessa Nicolson and Robert Sackville West; my nieces Flora and Clemmie Macmillan-Scott; as well as the irreplaceable Charles Anson and David O'Rourke.

Many friends have helped in different ways: Simon Bishop; Charlie Boxer; Emma Bridgewater; Helen Browning; Jonathan Buckley; Carla Carlisle; Antonio Carluccio; Sue Clifford; Priscilla Conran; Harry Cory-Wright; Tim Dee; Sheila Dillon; Montagu and Sarah Don; Martin Drury; Jo Fairley; Hugh Fearnley-Whittingstall; Simon and Lucinda Fraser; Katrin Hochberg; Patrick Holden; Glenn Horowitz; Mary Keen; William Kendall; Angela King; Robin Leach; John and Kate Leigh-Pemberton; Tom Maynard; Pip Morrison; Tom Oliver; Andrew Palmer; Anna Pavord; Dan Pearson; Thomas and Flora Pennybacker; Sorley Pennybacker; Johann Perry; Sigrid Rausing; Matthew Rice; Norman Rose; Jacob Rothschild; Peter Rumley; Craig Sams; Claire Spottiswoode; Phil Stocker; Penny Tweedie; Guy Watson; Peter Weeden; Claire Whalley; Kim Wilkie; Fred Windsor-Clive; and Sofka Zinovieff.

Others who have unstintingly given their assistance are: Tony Allison; Nicola Bannister; Peter Brandon; Betty Carman; Hadrian Cook; Nicholas Cooper; George Ellis; Lorraine Flisher; Douglas Green; Paula Henderson; Mark Hoare; Jeremy Hodgkinson; Maurice Howard; Alastair Laing; Todd Longstaffe-Gowan; Tom Maynard; Nick Newell; Susan Pittman; Ernie Pollard; Lee Prosser; Jeremy Purseglove; Ben Raskin; Margaret Richardson; Kirsty Righton; Tony Singleton; Michael Zell.

Caroline Dawnay and Zoe Pagnamenta have been stalwart allies as ever. At HarperCollins Susan Watt, Pria Taneja, Vera Brice and Helen Ellis have worked their usual miracles. In particular I would like to thank Peter Wilkinson for drawing the maps. Derrick Bradbury's picture of Sissinghurst was only identified by chance. He very kindly had it photographed for this book. If there is anyone else who knows of images, artefacts, plans or pictures of Sissinghurst, please get in touch with the author on adam@shiantisles.net

ILLUSTRATIONS

308 June 2008: Sam Butler, the National Trust's Visitor Services Manager at Sissinghurst, in front of the gate (*National Trust/Penny Tweedie*)

312 June 2008: Ginny Coombes, manager of the National Trust restaurant at Sissinghurst (*National Trust/Penny Tweedie*)

315 June 2008: Amy Covey, vegetable grower, and Sarah Raven, Adam Nicolson's wife, with the first salads from the veg garden (*National Trust/Penny Tweedie*)

317 2000: Nigel Nicolson in the Bishops' Gate outside the White Garden at Sissinghurst (*Ray Hallett*)

319 2008: Sissinghurst (*Penny Tweedie*)

Endpapers: front: 1761: Anonymous drawing of a double murder by an English militiaman at Sissinghurst. See description at the beginning of the book (*Derrick Bradbury*)

end: One of the maps included in a large-scale 1903 sale of the Cornwallis estate. Sissinghurst land at that time included more wood to the north and more farmland beyond Bettenham to the east than it does today. The small tripod symbol indicates hop gardens. Orchards are shown by fluffy trees.

NOTE ON SOURCES

For the early history of Kent, articles in the volumes of *Archaeologia Cantiana* are invaluable. Many are now online at www.kentarchaeology.org.uk

Frans Vera's *Grazing Ecology and Forest History*, CABI Publishing 2000, provides a new and fascinating perspective on the early environmental history of the Kentish forest. Oliver Rackham's *Woodlands*, HarperCollins 2006 ties Vera's suggestions into a more traditional English frame. William Anderson, in *The Green Man*, HarperCollins 1990, is a source of rich speculation on the meaning and significance of that near-universal wood symbol and G. H. Garrad, *A Survey of the Agriculture of Kent*, Royal Agric. Soc., 1954 provides a detailed account of the Kentish farmer's response to his environment. Henry Cleere and David Crossley, *The Iron Industry of the Weald*, 2nd ed., Merton Priory Press, 1995 speculates fascinatingly on the Weald under Roman occupation and gives a full description of the early modern iron industry.

J. K. Wallenberg's study of *The Place-Names of Kent*, Uppsala, 1934 and K. P. Witney's *The Jutish Forest: A Study of the Weald of Kent 450–1380 AD*, Athlone Press 1976 are the classic accounts of the early medieval penetration of the Wealden forest around Sissinghurst. K. P. Witney's edition of *The Survey of Archbishop Peacham's Kentish Manors 1283–85*, Kent Arch. Soc., Maidstone 2000, takes that movement up into the high Middle Ages.

For Sissinghurst's social environment in the 16th century, see Michael Zell's *Industry in the countryside: Wealden society in the sixteenth century*, Cambridge 1994 and a volume of essays edited by him, *Early Modern Kent 1540–1640*, The Boydell Press 2000. Maurice Howard, *The Building of Elizabethan and Jacobean England*, Yale 2007 and Malcolm Airs, *The Tudor and Jacobean Country House: A building history*, Sutton Publishing 1995, combined with Caroline van Eck, *British Architectural Theory 1540–1750*, Ashgate 2003 describe the philosophical, political and practical world in which the new Sissinghurst was made. For the use and aesthetics of the park around it, see the essays in Robert Liddiard, editor, *The Medieval Park: New Perspectives*,

Windgather Press, 2007. Descriptions of Sir John Baker's murderous behaviour can be found in Foxe's Book of Martyrs which is online in a variorum edition at www.hrionline.ac.uk/johnfoxe/. Early modern histories of the Weald are William Lambarde, *A Perambulation of Kent*, London 1570, John Philipott, *Villare Cantianum or Kent surveyed and illustrated*, 1659 and the great Edward Hasted's *History of the County of Kent*, 1790. The three-volume *History of the Weald of Kent* by Robert Furley, Ashford 1871, although often muddly, is full of fascinating sidelights. Nigel Nicolson's short *Sissinghurst Castle, An Illustrated History*, National Trust, 1964 has remained in print for over 40 years. Contemporary accounts of Elizabeth's progresses were gathered by John Nichols in the late 18th century. Many, including the list of those who came to stay at Sissinghurst in 1573, are now online at www2.warwick.ac.uk/fac/arts/ren/projects/nichols/progresses/

Papers of the Mann estate, including many relating to Sissinghurst, are kept in the Centre for Kentish Studies in Maidstone (U24). Quarter Session Records, detailing the Elizabethan park invasions, are there too. Accounts of the plot to destroy the ironworks at Hammer Mill are in the Staffordshire County Record Office. References are all available on www.a2a.org.uk

A printed copy of the sermon by Robert Abbott, vicar of Cranbrook, *The holinesse of Chrisian [sic] Churches, or a Sermon preached at the consecration of the chappell of Sr. Iohn Baker: of Sussing-herst in Cranbrooke in Kent, Baronet*, London 1638, is in the library of St John's College, Cambridge. For papers relating to the sequestration of the Baker estates in the Civil War, see SP/19, 20, 23 and 28 in the National Archives in Kew. The probate Inventory of Dame Elizabeth Howard's possessions at Sissinghurst in 1694 is also there under PROB 5/3715.

Sissinghurst as an eighteenth-century prisoner-of war camp is described in Francis Abell, *Prisoners of War in Britain 1756–1815*, Oxford UP 1914 and referred to by Edward Gibbon in his *Journal*, ed D. M. Low, Chatto & Windus 1929. The Admiralty files in the National Archives contain the long and fascinating transcript of an 'Examination of complaints of prisoners at Sissinghurst' (ADM 105/42) held in 1761 and under ADM 97/114/2 'Letters to and from French prisoners held in England 1756–63', many of them at Sissinghurst.

C. C. R. Pile's short leaflet on *The Parish Farm at Sissinghurst Castle*, Cranbrook and Sissinghurst Local History Society, 1952 remains the best account of Sissinghurst Castle Farm as Cranbrook's 'Old Cow'. MAF 32/1022/101 in the National Archives contains the 1941 Farm Survey

Records for Cranbrook in which Captain Beale's farm is revealed in all its perfection.

The Vita Sackville-West and Harold Nicolson years at Sissinghurst have been written about more than any other. Vita herself wrote *Country Notes*, Michael Joseph 1939, and many collections of her *Observer* articles have been in print since the 1950s. Anne Scott-James's *Sissinghurst: The Making of a Garden* was published by Michael Joseph in 1975. Jane Brown's *Vita's Other World: a gardening biography of V. Sackville-West*, Viking 1985 set Sissinghurst in wider context. Tony Lord, *Gardening at Sissinghurst*, Frances Lincoln 1995 focused tightly on the garden here, bed by bed. Nigel Nicolson edited Harold Nicolson's *Diaries and Letters*, in 3 volumes, Collins 1966–8 and in 1973 published *Portrait of a Marriage* (Weidenfeld & Nicolson), about his parents' marriage and homosexual infidelities. His own autobiography *Long Life*, Weidenfeld & Nicolson 1997, describes among much else his own deep attachment to Sissinghurst. Two biographies of Harold (James Lees-Milne, *Harold Nicolson*, 2 vols, Chatto & Windus 1980–81 and Norman Rose, *Harold Nicolson*, Pimlico 2006) match two of Vita (Michael Stevens, *V. Sackville-West*, Michael Joseph 1973 and Victoria Glendinning, *Vita*, Weidenfeld & Nicolson 1983). Susan Mary Alsop, wrote about Vita's mother in *Lady Sackville*, Weidenfeld & Nicolson 1978.

Most of the manuscripts on which these books were based are now to be found in the Lilly Library in Indiana (Harold's and Vita's letters – www.indiana.edu/~liblilly) or Balliol College, Oxford (the three million words of Harold's diaries).

INDEX

Middle Ages 126, 128
Milestone Wood 136
Milkhouse 128, 136
Monday, June 50
Monmatre de Petham, Elie 144
Morgan, Shirley 73, 74
Mottenden friary 144–5, 147, 170
Munday, June 210
Murray, Simon 153, 154

National Trust: aesthetic ideals of 39, 49,
  66, 210, 286, 310; AGM 104; A N's
  relationship with 49–50, 59–61,
  66–9, 100–5, 107, 115, 143, 149–66,
  209–10, 255–60; approve A N's plans
  for Sissinghurst 259; Central
  Projects & Acquisitions Group 258;
  Country House Scheme 39; donor
  families meeting, Spencer House
  152–5; Draft Occupancy Agreement
  62–3; Enterprises 113, 162; financial
  management and rules 43, 102–3,
  104, 106, 107, 108, 150–1, 159, 162, 164,
  209–10; Gardens Panel 66; Historic
  Buildings Committee 39; history of
  38–40; nature of institution 38–40,
  49, 153–5, 158–9; Nigel Nicolson
  hands Sissinghurst over to 40–9;
  organic farming, approach to 152;
  reaction to A N's proposals for
  Sissinghurst 49–50, 59–61, 66–9,
  100–5, 107, 115, 143, 149–66, 209–10,
  255–60; Regional Committee 152,
  255, 257; Regional Planning Group
  164; reject A N's plans for
  Sissinghurst 163–6, 209–11, 255–8;
  resident donor' status 62–4, 66,
  152–5; Sissinghurst, ownership of 11,
  38, 40–9, 253, 286; Special Trust in
  Credit 107–8; target market 60–1
Neve, Frederick William 244
Neve, George 73, 97, 99, 148, 241, 242,
  244, 246
Nicolson, Adam 26, 27; boarding school
  22, 45; childhood 1, 2–22, 23–6, 33–4,
  46–7, 75, 82, 177, 180–2; father,
  relationship with 2, 3, 4, 5, 19, 22,

23–4, 25, 26, 31–4, 46–7, 61–2, 70, 82,
  180–2, 316; grandfather, childhood
  memories of 17–18, 19–20; Homer,
  on nature of homecoming in 295–6;
  National Trust, negotiations and
  relationship with 49–50, 59–61, 62–4,
  66–9, 100–17, 149–66, 209–11,
  255–60; plan and vision for
  Sissinghurst 36–7, 49–50, 59–61,
  64–9, 100–17, 149–66, 209–11,
  255–60, 296–318; plans for
  Sissinghurst approved by National
  Trust 259; plans for Sissinghurst
  rejected by National Trust 163–6,
  209–11, 255–8; returns to live in
  Sissinghurst with family, 2004 29–31,
  61–2; Sissinghurst, attachment to
  1–2; puts plan for Sissinghurst into
  action, 2008 296–318; Weald,
  explores as a child 3–4, 15
Nicolson, Ben (A N's uncle) 23, 33, 262,
  263, 269, 279, 283
Nicolson, Harold (A N's grandfather) 44,
  75, 251; affairs 22, 276; A N's
  childhood memories of 17–18, 19–20;
  arrival at Sissinghurst 190, 191, 261,
  272–3, 277, 318; character 276; civil
  servant 262, 266–7; debts 41; diaries
  23; garden and ii, 90–1, 188, 277, 278,
  279, 282, 284, 285; letters 23, 262, 276,
  281; living arrangements 16; MP 262;
  National Trust, relationship with
  40; old age 17–18, 18, 19–20; papers
  276; photographs of 18, 26, 286, 288,
  292; son, relationship with 262, 263,
  267; Vita Sackville-West, marriage
  to and relationship with 17, 18,
  19–20, 263, 266–7, 268, 271, 277, 285,
  286, 293
Nicolson, Juliet (A N's sister) 2, 17, 19, 22,
  32, 48, 114, 261–2
Nicolson, Nigel (A N's father) 26, 27, 173;
  America, love of 24; A N's
  relationship with 2, 3, 4, 5, 19, 22,
  23–4, 25, 26, 33–4, 61–2, 82, 180–2,
  316; bedroom, childhood 180;
  building history of Sissinghurst and

Sissinghurst Castle Farm – *cont.*
307, 318; hedges 235, 236, 258, 318;
hops 11, 12–14, *13*, 27–8, 51, 53, 55, 57,
59, 71, 102, 130, 138, 142, 143, 168, 209,
242, 243, 247, 248, 249, 251, 252, 275,
283; Horse Race Field 42, 52, 73, 97,
108, 242; horses 53; hunting on 126,
193–4, 205, 211, 235, 243; Large Field
51, 111, 112, 241, 294; leased by parish
of Cranbrook, 1796 (poor relief
scheme) 234–41; Legge Wood 233;
Lodge Field 11, 51, 111, 192, 241, 247,
294; Long Orchard 75; Lower Moat
294; Lower Tassells 112, 210–11, 303;
meadows 4, 128–9, 132, 138, 141–2,
143, 202, 204, 235, 307; medieval strip
cultivation 132; Middle Ages 138–43;
Mount Cottage 50, 316; Nine Acres
52; 19th century 235–43; 1940s 52–5,
283; 1950s 55–8; 1960s 2–15, 41–9;
1960s-2004 26–37; oast houses 27, 28,
30, 241, 251, 253; oats 168; oilseed rape
165; Old Hop Garden 318; orchards
11, 12, 28, 42, 53, 75, 108, 111, 141, 147,
150, 157, 164, 173, 174, 175, 179, 184,
190, 243, 251, 255, 258, 277, 283, 307,
310, 318; organic 56, 66, 108–13, 151,
152, 163, 209, 211, 316; oxen 243; Park
ii, 52, 81, 89, 91, 132, 184, 191–6, 202,
204, 205, 207, 208, 216, 217, 227, 241,
243; pale 192, 195, 217, 218, 233; peas
53, 102, 303; Perch Hill 157, 313; pigs
11, 15, 19, 28, 53, 55, 105, 124–5, 127,
138, 209, 242; present day 299–303,
304–5; rabbits 62, 195, 207, 211, 283,
303; restaurant, as a supplier of food
for 65–6, 68, 102, 150, 151, 159–61, 165,
306, 311–15, *315*, 318; roughness of
14–15; Roughter 241; 17th century
211–18; sheep 11, 28, 53, 55, 164, 168,
209, *249*, 255, 299, 300, 301, 318;
Survey Record, 1941 52–5; tenant
farmers 50–1, 67, 104, 210–11, 247–51,
253, 259; trees *see* trees; Twelve Acres
318; 20th century 244–5, 247–54, 283;
2005 50–2; 2008 296–319; Upper
Tassells 210–11; vegetable growing

42, 112, 150, 162, 164, 209, 255, 296,
298–9, *298*, 301, 302, 303, 306, 317–18;
Victorian 241–5; Vita Sackville-West
and 283; Well Fields 52, 132, 217;
wheat 11, 51, 52, 57, 165, 168, 242, 317;
Whitegate Farm 210, 256, 301, 307;
wildlife 7, 8, 10–11, 32, 79, 111, 119,
120, 162–3, 184–5, 190, 195, 207, 211,
217, 243, 275, 283, 294–5, 296, 303,
307; woods 8–10, 30, 32, 73, 81, 84,
84, 85–9, *85*, *86*, *88*, 91–2, 102, 109–10,
110, 120, 125, 126, 138–41, 163, 184,
199–201, 215–16, 233–4, 241, 243, 253,
316
Sissinghurst Castle Garden iii, *161*, 183;
Cottage Garden 278; Delos 42, 108,
226, 277; design of 102, 277–9;
Elizabethan 183, 190, 226;
Erechtheum 188; Moat Walk 42, 148,
279; gardeners 113–14, 261, 285; Herb
Garden 18, 42, 90; iconic status of
160; Lime Walk 18, 42; 1960s 18–19,
18; Nuttery 18, 188; oak tree in 2;
Priest's House 16, 45, 50, 65, 155, 188,
213, 242, 277, 279, 307; Rose Garden
18, 19, 42, 226, 277, 285; 'Sissinghurst
Castle', Vita Sackville-West
discovers ii, 190, 202; Spring
Garden 278, 279; statues in 279;
Tower Lawn 278; vegetable garden
42, 66, 112, 150, 162, 164, 209, 255,
296, 298–9, *298*, 301, 302, 303, 306,
317–18; visitors, public 8, 11, 27–9, 31,
41, 43, 103, 113, 114–15, 149, 150, 161,
165, 244, 253, 261, 282, 310, 318; Vita
Sackville-West and ii, 190, 202, 275,
276, 277–9, *278*, 282, *282*, 284–5;
White Garden 32, 42, 108, 156, 188,
190, 278, 279, 285; Yew Walk 19, 277,
279
Sissinghurst Flower Show 285
Sissinghurst House Case 218
Smarden 121, 144
Smith, John 39
Smyth, Ethel 288
Snoad 123, 128
Soane Museum 186

Plan of
THE SISSINGHURST CASTLE
E·S·T·A·T·E·
TO BE SOLD BY
Messrs WINCH & SONS.
JUNE 25TH 1903.